The Scandal
of a
Crucified World

✝

The Scandal
of a
Crucified World

Perspectives on the Cross
and Suffering

✝

Edited by

Yacob Tesfai

ORBIS BOOKS

Maryknoll, New York 10545

The Catholic Foreign Mission Society of America (Maryknoll) recruits and trains people for overseas missionary service. Through Orbis Books, Maryknoll aims to foster the international dialogue that is essential to mission. The books published, however, reflect the opinions of their authors and are not meant to represent the official position of the society.

Published in the United States by Orbis Books, Maryknoll, NY 10545
Manufactured in the United States of America

All biblical quotations, unless otherwise noted, are taken from *The New Revised Standard Version,* copyright © 1989 by the Division of Christian Education of the National Council of the Churches of Christ in the United States of America.

Library of Congress Cataloging-in-Publication Data

The scandal of a crucified world : perspectives on the Cross and
    suffering / edited by Yacob Tesfai.
        p.   cm.
    Includes bibliographical references and index.
    ISBN 0-88344-976-5 (pbk.)
      1. Suffering—Religious aspects—Christianity.   2. Holy Cross.
  3. Christianity and culture.   4. Christianity—Developing countries.
  I. Tesfai, Yacob.
  BT732.7.S338   1994
  231'.8—dc20   94-17224
                                       CIP

Contents

Preface   vii

Chapter 1
Introduction
     YAGOB TESFAI   1

Chapter 2
The Memory of the African People and the Cross
of Christ
     JEAN-MARC ÉLA   17

Chapter 3
The Suffering of Human Divisions and the Cross
     SIMON S. MAIMELA   36

Chapter 4
An African-American Perspective on the Cross
and Suffering
     JAMES H. CONE   48

Chapter 5
An Asian Perspective on the Cross and Suffering
     ANDREAS A. YEWANGOE   61

Chapter 6
A Latin American Perspective on the Cross
and Suffering
     WALTER ALTMANN   75

Chapter 7
Is There a Feminist Theology of the Cross?
ELISABETH MOLTMANN-WENDEL   87

Chapter 8
Contextualizing Luther's Theology of the Cross
THEO SUNDERMEIER   99

Chapter 9
The Cross of Jesus Christ, the Unity of the Church,
and Human Suffering
WINSTON D. PERSAUD   111

Chapter 10
Christian Mission toward Abolition of the Cross
CHOAN SENG SONG   130

Contributors   149

Index   151

Preface

The Institute for Ecumenical Research had been engaged in a research project on the theology of the cross for the last four years. This research was divided into three lines of investigation: the first and the second were concerned with the ecumenical and traditional Western theological understandings of the cross. The first consultation was organized on these two lines of investigation in 1990. The second consultation was held May 17–22, 1992, in Nice, France. It dealt with the third line of investigation, which focused mostly on Third World understandings of the cross and suffering, with an opening to dialogue with others who have similar concerns, in this particular case, feminist and Lutheran. There was a guiding concern that underlined the consultation: to address the division and unity of humanity in the face of suffering. Our special angle was to assess the implications of the question of the cross and suffering on the unity of the church and humankind at a time when a significant number of theologians from the South (as well as others) are of the opinion that "the division between rich and poor is the major phenomenon of contemporary history."[1] We have constantly been conscious of the mind-boggling division of humanity between rich and poor, the grinding poverty that locks out millions of people from life, and all the ills that divide people in the contemporary world in a de facto system of apartheid. This collection of essays is an outcome of a consultation that attempted to struggle with this reality.

The contributors came from various countries and confessional backgrounds. There was a special intention to hear voices from the three Third World continents as well as those of African-American and feminist thinking on this issue. Luther was included because the theology of the cross elaborated by him had become a central theological point for reflection in recent years and because he had come under criticism from some Third World theologians. All the contributors had of course earlier dealt with and written extensively on the issue of the cross and suffering.

Yacob Tesfai introduces the discussion by giving an overview of the attempt of Third World theologians to come to terms with the cross of Jesus and the

---

1. Sergio Torres and Virginia Fabella, M.M., eds., *The Emergent Gospel: A Theology from the Underside of History* (Maryknoll, N.Y.: Orbis Books, 1978), vii.

immense suffering of the Third World. He shows that the cross is becoming increasingly the center of reflection in these theologies. In the life of Jesus as related in the gospels and in his death on the cross, the life of the God that Jesus reveals is intimately tied to the suffering of people. This takes form in the identification with the victims of oppression and their liberation.

Jean-Marc Éla struggles with the historical memories that shape the African people and relates them to the question of who Jesus Christ is. This reflection is done in the light of the growing significance of the shift of the center of Christianity from Europe to the Third World. In this context, it is imperative to think through anew the identity of Jesus Christ in the light of the experience of the African peoples and not parrot received traditions. The result is a new reading of the life and passion of Jesus Christ that speaks to Africans through their proper history and experience, especially that of slavery and the spiritual and material dislocation caused and still being caused by it.

In the light of the cross, *Simon Maimela* tackles the issue of apartheid, the ideology of separate development in South Africa that imposes immense suffering on the native population. He cautions that the cross can be ambiguous: it can either be used to lull people to accept their suffering without resistance or serve as an instrument of liberation. He outlines Luther's theology of the cross and sketches its relevance for present-day struggle in South Africa. In addition, he grapples with the theological problem posed by the separation of people on the basis of the color of their skin.

James Cone's essay links up with that of Éla in its focus on the continuing impact of the tragedy of slavery. Cone begins his reflection on the suffering felt by the torn personality that characterizes the African-American. He finds the source of this tension in the "African" and "Christian" heritages of the African-American. He traces this feeling of rupture in the African-American's "soul" through the spiritual journey of his people — the phases of slavery, the civil rights and black power movements, and finally the development of black theology.

Andreas Yewangoe leads us into the religious plurality of the Asian continent. He connects this with the realities of human suffering that are manifested there. First, he gives an overview of the views of suffering in the various religions of this continent and then concentrates on the discussions of cross and suffering by Asian Christian theologians. Reference is made to the theology of the pain of God from Japan and the *minjung* theology of South Korea. The essay finally zeroes in on the issues of suffering and poverty and some of the churches' thoughts on these problems.

Walter Altmann begins by highlighting the suffering of native Latin Americans, which came to light especially in 1992 on the occasion of the celebration of five hundred years of resistance. He argues that reflection on the cross today has to deal with this reality of the suffering of indigenous peoples in the execution and perpetuation of which the cross and the sword went hand in hand. He explores the images of Christ that accompanied the various phases of this history. Finally, he poses the challenges that the present situation of hopelessness poses to present-day Christians in Latin America and the Third World.

Elisabeth Moltmann-Wendel begins by reminding us that the cross of Jesus has come under severe attack by feminist theologians. To some, it has lost all meaning because it represents negative ideas of sado-masochism, a legitimation of force by men against women and the latter's subjection to the former. While taking serious note of these criticisms, she counters them by presenting a feminist theology of the cross as solidarity in suffering, as a place for the struggle against structural sin, and as a paradoxical symbol of life.

Martin Luther is acknowledged for picking up the cross and making it a central element in his theology. But as one observes in the contributions of Éla and Cone, Luther's theology has been sharply criticized by some Third World theologians. *Theo Sundermeier* takes it upon himself to elaborate Luther's theology. He discusses the question of whether one can universalize a contextual theology such as Luther's. He tests this possibility by taking examples from non-European artistic attempts to think through the meaning of the cross.

Winston Persaud explores the place of the cross in the life of the individual Christian as well as in the life of the church. He tackles the question of relating the "historical conditionedness" of individuals and communities with the search for universalism called for by the Christian message. The question is complicated by the various and sometimes conflicting interpretations of this gospel. This leads him to a discussion in the Latin American context of the place of the church in the confrontation with the plight of those who suffer.

Finally, *C. S. Song* reviews some aspects of the role and the place of the cross in the history of Christian missions. He struggles with the anomaly of the cross that became a means of conquest in the hands of Christians. He notes that the cross has not conquered the world, for example, in Japan. It is a case of "mission impossible" in such situations. The Christian faith finds itself in a dilemma because it continues to think in old categories while tremendous changes have occurred. The role of the South in the questioning of the Christian past is introducing a radical element that has to be taken seriously in the rethinking of mission and the cross. The final result should be the abolition of the cross.

It remains for me to thank my colleagues at the Institute for Ecumenical Research and the board who accorded me all the necessary cooperation and support in the process of the consultation and in the production of this book. A special word of thanks goes to Ms. Elke Leypold, our administrative secretary, for her efficiency in the organization of the consultation and the retyping of the manuscripts.

Yacob Tesfai
Strasbourg, France, 1992

Chapter 1

Introduction

Yacob Tesfai

✝

The manifestations of suffering on a large scale in the contemporary world are hard to miss. Sometimes, if we are far from the scene and not directly touched by them, they traverse our television screens and seem to come from another world. Women, men, and children ravaged by the effects of drought and famine sometimes reach us through secondary means. Victims of wars haunt our memories. The helpless cries of people caught up in situations of abandonment by a world that does not seem to care enough about their fate are heard mainly through the news media, and then only once in a while. Racially motivated killings, disturbances arising out of poverty and hopelessness sustained by political violence show us the faces of anarchy. All such fleeting occasions often hide the immense sufferings that people undergo, the people who are directly affected by these human tragedies and become their victims. Most often, such human sufferings are also reduced to cold statistics. Still, their numbers are staggering. We are told that 40,000 children under the age of five die every day due to lack of basic vaccines that prevent childhood diseases; each day 500 million people go hungry; over one billion people live in extreme poverty; 40 million people die yearly of malnutrition and hunger; more than three-fourths of the earth's population is condemned to share only 15 percent of its resources. And the list of such concrete sufferings and their devastating consequences goes on.[1]

Hidden under such statistical abstractions, the millions of people become faceless. But they are indeed individuals, with personal goals in life, children with hopes of growing up, and parents with prospects for their children. Even though they become victims of suffering en masse, they still do feel their pains individually and in their own specific ways. But such individual pains are lost within the faceless crowd. Being swallowed up in numbers, the persons become

---

1. *Croissance* (special issue) 8 (1992).

1

nameless and lose that which makes them specific. They are, as it were, buried
in mass graves where the individuality of each person is effaced beyond recognition and where it ceases to matter. Such faceless millions who suffer without
recognition are the peculiar and strange marks of the contemporary world.

Awareness of the Situation

This form of suffering is increasingly raising deep questions. The local manifestations of such a suffering are becoming the sources of intensive theological
engagement and thinking. The immense suffering to which people are subjected
in their millions in various parts of the world has begun to become the basis
of serious interrogations. "How can God be discussed from the perspective of
Ayacucho?" asks Gustavo Gutiérrez from the Peruvian city "buffeted by poverty and violence."[2] How can one make sense of suffering and know God's
place from Ayacucho, meaning "the corner of the dead?"[3] The suffering of the
marginalized, the poor, those who have been abandoned by the "powers that be,"
those who have been forced to live on the periphery of life and who have given
up their legitimate claims on life do not cease to utter the cry of desperation.

Such questioning in the face of concrete manifestations of suffering arising
in a variety of situations is echoed by other theologians coming from different
contexts. Bishop Desmond Tutu of South Africa, a Nobel peace prize winner,
muses about the problem of suffering in a pointed manner. In his case, it is the
question of suffering tied to the color of a person's skin that becomes the basis of the questioning. "In a country where blackness is non-beingness, where
people have no rights, no dignity, no respect; where an extremely refined system
of racial laws shouts inferiority at the black person on every level," the question of the suffering of people of color becomes important.[4] In the light of such
a situation, Bishop Tutu asks: "Why do we suffer so?"[5] The question is why
a human being, simply because of one's God-given color, suffers humiliation,
slavery, denial of basic human rights, segregation, extreme violence. The question again reverberates in the face of the poverty, famine, displacement, refugee
situations, and the resultant violence that has become the daily lot for millions
of Africans living as they are "in a continent which tends to become a veritable
empire of hunger."

In this light, Jean-Marc Éla poses the question: "How to speak about God
in the living conditions of the poor in African societies torn apart by many

---

2. "How Can God Be Discussed from the Perspective of Ayacucho?" *Concilium*, 1990/1, 103.
3. *A Theology of Liberation*, 15th anniversary edition (Maryknoll, N.Y.: Orbis Books, 1988),
177, note 24.
4. Allan A. Boesak, "Coming Out of the Wilderness," in Sergio Torres and Virginia Fabella,
M.M., eds., *The Emergent Gospel: A Theology from the Underside of History* (Maryknoll, N.Y.:
Orbis Books, 1978), 81.
5. "The Theology of Liberation in Africa," in Kofi Appiah-Kubi and Sergio Torres, eds.,
African Theology en Route (Maryknoll, N.Y.: Orbis Books, 1979), 163.

forms of neo-colonial violence?"[6] A similar question related to suffering but having a different source is asked in Asia. "Can we still believe in a God who is active in history in the midst of slum dwellers in Bombay, or in the midst of boat refugees from Vietnam?"[7] The sufferings caused by poverty, homelessness, death at an early age, refugee situations, hunger, and sickness on a hitherto unknown massive scale cannot be ignored any longer.

All these questionings on the issue of suffering have been the driving forces behind most of the theological reflections in the Third World. In fact, ever since its founding in the Tanzanian city of Dar-es-Salaam in 1976, the Ecumenical Association of Third World Theologians (EATWOT) has been trying to raise the issue of a different kind of suffering that is bedeviling the Third World, or the Two-Thirds World.[8] It has been attempting to bring into focus the suffering borne by millions of people around the globe. It has made their plight the context of its theological reflections. The challenge that needs to be addressed is to reflect on the relationship of the cross of Jesus and the immense suffering to which millions of people are subjected in the contemporary world. What do the cross and suffering mean in the context of such a tragedy and unacknowledged genocide?

Quincentennial and the Cross

The year 1992 happens to be an auspicious time to undertake such reflections. It is the five-hundredth anniversary of the arrival of Christopher Columbus in the Americas. It also happens to be a time when the cross became a point of reflection. It is a sign of the changing times that the case of Columbus continues to raise a great deal of heated debate with regard to its meaning, even in the churches. Columbus is related to the Christian church and the cross because of his alleged involvement in the evangelization and Christianization of the Americas. The manner in which the evangelization has been conducted is, of course, highly contested. There are sharply opposite opinions about it. In any case, the cross is in the center of the debate. Some celebrated the event with great fanfare in October 1992. The cross was at the center of the celebrations. In a sort of a repetition of the first act of Columbus, the inauguration of a memorial "lighthouse" in the form of a huge cross constituted part of the celebrations in Santo Domingo where the anniversary activities took place. There are two points that highlight the importance of the cross in this connection.

---

6. Jean-Marc Éla, *My Faith as an African* (Maryknoll, N.Y.: Orbis Books, 1988), xvii.

7. Andreas Yewangoe, *Theologia Crucis in Asia: Asian Christian Views on Suffering in the Face of Overwhelming Poverty and Multifaceted Religiosity in Asia,* Amsterdam Studies in Theology, vol. 6 (Amsterdam: Editions Rodpont, 1987), 285.

8. Virginia Fabella and Sergio Torres, eds., *Irruption of the Third World: Challenge to Theology* (Maryknoll, N.Y.: Orbis Books, 1983); Virginia Fabella, ed., *Asia's Struggle for Full Humanity* (Maryknoll, N.Y.: Orbis Books, 1980). See also notes 4 and 5.

First the story has it that one of the first acts of Columbus when he reached the shores of the New World was planting a cross. Recalling the significance of this first act, those who celebrate the anniversary of the so-called evangelization of the Americas are, in the words of Pope John Paul II, "commemorating the fifth centenary of the arrival of Christ's cross in those lands."[9] In a symposium held at the Vatican on the evangelization of the Americas, it was emphasized that the cross was the divine instrument that played an important role in the adventures of the explorers. As John Paul II again asserted, beginning from the embarkation of Columbus and his group of colonizers in the new world, "the cross of Christ was able to be planted in new lands, providing in this manner the beginning of the new World's evangelization. This Cross, planted in the heart of the New World, illuminated the ways of the explorers and colonists."[10]

Second, it is also necessary to remember that the use of the cross in the history of Western Christianity in general and in that of the colonizers in particular is very ambiguous indeed. This ambiguity characterizes too this time of so-called exploration and evangelization as well. The cross was not only an instrument and a sign of salvation and the well-being of the people to whom it was brought. It had a somber and violent aspect as well. One is reminded that the cross as a means of salvation or damnation triumphed in many instances because it went hand in hand with the sword. It was used not only to proclaim salvation to the peoples but it was also used in the process of crushing and subjugating others. As one writer put it, "the redeeming Cross was stained with blood. Not that of missionaries. Only that of the indigenous peoples."[11]

The indigenous population had a destructive meeting with the cross of the Christian conquistadors. The population had few opportunities to experience the cross as a redeeming instrument of God in view of the sufferings imposed on them by their conquerors. As a result, they had a distorted understanding of the cross of Jesus. "For the Indians, there was never much difference between the cross and the sword, not only because the conquistadors' swords were shaped like crosses, but also because the practices and customs which went with the preaching of the cross bore a closer resemblance to the use of the sword than to the proclaimed gentleness of a Gospel which they never really knew."[12] It is a symbolism of great magnitude that has its repercussions up to the present, for the "marginalization of the Indians merges with the marginalization of the vast mass of poor in Latin America, and it began with the conquest."[13]

---

9. Pope John Paul II, "Evangelization of the Americas — 500 years: Our Lady of Guadalupe Reveals Mary's Concern for Native Peoples," *L'Osservatore Romano,* weekly edition, no. 4, January 29, 1992, 16.

10. "Lumières et ombres," *A.R.M.* 101 (June 15, 1992): 10. Benoit Guillou, "Saint-Domingue: Le berceau des Amériques," *A.R.M.* 103 (September 15, 1992): 4ff.

11. Régis Debray, *Christoph Colomb: Le visiteur de l'aube* (Paris: La Différence, 1991), 36.

12. Julio Barreiro, "Rejection of Christianity by the Indigenous Peoples of Latin America," Julio de Santa Ana, ed., *Separation without Hope?* (Geneva: World Council of Churches, 1978), 128.

13. Ibid., 131.

This element increases the ambiguity of the interpretation of the cross in the history of the Christian churches and its relation to the suffering masses of the contemporary world. It is in view of this ambiguous history of the cross that pertinent questions are being posed regarding its meaning. In the name of the victims past and present of the conquest begun by Columbus, the use of the cross in it, and the consequent immense suffering of millions of people in our contemporary world, a deep questioning on the meaning of the cross and death of Jesus and suffering is in place. The conviction is of course that the ultimate meaning of the cross of Jesus has been missed by some traditional interpretations of it and, as a result, the message of the cross was turned completely upside down. In an ironic twist, the Jesus who himself fell into the hands of the powerful and was crucified by them ended up as an accomplice in the crucifixion of others. In the words of a theologian from Haiti: "This is perhaps the most serious question today: the Jesus who had been assassinated by a coalition of the powerful, tortured like a slave — how did he manage to become ... (as for example in Haiti) the God of the strong, the God of the powerful?"[14]

In the context of such situations of suffering, then, there is a profound rethinking of the cross going on. The traditional explanations of the meaning of the cross are being put to a severe test. They are even found to be inadequate. The theories of "satisfaction" and "reconciliation," which tried to explain why God became human, are being questioned. These theories were often constructed from the perspective of what went on in the heart of God. They were written, so to speak, from the perspective of heaven. They tried to describe the divine thoughts that led to the incarnation and the crucifixion of the Son of God. In the process, the sufferings of peoples played a marginal role in the attempt to understand the cross. But as James Cone insists, "How can we speak of Jesus' death on the cross without first speaking about the death of people?"[15]

In this light, a radical reversal of the understanding of the cross is now being called for. This understanding starts from below. Instead of speculating on the motives and the reasons behind the crucifixion as it happened in God's mind, it takes seriously the story of the passion of Jesus as related in the gospels and ties it to people's sufferings. The clearest formulation of this line of investigation calling for a totally new understanding of the cross is made by Hugo Assmann. In the context of such a rethinking of the meaning of the cross of Jesus and the suffering of millions of people, his words become a continuing challenge:

---

14. Gilles Danroc, "Haiti ou la question retournée," in Ignace Berten and René Luneau, eds., *Le rendezvous de Saint-Domingue: Enjeu d'un anniversaire 1492–1992* (Paris: Editions du Centurion, 1991), 225.

15. James Cone, "Black Theology: Its Origin, Methodology, and Relationship to Third World Theologies," in Virginia Fabella and Sergio Torres, eds., *Doing Theology in a Divided World* (Maryknoll, N.Y.: Orbis Books, 1984), 100. See also Rudolf R. Featherstone, "The Theology of the Cross: The Perspective of an African in America," in Albert Pero and Ambrose Moyo, eds., *Theology and the Black Experience: The Lutheran Heritage Interpreted by African and African-American Theologians* (Minneapolis: Augsburg Publishing House, 1988), 51.

The theology of liberation, as an effective process of critical reflection on historical practice, will have to go back to the theology of the cross. It will also have to strip it of the alienating mystifications that have accrued to it.... It will have to give back to the man Jesus his full integrity as a human being, and give his death the historical and political meaning that in fact it possessed. From there it can start to unravel the real meaning behind the symbolism of the New Testament: a whole line of challenge that has not yet been properly understood.[16]

Such renewed questioning in the light of the cross as a symbol and reality of suffering leads one back to the story of Jesus.

Rereading the Story of Jesus

It is being recognized now that the cross of Jesus cannot be understood without taking into consideration what went before it. This is to say that the life and message of Jesus are indispensable to finding a correct explanation of the phenomenon of his crucifixion. This takes one back to the story of Jesus as related by the evangelists. In the story, the passion narratives play a very significant role. In fact, in their light the entire life of Jesus is presented as an extended passion narrative. It begins with his poverty, which separates him from the rich. He is presented as a homeless wanderer who moves from one place to another and who does not possess a fixed domicile. His acts are indeed provocative viewed in the light of the religious expectations of his contemporaries. He ate with the outcasts, that is, the sinners, the prostitutes, the publicans, the tax-collectors. By so doing, he broke the laws of purity, the religious orders of the day, and provoked the suspicion and hostility of the Pharisees and the elders. By healing the sick on the Sabbath day and by breaking the laws that regulated cultic lives prescribed by the religious leaders, he earned their enmity. Above all else, through his actions and his message, Jesus aligned himself with the poor against the rich. He rubbed against the grain of the prevailing political situation by siding with the poor and the oppressed and by proclaiming the kingdom of God to them. Because of his life and message, Jesus was seen as a subversive who disturbed the political and religious order that held sway in his time. Finally, the authorities could no longer tolerate the challenge posed by him. He was condemned as a rebel and a criminal and ended up on the cross.

Jesus was crucified because he challenged the structures of power. His crucifixion is tied intimately with the kind of life he lived and the message he proclaimed within the context of a specific situation of injustice. His death on the cross was caused by specific political and social structures that were opposed to the kind of person Jesus was and to his message. In his life and message,

---

16. Hugo Assmann, *Theology for a Nomad Church* (Maryknoll, N.Y.: Orbis Books, 1976), 86.

Jesus was committed to the poor and made an option for the poor. The God who was proclaimed by Jesus is the God who decided in favor of the poor and took their side. It follows that this God is opposed to all forms of the oppression of the poor, be they religious, social, or economic. Jesus' standing on the side of the poor led him to the cross. This cross is thus the definite consequence of a life committed to the dregs of society and in favor of their liberation. It is a direct result of the commitment of Jesus to those who stand to lose within a system of exploitation. The cross followed a subversive life that confronted the status quo tilted unjustly in favor of the rich and the powerful. Jesus was crucified as a criminal among other criminals because he contradicted and opposed the unjust system that eventually felt threatened by him. Jesus' cross can be rightly understood only when viewed within the context of the historical "givens" of his time. "His life of solidarity with the poor and the rejected is the key to the credible interpretation of his death in the context of our life today. The death of Jesus is the inevitable denouement of a drama linked to the whole story of his life — an unending struggle against oppressive socioreligious forces and structures. A victim of repressive violence, Jesus pays for the boldness of his subversive ideas.... Jesus' death is the result of his option for the poor and the oppressed."[17] And Leonardo Boff concedes: "This denouement, namely, the shameful crucifixion, was a result of a commitment and a praxis that threatened the status quo of the time."[18]

Here the cross becomes the culmination of a life dedicated to the poor and against those powers that deny the rights of the poor. As a result, there is a radical transformation of the cross that takes place. Instead of being an ignominious end to an equally ignominious life, it becomes the crowning of a life of struggle against the systems that subjugate peoples. The cross is imposed upon or taken up by the person who challenges the existence of the structures that abuse the people created in the image of God and called to live as full human beings. It crowns a life that is committed to the advocacy of the liberation of the poor in solidarity with them. As a consequence, "Jesus transforms the cross from an instrument of humiliation into an instrument of struggle against slavery and death. For Christians and the church, the liberation of the poor, then, is the basic issue at stake in the death of Jesus."[19] The cross is viewed in this light: "In the end, the gospel confronts a strategy of domination leading to hunger, set in a world structure where the administration of the wealth of the earth is monopolized by those who control the economic and political apparatus. Jesus reveals God and his option for the poor and the little ones."[20]

---

17. Éla, *My Faith as an African*, 108.
18. Leonardo Boff, *Jesus Christ Liberator: A Critical Christology for Our Time* (Maryknoll, N.Y.: Orbis Books, 1980), 289.
19. Éla, *My Faith as an African*, 109.
20. Ibid., 107.

A Continuous Good Friday

In the light of such an understanding of the relationship between Jesus and the cross, the relationship of the resurrection to the cross is also reviewed. The ambiguity of their relationship becomes unsettling. It is true that the resurrection of Jesus Christ was central in the emergence of the Christian church. This is amply demonstrated in the New Testament.[21] But the resurrection has often been viewed as effacing the cross. The latter is seen as being overcome and superseded by the former. It is sometimes argued as if the resurrection has rendered the cross superfluous. It is often forgotten that the cross comes first and that there is no resurrection without the cross, that it is the way of the cross that leads to the resurrection. In this understanding, the cross is simply forgotten and relegated to the past. There is a rush to embrace the resurrection without the cross.

But the cross cannot be forgotten so easily, because it characterizes the lives of millions of people in the world. It is the cross as a symbol and reality of a horrible suffering that many experience at present. There are those who are united with Christ not in his resurrection but in his crucifixion. This situation of continuing suffering is expressed through the imagery provided by the passion narratives. In the words of Leonardo Boff and Virgil Elizondo, for example, the suffering of peoples that started during the conquest of the Americas is experienced as a continuous Good Friday: "12 October 1492 was the beginning of a long and bloody Good Friday for Latin America and the Caribbean. It is still Good Friday, and there is no sign of Easter Day."[22]

In such a view, the life marked by suffering is a continuous participation in a passion story characterized by daily crucifixion imposed from outside. In this case, the cross as an expression of suffering is not only a past event but one that determines life in the present. The tensions between Good Friday and Easter Sunday, the crucifixion and the resurrection, are visible here. The problem of viewing from the perspective of the resurrection a life that does not yet know any resurrection becomes acute. The question of the celebration of the resurrection by a people who find themselves daily confronted by the forces of death and subjection to death becomes crucial. In this kind of situation, where millions of people are given up to real deaths by hunger, famine, drought, and economic exploitation, the resurrection is as remote as the crucifixion is real. The passion and the cross thus claim the center stage. As Jean-Marc Éla expresses it: "How

---

21. Edward Schweizer, "Towards a Christology of Mark?" and Barnabas Lindars, "The Passion in the Fourth Gospel," in Jacob Jervell and Wayne A. Meeks, eds., *God's Christ and His People: Studies in Honour of Nils Alstrup Dahl* (Oslo: Universitetsforlaget, 1977), 37–39 and 71–83; C. K. Barrett, "Theologia Crucis — in Acts?" in Carl Andresen and Günther Klein, eds., *Theologia Crucis – Signum Crucis: Festschrift für Erich Dinkler zum 70 Geburtstag* (Tübingen: J. C. B. Mohr Paul Siebeck, 1979), 73–84.

22. Virgil Elizondo and Leonardo Boff, "1492–1992: The Voice of the Victims," editorial, *Concilium* 1990/6, vii.

can we celebrate the resurrection where millions of men and women live in suffering and oppression?...As Africans, how can we live and proclaim the Easter message today when we are already living out the passion of Jesus in history?"[23]

The crucifixion is not yet over but it continues in one way or another. It continues in any situation where people are deprived of their right to a life free from daily overshadowing by an impending death. This sentiment is echoed in South Africa, where it is said that "the crucifixion of God in Jesus Christ *is,* for us, the crucifixion of the oppressed people in our country....God is being crucified in South Africa today."[24] It is also taken up in Asia, when Yewangoe writes: "The cross also refers to the current suffering of people in this world."[25] The experience of Good Friday becomes a continuing and present experience. The experience of the resurrection becomes inadequate for the present, which is ruled, as it were, by the cross. Therefore, the question of the relationship of the cross to the resurrection becomes a serious issue. One cannot yet celebrate the resurrection. Easter is far away just as the crucifixion is here and now. As Mofokeng has said with reference to South African blacks,

> Good Friday comes normally to the black worshippers who pack the churches on this day....Jesus is being abused, tortured, humiliated and crucified in them in their country and in their time. They suffer a long Good Friday throughout their lives, a long Good Friday that relates very closely to Jesus' Good Friday. Jesus' cry of abandonment is their own daily cry.[26]

The people still live suspended, as it were, between the day of crucifixion and the resurrection. Resurrection will become a reality only when the oppression that denies their humanity and that subjects them to crucifixion is overcome once for all and they can share in the fruits of the resurrection, that is, in freedom from the threat of daily death. "Insofar as Jesus saw the presage of his coming passion in the poor, the oppressed and the marginalized, the resurrection is real and complete only when the poor pass from death to life."[27] There is the need, therefore, not to fall into the Corinthian temptation of elevating the resurrection to the point of ignoring the present situation. "We must reaffirm the scandal of the cross so that we do not fall into the Corinthian illusion that lies in wait for us as soon as we begin to think of the church as some 'Island of the Blessed.' "[28]

---

23. Éla, *My Faith as an African,* 110.

24. Albert Nolan, *God in South Africa: The Challenge of the Gospel* (Grand Rapids: Eerdmans, 1988), 67.

25. Yewangoe, *Theologia Crucis in Asia,* 7.

26. Takatso Mofokeng, "The Cross in Search for True Humanity," *Journal of Black Theology* 3 (1989): 47.

27. Éla, *My Faith as an African,* 111.

28. Ibid., 130; Jon Sobrino, *Christology at the Crossroads: A Latin American View* (Maryknoll, N.Y.: Orbis Books, 1978), 278.

The Crucified People

The contemporaneity of the cross of Jesus in the sufferings of the present is caught up by the pregnant phrase, "the crucified people." This phrase attempts to convey the idea that the cross of Jesus continues its presence in the current manifestations of suffering that afflict people. In this connection, the living out of the passion is emphasized. In the Latin American context, the phrase seems to have had its origin with the Jesuit priest murdered in El Salvador in 1989, Father Ignacio Ellacuría. It refers to all those who are marginalized, oppressed, poor, and abandoned by the powers that be. They find their relationship to Jesus in that "today, the crucified Lord is present in the crucified people."[29] The term is extensively used by Jon Sobrino as referring to the people who are still enduring the crucifixion in their everyday lives.[30] But such use of this term is not confined to the situation in Latin America. It is also used by the South African writers Takatso Mofokeng and Albert Nolan.[31]

The point is to emphasize the intimate connection between the cross of Jesus and the present crosses of people. They are not separate; instead, they meld into one. The identities of the cross of Jesus and those of the poor are not sharply divided; they are rather united in the suffering to which both Jesus and the crucified people are subjected. Jesus is thus to be found in *the crucified people* today. Wherever there is suffering, there are found not only *the crucified people* but the crucified Jesus as well. In a world of suffering, Jesus is actually present in it. "The Third World carries within itself the hidden Christ. It is the historic body of Jesus Christ today.... We must go and rediscover Christ in the slums, in the places of misery and domination, among the majority of the poor and the oppressed people."[32]

Furthermore, the crucified people are the "signs of the times." In the words of Ellacuría:

> This sign is always the people crucified in history whose sad existence *repeatedly undergoes various forms of crucifixion*. This crucified people is the continuation of the Servant of the Lord whom the sin of the world plunders now as before, the one whose life is robbed now as before, above all else, life itself.[33]

---

29. José Ignacio Gonzales, "Dankesschuld an Ignacio Ellacuría," *Orientierung* 20 (October 31, 1990): 220.

30. Jon Sobrino, "The Crucified Peoples: Yahweh's Suffering Servant Today — In Memory of Ignacio Ellacuría," *Concilium* 1990/6, 120–29; Sobrino, *Jesus in Latin America,* 159ff.

31. Mofokeng, "The Cross in Search for True Humanity," 47; Nolan, *God in South Africa,* 49ff.

32. Éla, *My Faith as an African,* 99.

33. Ignacio Ellacuría, "Discernir 'el signo' de los tiempos," *Diakonia* (April 17, 1981): 58; quoted in Jon Sobrino, "Der Glaube an den Sohn Gottes auf der Sicht eines gekreuzigten Volkes," *Der Christus der Armen: Das Christuszeugnis der lateinamerikanischen Befreiungstheologen* (Freiburg: Herder, 1988), 127. See also Sobrino, "Le Ressusité et le Crucifié: Lecture de

It follows from this that a proper understanding of the cross of Jesus can be arrived at only in the light of the sufferings experienced by people in the contemporary world. The cross of Jesus and the cross of the people cannot be separated; they explain one another. The true meaning of the cross of Jesus can be reached at only in view of "the situation of captivity and resistance in which so many human beings live today,...a situation of world injustice."[34]

A closely related extension of this idea is the solidarity and even identification that exists between the crucified Jesus and the crucified people. The crucifixion of Jesus is not an event in the past that happened to one person only. On the contrary, it is a cruel chastisement being meted out to all those who suffered and suffer still in various ways because of unjust and inhuman activities of people and the structures and systems created and sustained by them. Contemporary sufferers see in Jesus their own proper suffering. This idea is expressed in the now celebrated poem of the South African theologian Gabriel Setiloane:

> And yet for us it is when he is on the cross,
> This Jesus of Nazareth, with holed hands
> and open side, like a beast at a sacrifice:
> When he is stripped, naked like us,
> Browned and sweating water and blood
> in the heat of the sun,
> Yet silent,
> That we cannot resist him.[35]

In this understanding, there is a unity and solidarity between the crucified Jesus and those who are suffering in their daily existence from unjust structures created by human beings. Their cries meld into those of Jesus. He and the suffering people are one; he is one of them.

> Jesus suffered and died on a Roman cross because...he was horrified by the sufferings of the people, shared in their sufferings and was determined to do something about their plight. Jesus was one of the oppressed struggling to free all who suffered under the yoke of oppression. This is the meaning of the cross.[36]

In fact, in their suffering they become the privileged places where God is found. In the present world it is in the suffering millions that the crucified God is found. In the words of James Cone, "The oppressed are the presence of the

---

la Résurrection à partir de Jésus et à partir de Crucifié du Monde," in Jacques van Nieuwenhove, ed., *Jésus et la libération en Amérique Latine* (Paris: Desclée, 1986), 298.

34. Leonardo Boff, *Passion of Christ, Passion of the World: The Facts, Their Interpretation, and Their Meaning Yesterday and Today* (Maryknoll, N.Y.: Orbis Books, 1987), 1.

35. "I Am an African," quoted in Kwesi A. Dickson, *Theology in Africa* (Maryknoll, N.Y.: Orbis Books, 1984), 196.

36. Nolan, *God in South Africa*, 61.

crucified God.... It is in the deaths of the poor of the world that is found the suffering and even death of God."[37]

The Cross and Structures of Injustice

The meaning of the cross of Jesus and the crucified people can rightly be understood only within the context of specific unjust structures created and sustained by human beings. Ever since the 1960s, the conviction has grown gradually within various theologies that the suffering of the masses is also caused by structures, systems.[38] There is the growing conviction that there are ways of organizing human life that are lopsided and unjust and that feed on the oppression, marginalization, and exploitation of the majority of the world's population. They form part of what Míguez Bonino calls "a total system of death."[39] It is a system in which and by which "the poor are dying. They die from starvation, from deprivation, from oppression. But it is their life and labor which creates the wealth of the few."[40]

Far from being divinely instituted, these are structures created and sustained by human beings. These systems can be fashioned for diverse reasons, bases, and interests: economic, social, racial, sexist, political. These structures are characterized by the fact that they divide human beings into those who benefit from them and those who are oppressed by them and suffer under them. In the words of Allan Boesak regarding apartheid: "The situation was created by people. It is a system that is still maintained by people through various methods."[41] And Éla agrees: "We know today that the suffering of people is not natural; it does not result from any human limitations. Instead, it is produced by people, by groups in power, and by models of society and culture."[42] The sufferings on a large scale imposed by some on others have nothing fatalistic about them; they are caused by human beings intent on maintaining their own particular interests at the expense of fellow human beings. In this context, "the widening gap between the rich and the poor is an obvious challenge. The plight of the millions of

---

37. James Cone, "Reflections from the Perspective of U.S. Blacks: Black Theology and Third World Theology," *Irruption of the Third World,* 241.

38. Konrad Raiser, *Ecumenism in Transition: A Paradigm Shift in the Ecumenical Movement?* (Geneva: WCC, 1991), 18; Richard D. N. Dickinson, *To Set at Liberty the Oppressed: Towards an Understanding of Christian Responsibilities for Development/Liberation* (Geneva: World Council of Churches, 1975), 7, 51; David M. Paton, ed., *Breaking the Barriers,* Nairobi 1975: The Official Report of the Fifth Assembly of the World Council of Churches, Nairobi, 23 November–10 December 1975 (London: SPCK, 1976), 100ff.

39. José Míguez Bonino, "For Life and against Death: A Theology That Takes Sides," in James Wall, ed., *Theologians in Transition* (New York: Crossroad, 1981), 171.

40. Julio de Santa Ana, ed., *Towards a Church of the Poor: The Work of an Ecumenical Group on the Church and the Poor* (Geneva: World Council of Churches, 1979), 3.

41. "Liberation Theology in South Africa," *African Theology en Route,* 12.

42. Éla, *My Faith as an African,* 111.

poor people and their struggle for survival is another cause for alarm. So is the affluence of the rich which is part of the cause for the sufferings of the poor."[43]

This is where Jesus' cross and suffering tie together. Their connecting link is found in the structures of oppression that create crosses for both Jesus and the crucified people. The cross of Jesus finds its place here. It finds its place as a sociopolitical event. In the words of James Cone, "The *Victim,* Jesus of Nazareth, was crucified because he was a threat to the political and religious structures of his time."[44]

Two meanings of the cross then go together. On the one hand, the cross expresses the condition of suffering in which people find themselves. It is a condition that negates the God-given destiny of people. By subjecting them to undeserved suffering, it contradicts their humanity. It is the situation of those whose lives are annihilated by famines and human-made disasters. On the other hand, it becomes the end result of a provocative life, a life that challenges the systems or structures of oppression. It follows a life lived in solidarity with the poor, the downtrodden, the marginalized, those who live on the periphery and to whom the kingdom of God is proclaimed. It is the crowning of a life dedicated to pay any price in the service of those it loves dearly.

The Cross and Abandonment by God

But there is a further dimension of the cross of Jesus that needs to be considered here. One of the shrill and enigmatic cries uttered by Jesus from the cross was formulated in the form of a question to God. "My God, my God, why have you forsaken me?" (Mark 15:34). In the context provided for this cry, the passion narratives dwell on Jesus' loneliness in the face of his suffering. His disciples leave him alone at the very hour when he needed them most. This point is hammered home constantly: the disciples neither understand the suffering of Jesus nor are they prepared to share it in any way (Mark 14:27); they sleep when Jesus expects them to watch with him in his loneliest moment (Matt. 26:36–46; Mark 14:37; Luke 22:46); Peter even denies him (Matt. 26:69–75), and all the disciples flee in the face of the imminent danger that Jesus was facing from the authorities (Mark 14:50). In the absence of human friends and companions, the question is addressed to the God who should be present but who is felt as absent. In this sense, it is an enigmatic question because it is tied to the feeling of utter abandonment by Jesus. Furthermore, it is scandalous because it is addressed to God by the Jesus who called him "Abba," the intimate Aramaic word for "Father." No wonder then that the interpretation of this

---

43. C. I. Itty, "Introduction," in Julio de Santa Ana, ed., *Good News to the Poor: The Challenge of the Poor in the History of the Church* (Geneva: World Council of Churches, 1977), ix.

44. James H. Cone, "Christian Faith and Political Praxis," in Brian Mahan and L. Dale Richesin, eds., *The Challenge of Liberation Theology: A First World Response* (Maryknoll, N.Y.: Orbis Books, 1981), 55.

cry has often proven controversial. It cannot be denied, however, that in this question, there is expressed the feeling of abandonment, loneliness, and fear in the face of the abyss and failure of crucifixion. It is a disturbing question being posed in the face of suffering where God seemed to be far away, and even absent. "My God, you have forsaken me, but why?" We are faced here with the "offensive character of the saying" that expresses "uttermost desolation and profoundest distress."[45] The enigma of suffering is sharpened by this desperate call. The significance of this cry of dereliction is rightly contemplated by many theologians. It is a cry uttered in the wilderness without any possible hearer. It is here that the stark meaning of the cross is revealed. "Jesus experienced the Father's total abandonment on the cross."[46]

There are two points that need to be made. First, the weakness of God is revealed on the cross. Here is a situation of suffering where the evil structures have their say, a situation where the innocent sufferer is subjected to the fury of those in power. God is paradoxically revealed in the powerlessness of the victim. This is the occasion of the ultimate incarnation: God's presence in the weakest and most vulnerable form of suffering. It is the point where "God becomes genuinely other."[47] Furthermore, the question of God's silence in the face of the suffering of the innocent as well as that of the millions of people is raised in an acute manner. The seeming incapacity of God to deliver those who cry to God at the hour of their utmost helplessness is posed in a sharp way on the cross. The intriguing experience of a God who hides at a time when God is needed — when the powers of injustice hold sway and crush the weak victim — is exacerbated in the event of the cross. It is a haunting cry of loneliness that is picked up and carried over by the millions of human beings who are sacrificed on the altars of heartless systems. It is echoed in the cries of the multitudes left to themselves to perish in undeserved deaths. In the face of the harsh judgments and punishments experienced by the victims, the silence proves deafening. In this light, the cross of Jesus and the crosses of all those who suffer with him throughout history, as well as the crosses of those millions who perish without any apparent reason, are dumbfounded in the face of the silence of God. These crosses continue to challenge their easy dismissal. The cries from these crosses also continue to haunt the lives of those who disappear without a witness in a violent world, a world that annihilates them without being conscious of its heartlessness.

Second, the abandonment on the cross shows Jesus' determination to stick to his calling to the bitter end. Even though the passion narratives are open enough to acquaint us with the pain that was felt by Jesus regarding his mission, we see him obedient even to the cross. The cross shows Jesus' commitment to

---

45. E. S. Gerstenberger and W. Schrage, *Suffering,* trans. John E. Steely, Biblical Encounters Series (Nashville: Abingdon, 1977), 175.

46. Sobrino, *Christology at the Crossroads,* 107, 188; see also, Juan Luis Segundo, "Jesu und seine Gemeinde" in *Christus der Armen,* 115, and Claus Bussmann, *Befreiung durch Jesus? Die Christologie der lateinamerikanischen Befreiungstheologie* (Munich: Kösel Verlag, 1980), 123–32.

47. Boff, *Passion of Christ, Passion of the World,* 52.

his cause. Even when exposed to the harsh fact of death on the cross, Jesus stands firm. His steadfastness is seen not only in the fact that he is willing to endure physical suffering. He faces squarely even "historical failure." He gives himself totally to whatever the consequences may be for his life. "The cross demonstrates the conflict-ridden nature of every process of liberation undertaken when the structure of injustice has gained the upper hand. Under such conditions liberation can come about only through martyrdom and sacrifice on behalf of others and God's cause in the world. This is the route which Jesus consciously chose and accepted."[48]

The cry of abandonment of Jesus is a cry that reverberates throughout history and that does not seem to have found a definitive answer. It is picked up and carried forward in the cries of all the victims who are deprived of their humanity in one way or another by the various systems of exploitation of human beings by their fellow human beings. In this connection, the questionings of a feminist theologian become pertinent: "Does the resurrection allow us to deny this cry from the cross? Do we say that Jesus did not really intend this as a cry of despair, that all along he knew that God would raise him up on the third day?" Not indeed. "We should not stifle the cry of Jesus . . . but, instead, let it continue to ring out from the cross, from all the crosses of unjust suffering throughout history, as a question mark about the nature of present reality."[49]

The cross relates to the resurrection in a paradoxical way. The two cannot exist one without the other: the resurrection is presupposed and preceded by the cross and the resurrection follows the cross. The cry from the cross and the hope of the resurrection shape each other in a dialectical way. The cross is picked up in the hope of the resurrection, in the firm hope that the causes that make it happen in the first place will eventually be overcome in God's own good time. The hungry will be fed, the naked clothed, the prisoners will be set free, those who "live under the shadow of death will see a great light," those confined to the periphery will once again emerge from their isolation and claim the rights of the daughters and sons of God.

But the resurrection is that of the crucified and those on behalf of whom they died. It proclaims that the crosses borne by the crucified were after all not in vain. The crosses borne by the crucified pave the way for the resurrection of those who come after them. The crosses of the crucified hide in them the resurrection of those who follow them. As the cross of Jesus bore fruit in his resurrection, those who are crucified with him are also heirs of his resurrection. The cross and resurrection thus go together and overshadow one another. The cross is the road that leads to the resurrection, and the resurrection has no meaning without the cross. "The cross is the historical meaning of the resurrection. . . . This means that the resurrection should not be separated

---

48. Boff, *Jesus Christ Liberator*, 290.
49. Rosemary Radford Ruether, *To Change the World: Christology and Cultural Criticism* (New York: Crossroad, 1983), 28, 29.

from the cross.... Once it becomes separated from the cross, the resurrection divorces itself from history."[50] The cross must also be viewed in the light of the resurrection. Viewed so, it transcends itself and creates hope in the future born through its birthpangs. The resurrection vindicates the cross by revealing the ultimate meaning of its pain. The resurrection leaves open the possibility of the final conquest and removal of the cross. Resurrection and the cross thus illuminate one another and exist together. In this way, the resurrection has the power to kindle hope even in the midst of the most meaningless crosses.

---

50. Choan-Seng Song, *Third-Eye Theology: Theology in Formation in Asian Settings* (Maryknoll, N.Y.: Orbis Books, 1991), 206.

Chapter 2

The Memory
of the African People
and the Cross of Christ

Jean-Marc Éla

✝

"I decided to know nothing among you except Jesus Christ, and him cruci-fied" (1 Cor. 2:2). Such is the core from which we have to verify our faithfulness to the basic sources of the faith and examine the contents of any talk that claims to speak the gospel in African circles. For, "if one wants to summarize the con-tents of the gospel in one word, one needs to say Jesus Christ." The entire gospel goes back to the event of Jesus Christ. Even more, it is in him that the entire New Testament is centered. Jesus Christ is not only the subject announced by the message of the gospel; he is also the subject of the message proclaimed by the church. But the summary of the message is contained in the following few words: "Jesus is Lord." Taking into consideration the importance of such a basic formula, "Christology is no more than a conscientious elucidation of that proposition."[1] Even more, if the eyes of the New Testament are focused on Jesus Christ, every theological reflection begins and ends with Jesus of Nazareth. In a sense, Christology is theology itself, its center of gravity, its motive and its basic theme. In fact, as one notices at present, theological discussions tend to concentrate on Jesus Christ. Behind the questions concerning the church or the sacraments, one always returns to the central question of Jesus.[2]

It is a matter of demonstrating that the manner in which Jesus is and acts arises out of an original relationship that he maintains and manifests with God. For the designation of God as "father" is found in a symbolic network where

---

1. Walter Kasper, *Jesus the Christ* (New York: Paulist Press, 1977), 15.
2. See also Yves J. M. Congar, *Le Christ, Marie et L'Église* (Paris: Desclée, 1955).

the conduct of Jesus leads one back to the decisive question: Who is Jesus, this only Son of the Father born before all the centuries? This question is at the heart of the gospel. Jesus himself had posed the very question to his disciples: "And you, who do you say that I am?"

Given the fact that access to Jesus through the New Testament always involves a process of reading and interpreting from the perspective of the situation and problems with which the church is confronted in history, the version of Christianity received from the churches of the West cannot escape the risk of being reinterpreted in Africa. We cannot reproduce formulae that in no way respond to the questions that the gospel addresses to us in the conditions in which the Word of God finds us (1 Cor. 7:20). That is why we have to subject the totality of revelation to an open test and appropriate the confession of the faith from the vantage point of where we actually are. Who is Jesus Christ to the African? At a time when the future of Christianity will be decided less in Europe and America than in the countries of the South, where demography is itself — especially in Africa — one of the great challenges of the end of this century, we have to go beyond the Byzantine quarrels and weigh what is at stake in such a debate.

In this context, it is necessary to be sensitive to culture shock and to be aware of the ethnocentrism of theology that for many centuries has exercised a dominant hold over the questioning and understanding of the faith. But in order to avoid falling into the trap of culturalism, which does not take into consideration the concrete subjects of history, we cannot confront the shock of differences without at the same time taking up the challenge of the poor and the oppressed.[3] For the "irruption of the Third World" is shaking up theology. It is necessary to underline here the extent of the "shift" that is taking place in a turnaround of history where theology elaborated in the West is less assured of remaining the official theology of the entire church. The rupture with North Atlantic theology is henceforth imperative if we want to rediscover God from the "periphery."[4] Such an undertaking is thrust upon those in the countries of the Third World who are asking themselves about the mystery of the connection between the peculiarity of Jesus and the universality of Christ in the unique person of the Son of God. In short, a critical and responsible reappropriation of the scandal of Jesus obliges us to remain faithful to the places where the irruption of the poor in history questions our understanding of the faith.

If Christianity wishes to avoid the temptation of the priest and the Levite in the parable of the Good Samaritan (Luke 20:31–32), it must assume the tragedy in Africa of those whom Frantz Fanon has called "the wretched of the earth." In this situation, the return to Jesus makes it absolutely necessary that our Christian reflection becomes incessantly suspicious toward any God-talk that attempts to

---

3. See Jean-Marc Éla, "Identité d'une théologie africaine," *Théologie et choc de cultures* (Paris: Cerf, 1984), 23–54.

4. For the "Final Statement" of Dar-es-Salaam, see Sergio Torres and Virginia Fabella, eds., *The Emergent Gospel: Theology from the Developing World* (Maryknoll, N.Y.: Orbis Books, 1978), 259ff.

"pass on the other side" of the actual situation in Africa. How can one rediscover God from the perspective of "a crucified messiah" (1 Cor. 1:23) while at
the same time covering up the other scandal that is at the center of the human
adventure of our era? Here is this scandal: for five hundred years, the West has
chosen the Christ without the cross, while the people of Africa live the cross
without the Christ. It is this passion without redemption in which Africa continues to live that must question our understanding of Jesus Christ. Taking into
consideration such a basic situation, how can we articulate the crucifixion of
Jesus and the historical suffering of our people? In other words, how can we
reread in our own way the narratives of the Passion of our Lord Jesus Christ
taking into account the stations of our memory? Such is the question that comes
out of the black continent, where — if one really dares to admit it — God speaks
to the world and to the church.

The Dead-end of Ethnotheology

In order to situate properly the following reflections, we need to point out
the limits of approaches that risk emptying the scandal of the cross with which
every serious discussion of Jesus of Nazareth is confronted. It is imperative to
highlight all the ethnotheological dead-ends that dominate the greater part of the
research conducted on the relationship between Christianity and Africa.[5] One
realizes very well that "the next task of African theology is to grapple seriously
with the question of Christology: Who is Jesus."[6] But the attempts that aim
at reinterpreting faith in Christ in the African context lock themselves up in a
"theology of digging the sources," which is developed on the basis of concepts,
beliefs, or traditions of African culture. If we listen to the questions raised by the
development of the African independent churches, we find out that the question
of the significance of Jesus is raised mainly within the context of the traditional
world. We see how John Mbiti tries to comprehend the main events of the life
of Jesus with reference to African anthropology.

When we wish to understand from our sociocultural context the titles given
to Jesus by the New Testament, we realize immediately that such titles do not
correspond to traditional African concepts. For, writes Mbiti, "no parallels exist
in the African forms of thought, histories, and traditions."[7] While refusing to listen to God in the concrete challenges through which God speaks in our history,
some believe that they can find in black Africa clues leading to a deeper understanding of Jesus Christ. This is the problem faced by studies that limit the space

---

5. For this research, consult the small book of Elo Messi Metogo, *Théologie africaine et
ethnophilosophie* (Paris: L'Harmattan, 1985).

6. Gabriel M. Setiloane, "Where Are We in African Theology?" in K. Appiah-Kubi and
S. Torres, eds., *African Theology en Route,* (Maryknoll, N.Y.: Orbis Books, 1978), 64.

7. Quoted by P. Stadler, "Approches théologiques en Afrique," *Bulletin de Théologie Africaine*
9 (January–June 1983): 43.

of the encounter with the Christ to the sphere of the ancestral culture only. Such attempts based on local traditions, titles, names, or the vocabulary of a given society will succeed in providing us only with a Christ who is a chief, an ancestor or an elder, a master of initiation, or a healer, as one recent book shows.[8]

Faced by such so-called African representations, we recognize perhaps the insignificance of the Jesus Christ of the missionary churches who, instead of becoming a personal and tangible reality, is presented like an abstract entity locked within the conceptual framework of Greco-Latin philosophies. At a time when the urgent need for Christology is felt in Africa, it is imperative to liberate the faith of the local churches from formulae that have the effect of obscuring Jesus from being recognized by other people because they emanate from a sort of foreign cultural monopoly. Shouldn't we question the validity of approaches that take no consideration at all of the tensions and conflicts in the context of which the people of today hear the gospel in contemporary African traditional societies? In fact, if it behooves us to see Jesus Christ "beyond models,"[9] it is imperative to avoid the anachronism of figures who would propose to us an African Christ "outside the here and now." What seems harmful to us in the African churches, where the debate on Christ becomes a necessity, is that the desire for cultural adaptation more or less unintentionally succeeds in separating the cross from "the ways of African Christology." But can Jesus be really present among us without the cross? To be more precise, who is the One "whose mystery we confess" without ever joining him in the tragedy of his Passion? In short, can one claim the gospel when one presents an African Christ while at the same time remaining totally silent on this very tragedy? Must not we also see the crucified with our own African eyes? Here we cannot evade the question that still persists: "And you, what do you say? Who am I to you?" We have to get out of the dead-ends of ethnotheology in order to respond to this unavoidable question.

The Historical Experience of the African

The challenge that the African theologian should take up requires a double effort. We should remember Jesus Christ (2 Tim. 2:8) and rediscover his proper identity. To do so, it is sufficient to inquire into his life, words, and acts. We should also rediscover our proper identity in such a way that Jesus Christ becomes part and parcel of our memory. Given that the Bible speaks of God and human beings in the same breath, our view of Jesus Christ is inseparable from the understanding we have of ourselves. It is therefore imperative that we try to seize the core of the meaning of the faith in the very context in which we

---

8. See also Robert Schreiter, ed., *Faces of Jesus in Africa* (Maryknoll, N.Y.: Orbis Books, 1991).

9. François Kabasele, "L'au-delà des modèles," in F. Kabasele, J. Doré, and R. Luneau, eds., *Chemins de la Christologie africaine* (Paris: Desclée, 1986), 203.

recognize ourselves and our situation in the world. In such a perspective, we have to reject any talk that absolutizes Jesus by denying him any real rooting in the historical experiences that mark the life of the African.

The story of the gospel is the place from where there springs up a basic personality who has marked the foundational event of the faith. But our retelling of this event is always done in a particular context. We never speak out of nowhere. We need to come back to the traditions that Africa invents about its own self and avoid the many approaches that were distorted because they applied concepts of Western knowledge to the realities specific to Africa. Mudimbe has made an inventory of such approaches in an erudite book.[10]

It cannot be denied that, since the meeting of Africa with the West, a tradition has arisen about ourselves, about our African experience in history, in the midst of the tensions and conflicts that have marked our imagination. Life histories, songs and worship, myths and symbols, forms of struggle and resistance belong to this imagination that constitutes the privileged context where Africans recognize themselves and their condition. Whenever society is gripped by the crises and challenges of the day, it goes back to its imagination to construct a specific identity. Reconstructed each time, "the tradition" becomes a resource to update the materials used in art and music, languages belonging to the popular culture, the written and oral stories, the religious and political life. All these areas that the memory takes hold of lead us to the center of our historical consciousness. Taking into consideration the importance of the places where the profound imagination of a people is shaped, we ought to rediscover the African across these places where memory is invested. Our society never ceases maintaining its relationship with these stations. It finds there the ground for its own comprehension; it draws from them materials through which it makes sense of itself. African theologians cannot therefore spare the memory if they want to hear the narrative of the Passion of Jesus Christ in the specific places where the concrete and historical dimensions of the African imagination are rooted.

Without deepening the analyses, it suffices for us to determine the "place" from which springs up, in our view, the brutal and massive reality of a continent whose life and history are tied to a long, drawn-out agony. Africa is this ancient land where humanity has been treated with contempt for many centuries. In a sense, analyzing the experience of the African means to attempt to construct an anthropology of misfortune, to plunge deep into a history of suffering tied to the domination of this region of the planet by the West since the Renaissance. We need to come back here to the long debate on Africa that started from the point of view of the West. Beginning in the year 1492, which constitutes a sort of foundational myth on which the economy of our era, the shape of nations and the names of countries are based,[11] the world is no longer the West, but it is

---

10. V. Mudimbe, *The Invention of Africa: Gnosis, Philosophy, and the Order of Knowledge* (Bloomington: Indiana University Press, 1988).

11. See also "1492: État de lieux," *Magazine Littéraire* 296 (February 1992): 23–24.

rather the West that dominates the world. In this context, the meeting of the West with Africa takes place in the form of violence. It seems that "Western Reason has to subject one to violence as its condition and as its instrument, for whoever differs from it is found in a state of 'sin' and falls therefore into the unacceptable state of the irrational."[12] In order to situate properly the agony of the African in the history of modern times, it is necessary to bring this paradox to light: "we find in the spirit of our civilization," says P. Castres, "and coextensive with its history, the close interrelationship of violence and Reason, the latter succeeding in establishing its demanding rule only by means of the former."[13]

At the beginning of our historical experience, there has been since the Renaissance this incapacity of Western civilization "to recognize and accept the Other as such, its refusal to let live that which is not identical with it."[14] Ever since the West launched its technical know-how, its culture, and its faith for the conquest of the tropics, the different peoples that it met on its way have been given up to extinction and death. A sort of specific suffering is tied to the condition of peoples who clash with Western expansion beyond its frontiers. Deprivation of one's own self, massacres, annihilation of indigenous cultures, systems of exclusion or destruction do not constitute abnormalities of the system. They belong to this form of savagery that the West carries along with itself from a "culture of intolerance and violence" that belongs intrinsically to it. "The archaeology" of this culture brings to light the "places of memory" where our conscience is rooted.

Let us dwell on the enslavement of blacks, which comes out as one of the most profound and tragic wounds of humanity from which countries like England, Spain, France, Portugal, as well as the United States have profited immensely.[15] Linked directly to the genocide of millions of Indians who had perished in the wholesale massacre that was the conquest of the Americas by the Europeans, the African slave trade is the consequence of the development of the great colonial plantations. It came to an end only when it began to slow down the development of industrial capitalism. Up to the beginning of the nineteenth century, Africans were subjected to the reign of sugar and King Cotton, while the Atlantic slave trade was organized and became a profitable economic market. State monopoly established itself in Europe by means of the commercial companies that brought together public and private capital. We can imagine the immense demographic drainage provoked by the slave trade. It compromised drastically the future of the peoples of West Africa, who had attained a degree of economic development and a cultural level far superior to that of their masters. In the course of the centuries in which Africa became, in the words of Marx, "a sort of a rabbit warren of commerce for hunting black skins," the number

---

12. P. Castres, "Entre silence et dialogue," in *L'ARC* 26, 76.
13. Ibid.
14. Ibid.
15. See Eric Williams, *Capitalism and Slavery: The Caribbean* (London: Trafalgar Sq./David and Charles, 1964).

of African victims of slave trade reached about 200 million. While it paralyzed the growth of Africa through demographic bleeding and the resultant enormous loss of human resources, the slave trade enabled Europe to accumulate enormous capital, which contributed in turn in the nineteenth century to the take-off of the great Industrial Revolution. Cities in Europe like Nantes, Bordeaux, and La Rochelle, which traded blacks, owe their prosperity to the triangular trade. Marx has demonstrated the high level of tribute paid by Africa to the development of British capitalism. As the history of Liverpool shows, the slave trade laid the foundation for the greatness of Europe and constituted the entire method of primitive accumulation.[16] In other words, in a time of progress of commerce and transport, power, riches, and the funds of the metropolis in the West — all the fruit of the slave trade — the slaves experienced a long, drawn-out agony.

We need to recall that before their arrival in the New World the sick slaves, who ran the risk of not being sold and for whom the slave traders did not want to pay taxes, were thrown into the sea. This happened mainly to the babies, who were more susceptible to illness during the voyage. Before their sale in America, the slaves were fed by force and sometimes given drugs, in order to be presented in good shape, even if the size of their muscles and the brightness of their skin were artificial and did not last long. Once again there occurred the same scenes that occurred in the departure from Africa: inspection of teeth, eyes, sex, feet and hands, blows to test the resistance of the subject, or rather the object. Some went so far as to taste the sweat of the captive in order to verify whether the brilliance of the skin was due to an artificial polish.

The agony of the slaves was not over when they finally were purchased by a master in Brazil or Cuba or North America. A second chapter was only about to begin. The slave had no rights at all. We find such announcements as this: "For sale, a house ... with sixteen squares of land, kitchen, store, rabbit hutch, fully equipped, a horse, four niggers ... "[17] After Louis XIV enacted the slave laws, which in legal terms is one of the most monstrous texts of history, black persons were neither citizens, nor human beings, not even animals: they were things, furniture, payable and retrievable just like a sum of money or any other personal property. In the view of French law, the black person had become an object. The Black Code is a real journey to the extremes of infamy.[18] Captured in Africa and thrown into the squalid belly of a ship trading in blacks, the slaves were delivered to a whip in rhythm with the agony of the crossing of the sea.

To be ripped by the whip, to be mutilated by other much crueler punishments, these are the daily sufferings of the blacks, until their energy had been devoured by hunger, work, devilish treatments, misery, and

---

16. Karl Marx, *The Capital,* Book I, vol. 3.
17. J. Ki Zerbo, *L'Histoire de l'Afrique Noire* (Paris: Édition Hatier, 1978), 216.
18. See L. Sala-Molins, *Le Code Noir ou le Calvaire de Canaan* (Paris: P.U.F., 1987).

hopelessness. Alas! unfortunate mortals, how greatly you agonize! Your executioners are called Christians.[19]

To solve the problem of the shortage of sugar, cotton, and coffee for the European market, the blacks were subjected to the worst corporal punishment if they made the least attempt to run away. For running away was for a long time the only means of escaping the harsh conditions imposed by the slave holders, "terrifying conditions that, most often, exceeded the human capacity to bear suffering," notes a black Brazilian historian.[20] Wandering in the vicinity of the plantations in order to survive by undertaking small raids, the fugitives were soon captured by the headhunters, "the captains of the forest," who specialized in such a function. After their capture they were subjected to the cruelest tortures to serve as examples to others. A most severely repressive measure was prescribed against the slaves of Guinea and Angola who revolted by forming the nucleus of the resistance that organized the fugitive slaves.

On the African continent, "permanent insecurity, wars, and incessant raids that generated misery and famine became the characteristic traits of Black Africa."[21] This situation never changed as long as the interests of capitalism demanded new forms of ransacking. If slavery disappeared, oppression still continued. When the change from slavery to colonialism took place after the Berlin conference, the condition of blacks became nothing other than the continuation of slavery. Without doubt, the era of the slave trader was only the most brutal form, the most naked exploitation of human beings by human beings, which is at the heart of capitalism. But along with the colonial plantations, the forced labor, and the period of destitution that have their rightful places in the memory of the African peoples, we find the same violence, the same brutality, the same contempt that, since the sixteenth century, marks the meeting of Africa with Europe. "Suffer, poor nigger! Black like misery!" sings David Diop. In Africa, where disembarked

> Those who invented the compass,
> Those who were able to domesticate steam, electricity,
> Those who explored the seas, the sky.

With the history of sugar, coffee or rubber, bananas or cotton, what we recall is the misery — moral as well as physical. This misery is the result of a conflictual situation where, as demonstrated in the works of Césaire, we find these polemical couplets: master/slave; colonizer/colonized; oppressor/oppressed; reason/folly; dominant race/race that wailed in torture; good nigger/bad nigger. We find the concentration of the entire history of Africa in these opposites. This history has been called trade, colonization, lynching, whip, dungeon, red hot

---

19. S. Quartin, "L'esclavage de Noirs," in *L'Économie du Tiers-Monde* (May–June 1977).
20. Quoted by Quartin, "L'esclavage de Noirs."
21. J. Suret-Canale, *Afrique Noire* (Paris: Éditions Sociales, 1973), 203–4.

iron seal. It is a history of misfortune that in the final analysis, goes back to a long past. It was incarnated in the hard labors of the high Nile of ancient Egypt, and then in the raids carried out by Mauritanian traders; still later it was continued in the raids of the Arabs, an inexhaustible source of domestic workers, dockers for Baghdad, Istanbul, and other cities, and in the journey in the depths of slave ships to the New World. No one has journeyed as much as the blacks "since Élam, since Akkad, since Sumer," says Césaire. As a matter of fact, black people incarnate in their very selves the agony of all the exploited of the modern world. "There is no one in the world," says Césaire, "be it a poor lynched person, a poor tortured person in whom I am not assassinated and humiliated." In short, "I will be a Jew, a Hindu of Calcutta, a person from Harlem who cannot see. The person-starvation, the person-insult, the person-torture...."[22] Such are the Africans who have experienced in their bodies and in their spirits the consequences of the dialectic of master and slave in all their forms.

These are times of revisionism, when "advocacy on behalf of the Third World" is a beast to be "knocked down."[23] Such advocacy was the origin of the "sobs of the white man," when colonialism and imperialism questioned the innocence of the West in the face of the agony of the ancient slaves. In this context, some have been tempted to relativize what happened to Africans when persons became things. After all, Africans would not be the only case; other peoples have suffered as much as Africans. We ought to remember, for example, the extermination of the Jews during the Nazi era. In addition, should not Africans take their part of the blame as far as colonial violence is concerned? For nothing took place without their close "collaboration." In fact, colonial domination, like the slave trade, had become a lucrative "source" to the indigenous population when interest groups had known how to "use" the structures of inequality and oppression and, in this way, contributed to the martyrdom of their own people. But, as Achille Mbembe has noted, "the use of African 'dependence' by local agents as 'resources' in the control of the local market does not remove the reality of structural domination that weighs heavily on black societies."[24] From this point of view, whatever may have been the scale of the "complicity" of native agents, Gorée still remains the symbol of the historical suffering of the African. This historical fact on its own reintroduces in the center of the modern culture an essential evil that requires apology and penitence, as was recalled by Pope John Paul II during his latest visit to black Africa.[25]

What we cannot hide today is the impact of age-old conditions of alienation and oppression on the imagination of African societies. Such conditions have not lost their contemporary power. It is what happens when blacks accept and interiorize the stereotypes, the prejudices, and the myths of blackness, the false

---

22. Aimé Cesaire, *Discourse on Colonialism* (New York: Monthly Review Press, 1972).

23. See *Le Monde Diplomatique* (May 1985).

24. Achille Mbembe, *Afriques Indociles* (Paris: Karthala, 1988), 136.

25. Pope John Paul II came back to this topic during his trip to Cameroun and Senegal, especially during his visit to the island of Gorée.

images and the degrading portraits that the masters have inculcated in their sub-jects. If in relative terms colonization had been of short duration, slavery, in contrast, was practiced for more than three hundred years. This experience af-fects profoundly the life of a people and their culture. One cannot with impunity reduce a people to the status of an object, in a context where the masters of Western thought, as Hegel reminds us, have agreed to exclude Africans from the status of the human in order to throw them back to the status of animals, locked within biological and basic needs.[26] In a sense, the Africans are these "millions of people in whom one has knowingly inculcated fear, an inferiority complex, trembling, debasement, hopelessness, a servant mentality."[27] Across the diverse attitudes and behaviors, "stunned by a cultural invasion that marginalizes them, the confused Africans are today the deformed images of the other."[28] It is neces-sary to take into consideration here "the irrationality of mimicry," which is the consequence of a real social pathology rooted in the indigenous populations; in it the colonized end up by accepting the myths invented by the West to legit-imize its domination. Such a situation is analyzed in the book by Frantz Fanon, *Black Skins, White Masks.* It finds its place, in a profound way, in this sys-tem of "annihilation" and "anthropological poverty" of which Engelbert Mveng speaks.[29]

From such a point of view, the flag independences have in no way changed this situation. Under regimes where, for thirty years, power has been exercised in the context of a prison system and where these states have become deserts of human rights,[30] black persons persecute their brothers and sisters, pillage and ransom them. In a sense, the system of the dungeon has been restored by the postcolonial states, where access to power enables one not only to accumulate but also to kill.[31] Here and there, violence tends to become a real method of gov-ernment. Under the iron-fisted regimes and the absurd dictatorships that have led to the political emasculation of millions of Africans and to the strangulation of their societies, we find once again the weight of slavery, whose influence in the formation of the political systems of contemporary Africa should be underlined. Edem Kodjo has observed it well:

> In its conception as well as in its organization, postcolonial power in Af-rica gets its direct inspiration from the power imagined by the slave traders

---

26. See Hegel, *Reason in History: A General Introduction to the Philosophy of History* (New York: Macmillan, 1953).

27. Aimé Césaire, *Discourse on Colonialism* (New York: Monthly Review Press, 1972).

28. See also Engelbert Mveng, *L'Afrique dans L'Église: Paroles d'un croyant* (Paris: L'Harmattan, 1985), 85–87.

29. Engelbert Mveng, "Third World Theology — What Theology? What Third World?: Evalu-ation by an African Delegate," in V. Fabella and S. Torres, eds., *Irruption of the Third World: Challenge to Theology* (Maryknoll, N.Y.: Orbis Books, 1983), 220.

30. On this topic see, Jean-Marc Éla, *African Cry* (Maryknoll, N.Y.: Orbis Books, 1991).

31. *Politique Africaine* 7 (1982).

and relayed by colonization, whose practice it continues. It crystallizes itself in this phenomenon that we have called "obscure despotism."[32]

We find ourselves here in the midst of a history characterized by "the repetition of imbecility" taking into account the extent of mechanisms that reproduce the structures of inequality and domination.[33]

There is no doubt that Africa is not a tragic continent where all sense of dignity and joy of life have disappeared irretrievably. Beyond the Afro-pessimism nourished by the old myths of the curse of Ham, which never ceases enumerating the symptoms of African evils by exhibiting the specter of rampant tyrannies, of tribalism, of famines and violence, it is also imperative not only to see an exclusively suffering Africa, but also an Africa of struggle and resistance. We need to emphasize this side if we do not want to repeat the Western speeches by reappropriating the apocalyptic images of a drifting continent, "sinking," "a disaster area" — a modern reproduction of the title of a book that appeared in 1945, *Africa Commits Suicide*. In reality, Africa is a grouping of societies that are historical because they are societies that have suffered. In order to weigh exactly the extent of the historical suffering of this continent, it is necessary to go back to the original experiences, like the slave trade, colonialism, and the "postcolonial era," that have marked profoundly the subconscious of African societies. At a time when the rich nations do not cease pulling the cord that strangles Africa, strategists are busy finding ways and means of reducing our societies to outlets for the fury of the great powers, and even into an immense garbage can of the North. Thus stripped of folklore, reality appears dark and brutal. Like yesterday, Africa has not ceased being a land of poverty, oppression, and violence. Such is the place of our memory, as Césaire cries out:

> What blood in our memory,
>   In my memory are the lagoons.
>   They are covered by skulls of the dead.
>   My memory is wrapped up in blood.
> My memory has its girdle of corpses.[34]

Such a memory, which is the real dimension of our faithfulness to our very selves, the origin of all our other faithfulnesses, appears quite obviously like the memory of the agony of the African. For it refers itself back to the traumatic events whose consequences structure our imagination.

---

32. Edem Kodjo, *Et Demaine L'Afrique* (Paris: Stock, 1985). 157.
33. See Mbembes, *Afriques Indociles.*
34. On the works of Césaire, see M. and M. Ngal, *Aimé Césaire: Un homme à la recherche d'une patrie* (Dakar: Nea, 1975).

Jesus, the Crucified

In this context, what does a Christ dressed up in a leopard's skin like a Bantu chief signify? In order to define the stakes of the theological debate in Africa, it is necessary to ask which God has been preached in the missionary churches that had remained over the centuries an integral part of the dominant society. For it is not self-evident that the Christ of the gospels identifies himself with the Christ of the slave traders proposed by the churches. The churches have had the tendency to cover up the concrete and historical dimensions of the message of God so that "the theology of the salvation of souls" has triumphed.[35] The meaning of Christianity is called into question in situations lived out by blacks where for many years Voodoo was the only means of protest in the land of slavery.[36] If we do not wish to leave in the hands of the prophetic movements that have proliferated since the era of colonialism the monopoly of recapturing the liberating potential of the gospel through the irruption of "Black Christs,"[37] shouldn't we turn toward the crucified of Golgotha through whom we question ourselves regarding our own destiny? Finding its place in the center of the religious drama, the historical experience of the black person is a theological *locus* that we should pick up in order to read the passion story on the paths of suffering where the crucified Jesus appears as the prototype of the African.[38] In societies where the meeting of Africa and the gospel is tarnished by a great deal of misunderstanding[39] and raises questions that should neither be eluded nor dodged, what has been sought for many generations is a face-to-face encounter with Jesus Christ on the basis of a history of the servitude and oppression that sheds light on our history. "On the day of truth," writes Father Mveng, "all these noises will disappear, leaving us alone crucified with Jesus Christ. Then from our cross to his cross rises one and the same clamor: "Eli! Eli! Lema Sabachthani?" (My God, my God, why have you forsaken me?)[40]

If it is impossible for us to throw a veil of shame over our real condition in history, it is because this is the very place from where the "great black cry" springs, the cry that joins the anguished appeal of the crucified of Golgotha. African theologians have the urgent task of integrating the most profound aspects of the Passion of Christ; otherwise they will "pass by on the other side" of their historic mission. We need to extract ourselves from pious abstractions

---

35. See O. M. Bimwenyi-Kweshi, *Discours théologique Négro-Africaine* (Paris: Présence Africaine, 1981).

36. Éla, *African Cry,* 60.

37. On this topic, read the preface of R. Bastide to the book of M. Sinda, *Le Messianisme Conglais et ses incidences politiques* (Paris: Payot, 1972).

38. Bénézet Bujo, "Pour une éthique africaino-christocentrique," *Bulletin de Théologie Africaine* 3, no. 5 (January–June 1981): 41–52.

39. On this misunderstanding, read the novel of Mongo Beti, *The Poor Christ of Bomba* (Oxford: Heinemann, 1971).

40. Mveng, *L'Afrique dans L'Église: Paroles d'un croyant,* 5.

that compromise the truth of the gospel and constitute a real obstacle in the encounter between Africa and Jesus of Nazareth. Instead of soaring in the absolute and thus evading our historic responsibilities by hiding ourselves in the reproduction of hollow formulae or the resumption of old myths and symbols, it is a matter of following the Christ in his "Kenosis" to grasp the features of his face through the historical experiences of the black person. "In truth," notes Father Hebga, "Jesus is ours through the depth of his human humiliation.... We are related to Christ in humiliation."[41]

With St. Augustine, we need to emphasize the realism of the incarnation that is the basis of our relationship with Jesus on the cross:

> It was necessary that he become human to be arrested, human to be seen, human to be struck, human finally to be crucified and die. It is therefore as a human being that he came close to all these sufferings that would have not affected him had he not become human.[42]

In a sense, the cross completes the incarnation. "Put to death in the flesh" (1 Pet. 3:18–22), the crucified is truly the one who "in coming into the world says: ... a body you have prepared for me ... to do your will" (Heb. 10:5, 7, 9). Since the agony when he began "to be greatly distressed and agitated" (Mark 14:33) and "his sweat became like great drops of blood falling down on the ground" (Luke 22:44), it is truly "this man" (Acts 2:23) who, through the testing of the Passion, has passed through "the pangs of death" (Acts 2:24). Never has the communion of Christ with the human condition been so total as in this moment of his life where he "in every respect has been tested as we are" (Heb. 4:15), where, in the final analysis, he himself "became a curse for us" (Gal. 3:13).

But what happened to "Jesus of Nazareth, who was Crucified" (Mark 16:6) finds its place in the history of salvation. To understand properly the agony of his death, it has to be situated in God's own plan (Luke 24:7, 26, 46; cf. Acts 2:23). In this decisive turning point where "it is finished" (John 19:30), shouldn't we understand the meaning of the engagement of Jesus in "the death on a cross" (Phil. 2:8) on the basis of the specific ties that the poor and exploited have with him, taking into account a secret complicity with the tortured of Golgotha, which a rereading of the Bible suggests? Beyond the historical-critical studies that attempt to understand Jesus by concentrating on the relationship between the meaning of the gospels and history,[43] it seems necessary to explore how Jesus Christ is our contemporary by examining his radical choices, his convictions, his faith and message that tie his destiny to that of the poor and

---

41. Meinrad Hebga, "Un malaise grave," in *Personalité africaine et Catholicisme* (Paris: Présence Africaine, 1963), 10.

42. See Saint Augustine, *On Psalms.*

43. From among the numerous publications, one may refer to examples such as Kasper, *Jesus the Christ* (New York: Paulist Press, 1977).

the little ones (Matt. 25:32, 46). Is it a pure coincidence that the Gospel of Matthew announces the drama of the passion (Matt. 26:1–4) right after the section where the Christ identifies himself with the poor? Everything takes place as if the suffering and the death of the one who had been "handed over and rejected in the presence of Pilate" (Acts 3:13) would attain their true dimension and full significance only with reference to the plight of the poor and the excluded. In the view of the scriptures that clarify it, the sacrificial death of Jesus (Heb. 9:11–14; 10:10) is that of the "suffering servant," whose image, with reference to the oracle of Isaiah (52–53), has played a major role in the understanding and the preaching of the early church (Acts 3:12, 26; 8:28–36; Luke 22:37; Matt. 8:17; Rom. 10:16; 15:21; 1 Pet 2:24–25). This man, whose "destruction" (Luke 18) and crucifixion (Luke 23:21; Mark 15:13–14; Matt. 27:22–23) the people demanded, is "the Holy and Righteous One" (Acts 3:14) whose innocence is recognized by Pilate (Luke 23:4, 14, 22; Acts 13:28; John 18:38; 19:4, 6; Matt. 27:24–25).

The violence to which Jesus was subjected after being condemned is that of the one who "did not open his mouth like a lamb that is led to the slaughter" (Isa. 53:7; Acts 8:32). Jesus was confronted with this violence as early as his birth when he was forced to be a refugee in Egypt to flee from Herod, who was looking for him "to destroy him" (Matt. 2:13–15). In the course of his life he was exposed to violence in the conflicts that arose because of his disturbing words (Luke 20:21; Matt. 14:57–58; John 11:47–50). "The case of Jesus" reminds us of the biblical story of Joseph, who was sold by his brothers (Acts 7:9). If Moses had been "pushed aside" (Acts 7:27) and persecuted (v. 52), Jesus was "betrayed and murdered" (v. 52). As noted by Stephen, Jesus identified himself with the Righteous One announced by the prophets because he had to (v. 52). In addition, it was necessary that he be one of the prophets who were persecuted and killed (v. 52).

If the passion of Jesus is the fulfillment of the scriptures (Luke 24:25–27, 44–46; John 19:36, 37), the suffering of Jesus must be considered as the suffering and death of the poor and the oppressed. Such is the meaning of Psalm 22:2, which the crucified of Golgotha recites (Matt. 27:46; Mark 15:34). "They crucified him" (Mark 15:24): such is the utter humiliation imposed on the One who is condemned, whose innocence however is acknowledged. Originating in the East, such torture had been reserved by the Romans to seditious foreigners, to criminals, and to ruffians.[44] "In a place called the Skull," Jesus was crucified between two criminals, "one on his right and one on his left" (Luke 23:33). Beginning with the Roman occupation, the Jews had known such a punishment, especially in connection with the revolts in Galilee. The crowd thus demanded that Jesus be subjected to the punishment given to rebels (Mark 15:15). But

---

44. See F. Varillon, *L'Humilité de Dieu* (Paris: Le Centurion, 1974). One would profit from reading the works of M. Hengel, *Crucifixion in the Ancient World and the Folly of the Message of the Cross* (Philadelphia: Fortress Press, 1977) and Hans-Ruedi Weber, *The Cross: Tradition and Interpretation* (London: SPCK, 1979).

crucifixion was also the punishment for slaves in the Roman Empire. In this context, where the revolt of slaves sapped the energy of Roman capitalism, this torture was meted out as a shameful example to discourage any attempt at sedition. For the execution on the cross, said Cicero, "is the most cruel and the most shameful torture."

The death of Jesus finds its place in the context of a culture of violence, which, according to Roman law, punished those who were condemned to cruelty and shame on account of their social status. Crucifixion was a form of "barbaric" execution of the highest cruelty, violence, torture, and, definitely, shame. In this sense, Jesus the Crucified took upon himself the agony of the history of slavery that takes place in the countries where the local despots reinvent the "Black Code" against their peoples. Death on a cross is the ultimate humiliation of the One who "emptied himself, taking the form of a slave" (Phil. 2:7). What is at stake here is the agony of the humiliated. In uttering "a loud cry" (Mark 15:37; Luke 23:46), Jesus on the cross actualized the cry of the poor and the wretched (Pss. 34:7, 69, 70, 72, 77). In his passion he took upon himself the oppression and the injustice born by the Black Continent. In modern societies where the fact of being an African is a great challenge, tied as it is to a tragic and shameful history, we find here "a memory of the suffering" of the African. The slaughtered Lamb "recapitulates" the history of suffering in Africa, where the powers of death have been active for many centuries. The scourging of Jesus (Mark 15:15), the insults and the gestures of contempt, the scenes of derision and mockery (Luke 23:35, 39; Matt. 27:39–42) have meaning in the imagination of black persons. We cannot read the story of the Passion without finding ourselves in this history of contempt and of servitude that characterizes the destiny of blacks. In a sense, Jesus the Crucified is the African humiliated and oppressed for centuries.

It is necessary to understand here the depth of the humiliation of Jesus Christ (Phil. 2:8). Beyond his incarnation, which is already in itself "a living among us" (John 1:14), the Christ roots pain in the being of God through his body, which he subjected to outrageous shame on the cross. Such is the message of the gospel "in these last days when he [God] has spoken to us by a Son" (Heb. 1:2). The New Testament invites us to understand the destiny and history of Jesus in this "descent," which is death on the cross. But he who humiliates himself to such an extent is the one who is "in the form of God" (Phil. 2:6). Through the drama of the Passion, we recognize the suffering humanity of Jesus who said: "Whoever has seen me has seen the Father" (John 14:9). The crucifixion is the application of a tradition of sonship (Phil. 2:6; Luke 22:42). The crucified places his death under the sign of abandonment by God: "Father, into your hands I commend my spirit" (Luke 23:46).

We have to see God in this personal relationship with the Father that remains true "up to death on a cross." Jesus lived this unique relationship "up to the end," in a concrete way, in the death in which God's sympathy and passion for humanity are unveiled. Through Jesus of Nazareth, who is in fact the presence of God in the world, the love of God is manifested definitively in the agony in which he suffered his passion "under Pontius Pilate" and was buried. In short, Jesus accepts the task of perfecting the revelation of God to humanity through the mystery of the cross, which makes us understand the meaning of suffering of the black person in history. Taking into consideration the image that one has of God outside the gospel, "the word of the cross" can only be "a stumbling block to Jews and foolishness to Gentiles" (1 Cor. 1:23–24). But it is in weakness that God reveals his power. In other words, it is necessary to learn to contemplate God from "below," in the humiliation in which God is engaged in the drama of the crucified throughout history.

We need to deepen the meaning of the scandal that is at the heart of the gospel by emphasizing the destiny of the poor in the revelation of God in the crucified Jesus. For as St. Paul reminds us, "God chose what is foolish in the world to shame the wise; God chose what is weak in the world to shame the strong; God chose what is low and despised in the world, things that are not, to reduce to nothing things that are" (1 Cor. 1:27–28). Because the rich and the powerful of this world have the tendency to confiscate God, it is necessary to reread the gospel from the side of "the people who have no importance": the crucified messiah has linked once for all the mystery of God to the agony of those "without dignity."

Theology under the Tree

On the basis of these reflections we measure "the stakes of God" in a world of domination and servitude by taking into consideration the specific relationship of the Crucified with the "powerless." It is not self-evident that the church has always shouldered fully this "scandal." Since the conversion of Constantine, when Christianity was transformed from a religion of the people into a civil religion, integrating itself perfectly into the mechanisms of domination, theologians have avoided the reference to Jesus as "the suffering servant," preferring instead other titles such as "the Son of God," "Lord," and "Logos." As Cullmann has demonstrated well, the title of "servant," frequently applied to Jesus by the gospels, has not given rise here to any theological elaboration, while that of "Lord" (*Kurios*) has played a well-known role.[45] Given the conditions following the fourth century, in which the great dogmas were elaborated, taking an emperor's title and applying it to Christ was not innocent. Is not the transfer of terms here the reflection of the established order, serving in fact the preservation of the order?

Seized by the powers and without wishing it or recognizing it, with a sort of naiveté related to its places of production, theology became one of the building

---

45. See Oscar Cullmann, *Christology of the New Testament* (Philadelphia: Westminster, 1963; London: SCM, 1963), chap. 3.

blocks of the imperial order. An imperial image of Jesus Christ has served as an alibi for all the crusades and colonial enterprises in places designated pagan, where the "Christian" nations were more preoccupied with the accumulation of riches than with spreading the light of the gospel. One finds without difficulty the features of a slave-trading Christ in Christian institutions created during the period of the Enlightenment, when it was no scandal at all to give the name "Liberty," "Jean-Jacques Rousseau," or "Social Contract" to the ships in which blacks began their agony.

We should reexamine colonial Christianity to articulate how the evangelization of Africa reappropriated the critical function of the cross in a context where the exploitation of blacks attained a scale never seen before. Within the slave-trading states, the type of sermons that the missionary churches tolerated was a form of the proclamation of the gospel that emphasized internal conversion, penitence, suffering in hell, and the salvation of souls. Even today, do not the neo-colonial churches run the risk of transforming the miserable villages and the popular sectors into a vast religious market where the Great Capital does not hesitate to finance sects and manipulate the credulous in order to control the galley slaves of famine and to hinder the poor from committing acts of folly in the conflicts where they have nothing to lose? There seems to be an urgency to pull down Christianity in Africa by an effort to separate it from all the attempts that the local churches make to promote the ambiguous ties between "Revelation and Domination."[46] For if Christianity is to avoid falling into the tragedy of being insignificant, it must take up the challenge posed by poverty and oppression in societies where it is imperative today to dare rethink the gospel from the perspective of the suffering of "the strangled Africa."

We cannot permit ourselves to limit the debate on the meaning of the death of Jesus to the theology of the salvation of unbelievers. To be faithful to the gospel, we are called to bring the Crucified to memory through the resources of Africa, on the basis of fundamental situations where we rediscover the actuality of God "who has brought down the mighty from their thrones, and lifted up the lowly" (Luke 1:52). From this moment on, African theology will be born from the ashes of colonial Christianity. It springs up out of a genuine "descent into hell" in a context where the gospel of Jesus Christ is Good News for slaves. A new understanding of the cross that transcends dogmatic fences behind which it is no longer possible to "let God be God" imposes itself on the Christian churches. In this connection, Martin Luther seems to have locked up the theology of the cross in the temples. It is a question here of opposing the scandal of the cross to justification through the works of the law. The task consists in liberating humanity from its excessiveness and in submitting it to the grasp of the cross with the aim of preventing human beings from manipulating God.[47] Absorbed as it is by the problem of individual salvation, such a theology proves incapable

---

46. See F. Eboussi-Boulaga, *Christianity without Fetishes: An African Critique and Recapture of Christianity* (Maryknoll, N.Y.: Orbis Books, 1991).

47. On this problem, refer to my doctoral dissertation: "Transcendence de Dieu et existence

of bringing out the critical and liberating power of the cross. Consequently, we need to go out of the temples and learn to "see the world from the perspective of the cross."[48] In this view, everything takes place as if the Spirit had given the churches fresh possibilities to reread the gospel from the perspective of the forgotten of the earth. As Moltmann has proposed,

> The task therefore remained of developing the theology of the cross in the direction of an understanding of the world and of history. The theology of the cross had to be worked out not merely for the reform of the church but as social criticism, in association with practical actions to set free both the wretched and their rulers.[49]

In fact, taking into consideration the "collusion" of Jesus with the weak and the excluded of history in Golgotha, God is revealed through marginalization and subjects the world to judgment.

If Jesus Christ is not this depraved God used to tranquilize the poor and the humiliated, we need to tell the story of the agony of the passion in remembering this basic fact: on the cross, Jesus changed an instrument of humiliation into an instrument of struggle for life. This interpretation puts to a severe test the dogmatics viewed from above with universalist aims — a dogmatics that has been imposed on dominated and marginalized peoples and enabling the poor blacks to withstand their pain better in the hope of a heavenly bliss. Faced by the great challenges of contemporary Africa, we are called from the places where, in Christ, our history opens up the eyes of our faith to a God struggling to abolish all sorts of inhumanity from the land of Africa. We need therefore to come back to the foot of the tree of the cross to let the liberating potential of the gospel shine.

One thing is sure:

> When our church does not consent to live a life generously surrendered for the cause of God in the cause of today's exploited and oppressed classes, when it allows itself to be paralyzed with fear and does not remember its martyrs in solidarity with the people, we have the right to ask if it has new eyes to recognize the crucified Lord in the disfigured faces of the impoverished people of the Third World (see Puebla, nos. 31–39).[50]

In this case, the challenge that needs to be taken up today is that of "theology under the tree" — that theology elaborated where Christians and churches,

---

humain selon Luther: Essai d'introduction à la logique d'une théologie," University of Strasbourg, 1969.

48. Jean-Marc Éla, *My Faith as an African* (Maryknoll, N.Y.: Orbis Books, 1988).

49. Jürgen Moltmann, *The Crucified God: The Cross of Christ as the Foundation and Criticism of Christian Theology* (New York: Harper & Row, 1974), 72, 73.

50. "Final Document," in S. Torres and J. Eagleson, eds., *The Challenge of Basic Christian Communities* (Maryknoll, N.Y.: Orbis Books, 1981), 243.

based on the cross, listen to the "African Cry."[51] How can one believe in the Lord of life in African countries where "creation has been groaning... while we wait for adoption?" (Rom. 8:22–23). Such is the fundamental question that the understanding of the "language of the cross" on the basis of our experience in history imposes upon us. We catch a glimpse of the task of an African theology that should rethink the gospel from the perspective of "the table of the Magnificat," where God "has filled the hungry with good things, and sent the rich away empty" (Luke 1:47–56). This task is gargantuan; it has only just begun! One finds here only an outline, which may help in regiving this theology's entire strength to the scandal of Golgotha in our understanding of the faith. We cannot remember this man of Nazareth, crucified under Pontius Pilate, without questioning a society that tramples underfoot so many corpses and without awakening the hope that lives in the heart of the poor.

—Translated from the French by Yacob Tesfai

---

51. On this topic, Éla, *African Cry*; refer also to John M. Waliggo, "African Christology in a Situation of Suffering," in Robert S. Schreiter, ed., *Faces of Jesus in Africa* (Maryknoll, N.Y.: Orbis Books, 1991), 164–80.

Chapter 3

The Suffering of Human Divisions and the Cross

Simon S. Maimela

✝

Introduction

It is indeed a great honor for me to write this essay on one of the most fundamental concepts in Christian theology, namely, the cross and its implications for human suffering of divisions on the basis of race. However, I must also confess that it was with mixed feelings that I write on this theme because, for us as black South Africans, the questions of the cross and suffering are not issues that we can discuss in an abstract and theoretical way. For black people, the cross and suffering are experienced daily as a concrete and existential communal way of being in the white-dominated world. Indeed, for black South Africans who have been subjected to untold white racial hatred, contempt, and wanton violence simply because of their blackness, the theme of the cross and suffering raises the problem of theodicy, namely, how is God really there amid black oppression? How can God be justified before black suffering, which has been going on for such a long time?

Blacks have again and again experienced this perplexing feeling of abandonment by God when they are unable to discern God's presence in the midst of white racial oppression. Perhaps no one has expressed this better than Karl Goerdeler, a German conspirator against Hitler who, shortly before his execution, wrote:

> In sleepless nights I have often asked myself whether a God exists who shares in the personal fate of men. It is becoming hard to believe this. For this God must for years have allowed rivers of blood and suffering, and

mountains of horrors and despair for mankind to take place...He must have allowed millions of decent men to die and suffer without lifting a finger. Is this meant to be a judgment?...Like the psalmist, I am angry with God, because I cannot understand him....And yet through Christ I am still looking for the merciful God. I have not yet found him. O Christ, where is truth? Where is there any consolation?[1]

Black South Africans can easily identify with the sentiments expressed by Goerdeler as he languished in jail awaiting his appointment with death at the hands of Hitler's executioners. The cross and suffering are for us historical and given realities because we exist as victims of ongoing and, indeed, a long "Good Friday" of racial oppression and domination at the hands of white Christian settlers.[2] What is particularly painful in all this is not so much that black people have been experiencing this seemingly unending Good Friday but rather that racist white Christians attempted to abuse the theology of the cross by encouraging their black victims to carry their cross of suffering with dignity and without complaint as Jesus Christ carried his.[3] Indeed, we cannot but agree fully with Moltmann when he perceptively writes:

> The church has much abused the theology of the cross and the mysticism of the passion in the interest of those who cause the suffering. Too often, peasants, Indians and black slaves have been called upon by the representatives of the dominant religion to accept their sufferings as "their cross" and not to rebel against them. Luther need not have recommended the peasants to accept their sufferings as their cross. They already bore the burdens their masters imposed upon them. Instead, a sermon on the cross would have done the princes and the bourgeoisie who ruled them a great deal of good, if it was aimed at setting them free from their pride and moving them to an attitude of solidarity with their victims.[4]

Therefore, even as I accept the biblical proclamation that the birth, life, suffering, and death of Jesus Christ on the cross as well as his glorious resurrection provide the ultimate answer to all human suffering, I cannot for a moment forget that the theology of the cross is a double-edged sword that could be either a blessing or a curse. It all depends on who is talking about the theology of the cross, to whom it is addressed, and whose interests it intends serving. It could be a source of solace if it is proclaimed that Jesus suffered and died on the cross

---

1. Quoted in A. E. McGrath, *Luther's Theology of the Cross: Martin Luther's Theological Breakthrough* (London: Basil Blackwell, 1985), 179–80.
2. Simon S. Maimela, "The Crucified among the Crossbearers," *Missionalia* 13, no. 2 (August 1985): 85.
3. Manas Buthelezi, "Reconciliation and Liberation in South Africa," in Kenneth Y. Best, ed., *African Challenge* (Nairobi: Transafrica Publishers, 1975), 46.
4. Jürgen Moltmann, *The Crucified God: The Cross of Christ as the Foundation and Criticism of Christian Theology* (New York: Harper & Row, 1974), 49.

as an expression of God's solidarity with the poor and oppressed, taking their side, accompanying them in their search for their humanity, and assuring them that the crosses they bear at present will not be in vain but will be rewarded with victory — in the same manner that Jesus triumphed over evil by his resurrection from the dead.[5]

But it could also be a curse if the theology of the cross is used as "opium for the people," produced by those who have caused the suffering with a view to encouraging the victims of oppression to accept, in fatalistic resignation, their suffering under oppressive social structures as their fate, a way of life. As Buthelezi correctly points out, an endurance of such suffering, which cripples the initiatives of oppressed groups that are aimed at overcoming of it, serves no meaningful or redemptive purpose other than to cultivate a "cult, a form of idolatry and a sabotage of the design of God for the victims."[6]

Therefore, while the carrying of the cross and Christian suffering for the sake of our fellows is unavoidable in Christian life, it is absolutely essential that two kinds of suffering be distinguished in theological discourse. On the one hand, there is what could be referred to as an oppressive suffering, one not due just to the fateful cruelty of nature but is human made. In racial societies this form of suffering comes about as the result of the fact that society is designed by the dominant white group in such a way that blacks are perpetually dominated, exploited, and humiliated when they are denied political, social, and economic opportunities. On the other hand, there is redemptive suffering. This form of suffering is one that Christians take upon themselves after the model of Christ's suffering. Here suffering is not an end in itself, rather one suffers in order to realize the well-being of one's fellow human beings. It is suffering that flows out of love for others and is taken up by Christians who resolve to realize objectives that lie beyond suffering. Looked at from another angle, such a redemptive suffering is an expression of power over one's own suffering because it equips one to set aside one's own security and self-interests in order to serve the interests and security of one's fellow human beings. In South Africa, such redemptive suffering is exemplified by modern "martyrs" such as Nelson Mandela, Robert Sobukwe, and Steve Biko, who set aside their security and comforts by sacrificing themselves for their oppressed black masses. Their sacrifices and suffering are redemptive because they were meant to serve a higher cause beyond suffering itself, namely, the liberation of the oppressed blacks.[7]

In the light of the foregoing, any theology of the cross that tries to turn human suffering — which in the first place is evil — into some sort of virtue that is an end in itself must be rejected. It is highly oppressive of those it tries to train to regard as normal the state of being victims of evil and human oppression. Put

---

5. Maimela, "The Crucified among the Crossbearers," 83; Maimela, *Proclaim Freedom to My People* (Johannesburg: Skotaville Publishers, 1987), 105–8, 114–20.

6. Manas Buthelezi, "Daring to Live for Christ," *Journal of Theology for Southern Africa* 11 (June 1975): 9.

7. Ibid., 8–10.

somewhat differently, the theology of the cross, like every other theology, has been and is always open to distortion and misuse depending on who uses it and for what purposes. Over against this possible misuse of the theology of the cross, it is my contention that the cross must be understood as a symbol for the real human suffering and the crosses that are borne by the people of color in racist societies. These crosses must be overcome by those who take upon themselves Christian suffering after the model of Christ's suffering in order to save humanity from sin. We must not justify perpetual oppressive human suffering on theological grounds.

A Brief Outline of Luther's Theology of the Cross

It is generally acknowledged that St. Paul was the first theologian to construct and use the theology of the cross to express his rejection of all kinds of human exaltation, which often tempts human beings to use reason and works to justify themselves before God. Thus, in the same way in which he developed the doctrine of justification by faith in critical opposition to the doctrine of justification by works in Romans 1:17ff., Paul developed the theology of the cross in 1 Corinthians 1:1ff. against human wisdom and indirect knowledge of God that might be gained from human contemplation of God's works of creation.

Taking his cue from St. Paul, Luther formulated his theology of the cross in its explicit form in 1518 in the Heidelberg Disputation. In his most important statements in theses 19 and 20, Luther, laying perimeters within which a person may rightly be called a theologian, writes: "That person does not deserve to be called a theologian who looks upon the invisible things of God as though they were clearly perceptible in those things which have actually happened. He deserves to be called a theologian, however, who comprehends the visible and manifest things of God seen through suffering and the cross."[8]

In formulating the theology of the cross Luther wanted to achieve two purposes: first, he uses *theologia crucis* to oppose what he referred to as a *theologia gloriae,* which he identified with scholastic theology. In his view, the theology of glory was nothing but a theology of human self-exaltation, because it propounded a wrong conception of human righteousness and what human beings must do in order to become justified before God. Rejecting the theology of glory, which encourages the attitude of human pride and striving after works righteousness as humanity's way to attaining salvation, Luther writes: "He is not righteous who does much, but he who, without works, believes much in Christ."[9] Second, the theology of the cross, as opposed to a theology of glory, was formulated by Luther to express the Reformation insight about the liberating gospel of Jesus Christ in and through whom God deals mercifully with sinful

---

8. *Luther's Works,* vol. 31, *Career of the Reformer: I,* ed. Harold H. Grimm (Philadelphia: Muhlenberg Press, 1957), 40.

9. Ibid., 41.

humanity as the crucified and hidden God. For it is in the "humility and shame of the cross"[10] that God unconditionally accepts sinful humanity, by virtue of the fact that our righteousness was achieved through the cross of Jesus and is now communicated to the sinner through the forgiveness of sins, the forgiveness that Jesus Christ earned for the sinner by his vicarious suffering and death.[11]

In other words, the deepest and most central questions that Luther wrestled with when he formulated the theology of the cross were the age-old questions that humans keep asking: What must we do to be saved? How can sinners be justified before a righteous judge? Luther's answer was that the true knowledge of God that is apprehended via the suffering and the cross of Jesus has nothing to do with human wisdom, indirect knowledge of works of creation, and ethical works, but has everything to do with what God wants to give and to do in order to deliver human beings from sin and death and thereby save them. That is, sinful human beings become just and righteous, not by developing an attitude of pride in their lawful behavior or laying claim to superior wisdom, both of which have no use for the cross of Christ, but by faith in the crucified Christ. For the truth of the matter is that "nobody finds salvation within oneself: it comes from outside, without any condition from our part, without any merit, gratuitously and freely granted"[12] to those who through faith accept God's forgiveness of their sins. Indeed as Luther with deep insight points out, the salvation of the sinner is possible only because "through a sweet exchange and a royal marriage, God takes our humanity with all its weakness, temptation and sinfulness and makes us share in God's justice, grace and life."[13]

It is because Jesus was crucified for us that he is now the only mediator between God and sinful humanity. Therefore, to know Christ is to know the cross and to understand God under the crucified flesh. To sum up: just as Paul contrasted the wisdom of this world and the folly of the cross and, in parallel with this, contrasted righteousness by works of the law and the scandal of the cross, similarly Luther brought together the religious way to knowledge through contemplation of the works of God and the moral way of self-affirmation through a person's own works, and directed the theology of the cross polemically against both. Luther correctly saw that insofar as ethical works and religious speculations are considered to be ways to God, they have to be equally rejected. Thus by using the term *theologia crucis* in opposition to *theologia gloriae*, Luther succeeded in unmasking the common root of both moralism and rationalism, the human self-glorification and desire to attain personal righteousness by works or knowledge rather than by faith in God's own action in the cross of Jesus.[14]

---

10. *Luther's Works* (31), 53.

11. Wolfhart Pannenberg, "A Theology of the Cross," *Word and World* 8, no. 2 (Spring 1988): 163.

12. J. E. Vercruysse, "Luther's Theology of the Cross — Its Relevance for Ecumenism," *Bulletin/Centro Pro Unione* 35 (Spring 1989): 50.

13. *Luther's Works* (31), 351ff.; *Weimar Addition* (7), 54ff.

14. Walter von Loewenich, *Luther's Theology of the Cross* (Minneapolis: Augsburg Publishing House, 1976), 18–24.

As a theologian of the cross, Luther recognized that the solution to the human quest for salvation lay not in self-glorification through human knowledge and virtue but in the knowledge of God via the suffering of Christ. This knowledge of the "crucified and hidden God" is capable of effectively destroying human pride and self-deification. Moltmann's perceptive comments in this connection are helpful and worth recalling, and we shall quote him at length:

> The knowledge of the cross is the knowledge of God in the suffering caused to him by dehumanized man, that is, in the contrary of everything which dehumanized man seeks and tries to attain as the deity in him. Consequently, this knowledge does not confirm him as what he is, but destroys him. It destroys the god, the miserable in his pride, which we would like to be, and restores to us our abandoned and despised humanity. The knowledge of the cross brings a conflict of interest between God who has become man and man who wishes to become God. It destroys the destruction of man. It alienates the alienated man. And in this way it restores the humanity of the dehumanized man.... The knowledge of God in the suffering of Christ destroys man who abandons his humanity, for it destroys his gods and destroys his supposed divinity. It sets him free from his inhuman hubris, to restore his true human nature. It makes the *homo incurvatus in se* once again open to God and his neighbor and gives Narcissus the power to love someone else.[15]

Human Racial Divisions as a Theological Problem

The diversity of the human race and its different cultural manifestations in themselves have not always been and need not be understood as problematic in the church, if they are accepted as gifts with which the creator has endowed human beings for their mutual enrichment. This was certainly true in the early church, which was an ethnic and social admixture of different races that reflected the pluralism of the Hellenistic world. This healthy coexistence of different races in the church of Christ — in which "there is no longer Jew or Greek, there is no longer slave or free, there is no longer male and female" (Gal. 3:28), because they are one in Jesus Christ — did not last for long for many reasons. Among others, we need to mention but two important ones. First, the church underwent a major transformation during the Constantinian era, when it changed from a scarcely tolerated and often persecuted minority missionary movement into an established, official institution with the power to determine life for its members as well as for society. Once the emperor became a Christian, he began to assert his power on behalf of the church, opening the entire society for Chris-

15. Moltmann, *The Crucified God*, 70–71.

tianization.[16] In gratitude to Constantine, the church and its religious authorities were taken over and coopted by the ruling class, which expected them to construct a theology whose purpose was to advance and legitimate the causes and interests of the Roman Empire.[17]

Second, the collapse of the churches in North Africa and Asia Minor under the assault of Islam transformed the church into "the church of the white nations, of the Christian Occident and Orient,"[18] with dire consequences for the colored people of the world. With deep insight, Gollwitzer points out that this transformation of the church from one of ethnic pluralism into a Western, white church offered

> the white people, endowed with the mobility and activity characteristic of the temperate zones and especially of that peculiar continent of Europe, an unheard of self-confidence which first proved itself in the struggle against Islam and in the crusades, but then reached out over the entire globe in the age of great discoveries "empowering" the Europeans to regard all non-Christian people as destined by God for domination and exploitation. So the coasts of Africa and India were plundered by the Portuguese. The Pope divided up the New World between the Spanish and the Portuguese. The Aztec and Inca peoples were destroyed in a manifold Auschwitz.[19]

The upshot of what is being claimed here is that racial problems have their roots in the Constantinian takeover of the church and its subsequent Christianization of the white nations. During the modern European colonial period, this resulted in a theological self-understanding of the Western world that equated Christianity with Western culture. Concomitant with this was the belief that those who belonged to Western Christianity were superior to non-Christians, who happened to be the people of color.[20] Once the religious privilege of belonging to the church of Jesus Christ, who is Savior and Lord of the universe, had been transformed into the political, economic, and social privilege of God's chosen people, who happened to be white, it was a matter of time before social structures were created through which white people would enforce white supremacy and thereby subject the people of color to white plunder, domination, exploitation and oppression. It was during the European colonization of Africa, Asia, and Latin America that a colonial theology was developed to provide religious sanction for slavery and sociopolitical and economic bondage, to which

---

16. J. Driver, *Understanding the Atonement for the Mission of the Church* (Scottdale, Pa.: Herald Press, 1986), 29.

17. Maimela, *Proclaim Freedom to My People,* 134.

18. H. Gollwitzer, "Why Black Theology?" in Gayraud S. Wilmore and James H. Cone, eds., *Black Theology: A Documentary History, 1966–1979* (Maryknoll, N.Y.: Orbis Books, 1979), 154.

19. Ibid.

20. Ibid., 155.

people of color have been subjected in racist societies over many centuries up to the present.[21]

Therefore, in order not to write on the problematic nature of racial divisions in general, I want now to focus attention on the South African racial situation — of which I speak as a product and victim — to illustrate how the Constantinian model of a triumphal church and state have worked hand in glove to create the racism from which we are still struggling to liberate ourselves. The problem of racial division was exacerbated by the fact that a white colonial tribe, which wields all the political and economic power, appropriated for itself the symbol of Israel, claiming that white people in South Africa were specially chosen by God for a mission in the world. Therefore, white people came to regard themselves as God's chosen race or anointed, called upon to govern and spread Western civilization and Christianity even at the cost of fanatical persecutions of those regarded as unworthy human beings, the so-called heathens, who happened to be the people of color.

The apartheid system of white racial domination had its origin during British rule in the seventeenth century and was merely perfected by the Afrikaners in 1948; it is important that we discuss the phases of its development. In the first phase, it was the British imperialists who undergirded their colonial activities by understanding the British people as the elect of God felt called to a mission of bringing freedom to humanity. This mission was expressed in political and messianic terms. Its best representative, Cecil Rhodes, declared that "only one race," his own, "was destined to help on God's work and fulfil His purpose in the world . . . and to bring nearer the reign of justice, liberty and peace," because they as English people qua people approached God's ideal type.[22]

Put simply, British imperialism was underpinned by the belief that the British people were a "new" Israel chosen to fulfil a divine mission and, more importantly, that their election was determined by their racial and cultural superiority over those they were destined to rule. In this view the British people had a certain right to be elected to dominate the world, to spread British civilization even at the cost of intolerable persecution of the "heathens," who must be made British at all costs or die at the hands of the anointed ones and with the approval of this domesticated British "God."[23] Commenting on the marriage between the throne and altar that enabled such a small island to rule over 500 million people during the height of its power, de Gruchy points out that there existed an inseparable relationship between God, the church, and the British Empire. As a consequence, de Gruchy could with justification conclude that "few, whether Anglicans nor Non-conformists, apparently found anything incongruous about the Union Jack coexisting alongside the Cross and Altar, even when tattered

---

21. Ibid., 156–67.
22. Quoted in F. A. van Jaarsveld, *The Afrikaner's Interpretation of South African History* (Cape Town: Simondium Publishers, 1964), 3–4.
23. Maimela, *Proclaim Freedom to My People,* 8f., 30, 38.

and blood-spattered from encounters with the natives . . . in the service of God and Queen."[24]

Of course, de Gruchy's perceptive observations refer to the brutal British rule that managed to bring both the Boers and blacks in South Africa to their knees by repressive forces, believing that the expansion of British imperialism and exploitation of the so-called inferior races were serving the divine providential purpose of bringing the gospel and civilization to the "pagans" and uncivilized Boers. In consequence, the God the British churches talked about was nothing but a fine and loyal "English" God who regarded the Crown and the British people as "God's" anointed or chosen race called upon to govern and spread British civilization.

In a second stage, the Afrikaners in a similar fashion too coopted the Dutch Reformed churches to provide themselves with spiritual resources to meet the threat of British imperialism, on the one hand, and, on the other, the black majority, who through intermarriage would dilute their white group identity. In the process, an Afrikaner nationalism emerged and the church, wishing to have unquestioning loyalty and authority over the lives of its followers, was all too willing to wed itself to this Afrikaner nationalism. Just as with the British, the theology that was propounded by the Dutch Reformed Church gave the Afrikaners a theological sense of being a chosen people with a mission, namely, to create a new "white" nation in dark Africa as a beacon of Christian civilization. The Afrikaner leaders became men of calling to fulfil God's will, and this was true from Piet Retief in the nineteenth century, in his struggle against the British "Pharaohs" to Dr. Hendrik Verwoerd, the architect of apartheid policy in the twentieth century, in his struggle to prevent the black majority from engulfing his "volk."[25] Believing that part of their mission was to preserve the chosen white race in its pure form and therefore that it is against the divine will to be cast into a melting-pot through interracial marriage, a leading Afrikaner, Dr. Mansvelt, in 1892 reminded the white race that "after their having opened a way for the spread of the Gospel and civilization, I do not believe that Providence has destined the Afrikaner to disappear from history without trace and to give it to others."[26]

It is against the background of the Afrikaners' understanding of their divine calling that apartheid was formulated and carried out. Theology was used to underpin this ideology; it was argued that God has sharply divided human races and the Afrikaner's calling was to help attain this goal of permanent separation, thereby preventing the admixture of races that would destroy "Western civilization" and the "God-given" identity of the white race. Rationalizing their subjugation and oppression of black people, the Afrikaners argued that they had been placed in Africa by God and commanded

---

24. John W. de Gruchy, "English-speaking South Africa and Civil Religion," *Journal of Theology for Southern Africa* 19 (June 1977): 45.

25. van Jaarsveld, *The Afrikaner's Interpretation of South African History,* 17.

26. Quoted in ibid., 22.

to act as the guardian, master and spiritual leader to the Black man. To do that the white man has to have at his command the authority needed to uplift, Christianize and evangelize the black man; the purpose is that the Black man who is still a child from the point of view of civilization, shall grow and develop in due course in his own area, with his own language according to his nature and traditions.[27]

Carrying out the policies of apartheid, which were believed to be in accordance with God's will, the Afrikaners could not, for a long time, understand why the entire world faulted them for what they were doing in the service of God. Here again, as with British imperialism, we are confronted with a triumphal white nationalism and a triumphal white church — both of which have tried to create God in their own image, a God who is a loyal, white-bearded Monarch giving "divine" tasks and missions only to white people. At the same time this God is not bothered about the enormous suffering to which the racial policy of apartheid has subjected black people.

Put somewhat differently, the racial divisions that South Africans have suffered over the years are a product of European cultural and religious triumphalism, which has given rise to and feeds on the theology of glory. This reflects the "success motif" of Western Christendom. It has forgotten its origin in the crucified Christ and has allowed Christianity to be transformed into a religion of the successful and the mighty who exercise power to determine life both in church and society. This theology of glory has encouraged South African whites to develop an attitude of pride in themselves as worthier persons than the people of color by virtue of belonging to Western civilization and of being the elect of God to promote Christianity. Thus, unable to pass judgment on white humanity, which has become proud and triumphant because of the alleged superiority of its cultural and educational achievements, the theology of glory has allowed itself to be used for the justification of the concrete and unjust suffering of the people of color.

Put somewhat differently, racial divisions have become a theological problem for the people of color. Racism is not merely racial prejudice or a negative attitude toward a person whose color differs from one's own. Nor is racism merely a vague feeling of racial superiority in relation to other people. Rather racism is a social, political, economic, and cultural system of domination that white people employ to subjugate the people of color. It creates beliefs and myths about the cultural and biological superiority of the dominant racial group in order to justify the unequal distribution of resources between the dominant and the dominated groups.[28] It exalts a particular biological characteristic to a universal principle that determines what it means to be human. Not surprisingly, the color of one's skin and one's race become salvation principles, determining

---

27. Ibid., 25.
28. Allan A. Boesak, "He Made Us All, But...," in John de Gruchy and Charles Villa-Vicencio, eds., *Apartheid Is a Heresy* (Grand Rapids: Eerdmans Publishing Co., 1983), 3.

whether a person is declared justified or unjustified to enjoy certain economic, political, and cultural rights and privileges. Because color and race are salvation principles, it is not enough to be baptized after confessing Jesus Christ as Lord and Savior. Rather a person is expected to possess yet another attribute, which in the nature of the case, is to be reserved only for a select few. Hence, apartheid was designed and practiced in such a way that the people of color would be continually reminded that they are *unworthy persons,* regardless of whether they are Christians, simply because they do not possess that extra attribute, namely, white skin. The consequence of elevating the genetic factor of race into the criterion for distinguishing between the worthy and unworthy and between superior and inferior human beings has been devastating for the people of color. Condemning the negative effects of the apartheid system on blacks, Archbishop Desmond Tutu, with deep insight, writes:

> Apartheid is intrinsically and irredeemably evil. For my part, its most vicious, indeed its most blasphemous aspect, is not the great suffering it causes its victims, but that it can make a child of God doubt that he is a child of God. For that alone, it deserves to be condemned as a heresy. Real peace and security will come to our beloved land only when Apartheid has been dismantled.[29]

At the same time, the apartheid system taught whites, regardless of whether or not they are Christians, that they deserve a particular life-style and enormous political and economic privileges, which are due to them by some natural right, that is, by virtue of their right color.

The Relevance of the Theology of the Cross

As much as it would be unacceptable to try to transform Luther's theology into a modern theology of liberation, it would be unfair to expect Luther's theology of the cross to give answers to the problems of the suffering of human divisions that modern racism has brought sharply into focus.[30] For even though Luther knew something about ethnocentrism and a vague human feeling of superiority over others, he certainly knew nothing about racism as a system of domination and attempts of the apostles of racialism to transform race and color into salvation principles that would compete with God's saving work in Christ. Nonetheless, I believe that Luther's theology has some relevance and can shed some light on the problem of human division as we have come to know it. Indeed, I am persuaded that if Luther were living in a racist society that oppresses and exploits others solely on the grounds of their color, his theology of the cross

---

29. Desmond Tutu, "Apartheid and Christianity," in *Apartheid Is a Heresy,* 46–47.
30. R. R. Featherstone, "The Theology of the Cross," in *Theology and the Black Experience,* 50.

and doctrine of justification by grace through faith alone would have forced him to make a preferential option for the downtrodden. Indeed, Luther's keen sensitivity to the many crosses and humiliations that millions of men and women have suffered throughout the world led him to speak of the God of the poor and the humble (*Deus pauperum/Deus humilium*) in his Commentary on Psalm 50. Here he speaks of God's preferential option for the oppressed and expresses the solidarity of God with the humble and the poor who, unlike the powerful and proud who are smug and secure, are aware that they are nothing before God.[31] Therefore, Luther's theology of the cross, which rejects human self-glorification of works righteousness or self-deification on the grounds of race, sex, and class, can meaningfully address the human suffering of divisions.

Our discussion of white racial domination in South Africa leads us to conclude that all the talk about divine election of white people, on the basis of which their domination of the people of color has been justified, is nothing but an attempt to theologize politics and thereby transform politics into an instrument of self-justification, self-salvation, and self-preservation for white people. Put simply, apartheid has taught whites to take their lives and future into their own hands and to believe that through some human wisdom and work they can save themselves in the face of real or imaginary dangers that the black majority has posed for them. In so doing, the system of racial domination was transformed into an idol from which white people would receive life, rather than from the true God, the Creator of life.

Over against the wrong conception of how persons can become righteous, the theology of the cross reminds us that all human beings are unworthy, unacceptable, and sinners before the righteous God and therefore that no race or group is any better than another. Therefore, instead of pleading one's racial worthiness, all human beings are challenged to confess that they need daily God's grace and mercy through which the righteousness of the Christ, the Crucified, is communicated to them. Directing itself against human concern for self-deification through knowledge and works, the knowledge of the cross of Christ destroys all human hubris and the divinity that is presumed to reside in the so-called superior races. For the cross compels sinful humanity to discover that all human beings equally live by God's grace, which challenges them to forgive and thereby be reconciled to one another.

While my brief was that of discussing the cross and its implications for human suffering of divisions on the basis of race, I trust the conclusions we have drawn are applicable to other problems of human suffering of divisions such as class domination, sexist domination, and denominational divisions that have prevented Christians from reconciling themselves to one another.

---

31. Vercruysse, "Luther's Theology of the Cross," 10.

Chapter 4

An African-American Perspective on the Cross and Suffering

James H. Cone

†

More than eighty years ago W. E. B. Du Bois wrote in *The Souls of Black Folk* his classic statement of the paradox of black life in America:

> It is a peculiar sensation, this double-consciousness, this sense of always looking at one's self through the eyes of others, of measuring one's soul by the tape of a world that looks on in amused contempt and pity. One ever feels his twoness, — an American, a Negro; two souls, two thoughts, two unreconciled strivings; two warring ideals in one dark body, whose dogged strength alone keeps it from being torn asunder.[1]

The "two warring ideals" that Du Bois described in 1903 have been at the center of black religious thought from its origin to the present day. They are found in the heated debates about "integration" and "nationalism" and in the attempt to name the community — beginning with the word "African" and using at different times such terms as "Colored," "Negro," "Afro-American," "black," and "African-American."

In considering black religious thought in this essay, let us give clearer names to the "two warring ideals" — clearer, that is, from the point of view of religion. I shall call them "African" and "Christian." Black religious thought is not identical with the Christian theology of white Americans; nor is it identical

---

1. W. E. B. Du Bois, *The Souls of Black Folk* (Greenwich, Conn.: Fawcett Premier Book, 1968), 16–17. Originally published 1903.

with traditional African beliefs, past or present. It is both — but reinterpreted for and adapted to the life-situation of black people's struggle for justice in a nation whose social, political, and economic structures are dominated by a white racist ideology. It was the "African" side of black religion that helped African-Americans to see beyond the white distortions of the gospel and to discover its true meaning as God's liberation of the oppressed from bondage. It was the "Christian" element in black religion that helped African-Americans to reorient their African past so that it would become useful in the struggle to survive with dignity in a society that they did not make.

Although the "African" and "Christian" elements have been found throughout the history of black religious thought, the Christian part gradually became dominant. Though less visible, the African element continued to play an important role in defining the core of black religion, thus preventing it from becoming merely an imitation of Protestant or Catholic theologies in the West.

Of course, there are many similarities between black religious thought and white Protestant and Catholic reflections on Christian tradition. But the *dissimilarities* between them are perhaps more important than the similarities. The similarities are found at the point of a common Christian identity, and the dissimilarities can best be understood in light of the differences between African and European cultures in the New World. While whites used their cultural perspective to dominate others, blacks used theirs to affirm their dignity and to empower themselves to struggle for justice. The major reason for the differences between black and white reflections on God is found at the point of the great differences in life. As white theology is largely defined by its response to modern and postmodern societies of Europe and America, usually ignoring the contradictions of slavery and oppression in black life, black religious thought is the thinking of slaves and of marginalized blacks whose understanding of God was shaped by the contradictions that white theologians ignored and regarded as unworthy of serious theological reflection. In this essay, I will analyze black religious thought in the light of Du Bois's "warring ideals" that emerged out of the struggle for justice — beginning with its origin in slavery and concentrating mainly on its twentieth-century development in the civil rights and black power movements, culminating with the rise of black theology.

Roots of Black Religious Thought: Slavery

The tension between the "African" and "Christian" elements acted to reorder traditional theological themes in black religion and to give them different substance when compared to other theologies in Europe and America. Five themes in particular defined the character of black religious thought during slavery and its subsequent development: justice, liberation, hope, love, and suffering.

No theme has been more prominent throughout the history of black religious thought than the justice of God. African-Americans have always believed in the living presence of the God who establishes the right by punishing the wicked and liberating their victims from oppression. Everyone will be rewarded and punished according to their deeds, and no one — absolutely no one — can escape the judgment of God, who alone is the sovereign of the universe. Evildoers may get by for a time, and good people may suffer unjustly under oppression, but "sooner or later ... we reap as we sow."[2]

The "sooner" referred to contemporary historically observable events: punishment of the oppressors and liberation of the oppressed. The "later" referred to the divine establishment of justice in the "next world" where God "gwineter rain down fire" on the wicked and where the liberated righteous will "walk in Jerusalem just like John." In the religion of African slaves, God's justice was identical with the punishment of the oppressors, and divine liberation was synonymous with the deliverance of the oppressed from the bondage of slavery — if not "now" then in the "not yet." Because whites continued to prosper materially as they increased their victimization of African-Americans, black religious thought spoke more often of the "later" than the "sooner."[3]

The themes of justice and liberation are closely related to the idea of hope. The God who establishes the right and puts down the wrong is the sole basis of the hope that the suffering of the victims will be eliminated. Although African slaves used the term "heaven" to describe their experience of hope, its primary meaning for them must not be reduced to the "pie-in-the-sky," otherworldly affirmation that often characterized white evangelical Protestantism. The idea of heaven was the means by which slaves affirmed their humanity in a world that did not recognize them as human beings.[4] It was their way of saying that they were made for freedom and not slavery.

> Oh Freedom! Oh Freedom!
> Oh Freedom, I love thee!
> And before I'll be a slave,
> I'll be buried in my grave,
> And go home to my Lord and be free.

---

2. A concise statement of black religious thought during and following slavery is found in a 1902 sermon of an ex-slave and Princeton Theological Seminary graduate, Francis J. Grimke: "God is not dead — nor is he an indifferent onlooker at what is going on in this world. One day He will make restitution for blood; He will call the oppressors to account. Justice may sleep, but it never dies. The individual, race, or nation which does wrong, which sets at defiance God's great law, especially God's great law of love of brotherhood, will be sure sooner or later, to pay the penalty. We reap as we sow. With that measure we mete, it shall be measured to us again." See C. G. Woodson, ed., *The Works of Francis J. Grimke, I* (1942), 354. Grimke's statement was undoubtedly influenced by the slave song, "You shall reap jes what you sow."

3. For an interpretation of the slaves' idea of justice and liberation, see my *The Spirituals and the Blues* (Maryknoll, N.Y.: Orbis Books, 1991). See also Albert Raboteau, *Slave Religion* (New York: Oxford University Press, 1978); Vincent Harding, *There Is a River* (New York: Harcourt Brace Jovanovich, 1981); and Gayraud S. Wilmore, *Black Religion and Black Radicalism* (Maryknoll, N.Y.: Orbis Books, 1983).

4. For a fuller discussion of the ideas of heaven in slave religion, see my *The Spirituals and the Blues,* chapter 5. See also John Lovell Jr., *Black Song* (New York: Macmillan, 1972), especially 310–12, 315–74.

Black slaves' hope was based on their faith in God's promise to "protect the needy" and to "defend the poor." Just as God delivered the Hebrew children from Egyptian bondage and raised Jesus from the dead, so God will also deliver African slaves from American slavery and "in due time" will bestow upon them the gift of eternal life. That was why they sang:

> Soon-a-will be done with the trouble of the world;
> Soon-a-will be done with the trouble of the world;
> Going home to live with God.

Black slaves' faith in the coming of justice of God was the chief reason why they could hold themselves together in servitude and sometimes fight back, even though the odds were against them.

The ideas of justice, liberation, and hope should be seen in relation to the important theme of love. Theologically God's love is prior to the other themes. But in order to separate black reflections on love from a similar theme in white theology it is important to emphasize that love in black religious thought is usually linked with God's justice, liberation, and hope. God's love is made known through divine righteousness, liberating the poor for a new future.

God's creation of all persons in the divine image bestows sacredness upon human beings and thus makes them the children of God. To violate any person's dignity is to transgress "God's great law of love."[5] We must love the neighbor because God has first loved us. And because slavery and racism are blatant denials of the dignity of the human person, God's justice means that "he will call the oppressors to account."[6]

Despite the strength of black faith, belief in God's coming justice and liberation was not easy for African slaves and their descendants. Their suffering created the most serious challenge to their faith. If God is good, why did God permit millions of blacks to be stolen from Africa and enslaved in a strange land? No black person has been able to escape the existential agony of that question.

In their attempt to resolve the theological dilemma that slavery and racism created, African-Americans turned to three texts — the Exodus, Psalm 68:31, and the story of Jesus' life, death, and resurrection.[7] They derived from the Exodus text the belief that God is the liberator of the oppressed. They interpreted Psalm 68:31 as an obscure reference to God's promise to redeem Africa: "Princes shall come out of Egypt, and Ethiopia shall soon stretch forth her hands unto God" (KJV).

---

5. Works of Grimke, 354.
6. Ibid.
7. For an interpretation of these texts, see Albert J. Raboteau, "Ethiopia Shall Soon Stretch Forth Her Hands: Black Destiny in Nineteenth Century America," University Lecture in Religion at Arizona State University (January 27, 1983); *The Spirituals and the Blues,* chap. 3.

The Jesus story was the key text. They were empowered by Jesus' ministry: "King Jesus preaching to the poor," "making the dumb to speak," "the cripple walk," and "giving the blind his sight." "Jesus," they said, can "do most anything." However, it was the cross of Jesus that attracted the most attention of black people. Oppressed blacks were moved by the Passion story because they too had been rejected, beaten, and shot without a chance to say a word in the defense of their humanity. In Jesus' death poor blacks saw themselves, and they unleashed their imagination, describing what they felt and saw:

> Oh, they whipped him up the hill,
>   and he never said a mumblin' word,
> He just hung down his head and cried.

They "nailed him to the cross," "pierced him in the side," and "the blood came twinkling down," but "he never said a mumblin' word," "he just hung down his head and he died." The death of Jesus meant that he died on the cross for black slaves. His death was a symbol of their suffering, their trials and tribulations in an unfriendly world. Because black slaves knew the significance of the pain and shame of Jesus' death on the cross, they found themselves by his side.

> Were you there when they crucified my Lord?
> Were you there when they crucified my Lord?
> Oh! Sometimes it causes me to tremble, tremble, tremble;
> Were you there when they crucified my Lord?

Through the blood of slavery, blacks transcended the limitations of space and time. Jesus' time became their time, and they encountered the theological significance of Jesus' death: through the crucifixion, Jesus makes an unqualified identification with the poor and the helpless and takes their pain upon himself. Jesus was not alone in his suffering; blacks were not alone in their oppression in the United States. Jesus was with them! He was God's Black Slave who has come to put an end to oppression. Herein lies the meaning of Jesus' resurrection. It means that the cross was not the end of God's drama of salvation.

Despite African-Americans' assurance that oppression was not the last word regarding their humanity, the contradictions remained between oppression and their faith.

Martin Luther King Jr.
and the Civil Rights Movement

No thinker has made a greater impact upon black religious thought than Martin Luther King Jr. He was a product of the black church tradition, and its faith determined the essence of his theology.[8] From the beginning of his role as the leader of the Montgomery bus boycott to his tragic death in Memphis, Tennessee, the heart of his beliefs revolved around the ideas of black religious thought — love, justice, liberation, hope, and redemptive suffering. The meaning of each is mutually dependent on the others. Though love may be appropriately placed at the center of his thought, he interpreted it in the light of justice for the poor, liberation for all, and the certain hope that God has not left this world in the hands of evil people.

Martin King took the American democratic tradition of freedom and combined it with the biblical tradition of justice and liberation as found in the Exodus and the prophets. Then he integrated both traditions with the New Testament idea of love and suffering as disclosed in Jesus' cross, and from all three, King developed a theology that was effective in challenging all Americans to create the beloved community in which all persons are equal. While it was the Gandhian method of nonviolence that provided the strategy for achieving justice, it was, as King said, the black church faith that empowered him to struggle.

As a Christian whose faith was derived from the cross of Jesus, Martin King believed that there could be no true liberation without suffering. Through nonviolent suffering, he contended, blacks would not only liberate themselves from the necessity of bitterness and feeling of inferiority toward whites, but would also prick the conscience of whites and liberate them from a feeling of superiority. The mutual liberation of blacks and whites lays the foundation for both to work together toward the creation of an entirely new world.

It was the faith of the black church that empowered King to take a stand against the war in Vietnam. Because the Civil Rights Act (1964) and the Voting Rights Bill (1965) did not affect significantly the life-chances of the poor, and because of the failure of President Johnson's War on Poverty, King became convinced that his dream of 1963 had been turned into a nightmare.[9] Gradually

---

8. The importance of the black religious tradition for King's theology has not received the attention that it deserves of scholars. See my "Martin Luther King, Jr.: Black Theology — Black Church," *Theology Today* (January 1984). See also the important essay of Lewis B. Baldwin, "Martin Luther King, Jr., the Black Church and the Black Messianic Vision," *Journal of the Interdenominational Theological Center* (forthcoming). David Barrow's definitive biography on Martin King is soon to be published under the title *Bearing the Cross: Martin Luther King, Jr. and the Southern Christian Leadership Conference 1955–1958.* It will show the important role of the black church tradition in King's life and thought.

9. On many occasions, Martin King talked about his dream of 1963 being turned into a nightmare. The most informative reference in this regard is his "Christian Sermon on Peace," delivered in Ebenezer Baptist Church at Atlanta, December 24, 1967. In that sermon he said: "In 1963 . . . in Washington, D.C. . . . I tried to talk to the nation about a dream that I had had, and I must confess . . . that not long after talking about that dream I started seeing it turn into a nightmare. I remember the first time I saw that dream turn into a nightmare, just a few weeks after I had talked about it. It was when four beautiful . . . Negro girls were murdered in a church in Birmingham, Alabama. I watched that dream turn into a nightmare as I moved through the ghettos of the nation and saw my Black brothers and sisters perishing on a lonely island of poverty in the midst of a vast ocean of material prosperity, and saw the nation doing nothing to grapple with the Negroes' problem of poverty. I saw that dream turn into a nightmare as I watched my

he began to see the connections between the failure of the war on poverty and the expenditures for the war in Vietnam. In the tradition of the Old Testament prophets and against the advice of many of his closest associates in black and white communities, King stood before a capacity crowd at Riverside Church and condemned America as "the greatest purveyor of violence in the world today."[10] He proclaimed God's judgment against America and insisted that God would break the backbone of U.S. power if this nation did not bring justice to the poor and peace to the world. Vicious criticisms came from blacks and whites in government, civil rights groups, media, and the nation generally as he proclaimed God's righteous indignation against the three great evils of our time — war, racism, and poverty.

During the severe crises of 1966–68, King turned to the faith of his own religious heritage. It was eschatological hope, derived from his slave grandparents and mediated through the black church, that sustained him in the midst of grief and disappointment. This hope also empowered him to "master [his] fears" of death and to "stand by the best in an evil time."[11] In a sermon preached at Ebenezer Baptist Church, he addressed the problem of violence at home and abroad:

> I've decided what I'm going to do; I ain't going to kill nobody...in Mississippi...and...in Vietnam, and I ain't going to study war no more. An you know what? I don't care who doesn't like what I say about it. I don't care who criticizes me in editorial; I don't care what white person or Negro criticizes me. I'm going to stick with the best....Every now and then we sing about it: "If you are right, God will fight your battle." I'm going to stick by the best during these evil times.[12]

It was not easy for King to "stand by the best," because he often stood alone. But he firmly believed that the God of black faith had said to him: "Martin Luther, stand up for righteousness. Stand up for justice. Stand up for truth. And lo, I will be with you, even until the end of the world."[13]

Black brothers and sisters in the midst of anger and understandable outrage...turn to misguided riots to try to solve that problem. I saw that dream turn into a nightmare as I watched the war in Vietnam escalating, and as I saw so-called military advisers, 16,000 strong, turn into fighting soldiers until today over 500,000 American boys are fighting on Asian soil. Yes, I am personally the victim of deferred dreams, of blasted hopes..." (see King, *The Trumpet of Conscience* [New York: Harper, 1971], 75–76). See also similar comments at an Operation Breadbasket Meeting, Chicago Theological Seminary (March 25, 1967) and during his appearance on the Arlene Francis Show (June 19, 1967), King Center Archives.

10. See Martin Luther King Jr., *Beyond Vietnam,* a pamphlet published by Clergy and Laity Concerned, 1982 reprint of his April 4, 1967, speech at Riverside Church in New York City, 2.

11. The most reliable sources for Martin King's theology are the unpublished sermons at the King Center Archives. They include "A Knock at Midnight," All Saints Community Church, Los Angeles (June 25, 1967); "Standing by the Best in an Evil Time," Ebenezer Baptist Church, Atlanta (August 6, 1967); "Thou Fool," Mount Pisgah Baptist Church, Chicago (August 27, 1967); "Mastering Our Fears," Ebenezer Baptist Church (September 10, 1967).

12. "Standing by the Best in an Evil Time," 7.

13. "Thou Fool," 14. This quotation is taken from King's account of his "conversion experi-

Martin King combined the exodus-liberation and cross-love themes with the message of hope found in the resurrection of Jesus. Hope for him was derived from his belief in the righteousness of God as defined by his reading of the Bible through the eyes of his slave foreparents. The result was the most powerful expression in black history of the essential themes of black religious thought from the integrationist viewpoint:

> Centuries ago Jeremiah raised a question, "Is there no balm in Gilead? Is there no physician?" He raised it because he saw the good people suffering so often and the evil people prospering. Centuries later our slave foreparents came along and they too saw the injustices of life and had nothing to look forward to, morning after morning, but the rawhide whip of the overseer, long rows of cotton and the sizzling heat; but they did an amazing thing. They looked back across the centuries, and they took Jeremiah's question mark and straightened it into an exclamation point. And they could sing, "There is a balm in Gilead to make the wounded whole. There is a balm in Gilead to heal the sinsick soul."[14]

Black Power and Black Theology

From the time of its origin in slavery to the present, black religious thought has been faced with the question of whether to advocate integration into American society or separation from it. The majority of the participants in the black churches and the civil rights movement have promoted integration, and they have interpreted justice, liberation, love, suffering, and hope in light of the goal of creating a society in which blacks and whites can live together in a "beloved community."

While integrationists have emphasized the American side of the double consciousness of African-Americans, there have also been nationalists who rejected any association with the United States and instead have turned toward Africa. Nationalists contend that blacks will never be accepted as equals in a white

---

ence," that is, his existential appropriation of the faith he was taught during his childhood. There is no doubt that the "kitchen experience," as it might be called, was the turning point in King's theological development. During the early stages of the Montgomery bus boycott, the constant threats of death to him and his family (about forty telephone calls per day) eventually caused him to admit that he was "weak,...faltering, [and]...losing [his] courage." In that crisis moment when the fear of death engulfed him, he said: "I pulled back on the theology and philosophy that I had just studied in the universities, trying to give philosophical and theological reasons for the existence and reality of sin and evil, but the answer didn't quite come there" (p. 13). The answer came in his dependence on the God of black faith. "Don't be a fool," he said in his climactic conclusion to this sermon. "Recognize your dependence on God. As the days become dark, and the nights become dreary, realize that there is a God, who rules above. And so I'm not worried about tomorrow. I get weary every now and then, the future looks difficult and dim, but I'm not worried ultimately because I have faith in God" (p. 14).

14. This is an often used conclusion of many of King's sermons. This quotation is taken from "Thou Fool."

racist church and society. Black freedom can be achieved only by black people separating themselves from whites — either by returning to Africa or by forcing the government to set aside a separate state in the United States so blacks can build their own society.[15]

The nationalist perspective on the black struggle for freedom is deeply embedded in the history of black religious thought. Some of its prominent advocates include: Bishop Henry McNeal Turner of the A.M.E. Church; Marcus Garvey, the founder of the Universal Negro Improvement Association; and Malcolm X of the religion of Islam. Black nationalism is centered in blackness, a repudiation of any value in white culture and religion. Nationalists reversed the values of the dominant society by attributing to black history and culture what whites had said about theirs. For example, Bishop Turner claimed that "we have as much right biblically and otherwise to believe that God is a Negro...as you...white people have to believe that God is a fine looking, symmetrical and ornamented white man."[16] Marcus Garvey held a similar view: "If the white man has the idea of a white God, let him worship his God as he desires....We negroes believe in the God of Ethiopia, the everlasting God — God the Father, God the Son and God the Holy Ghost, the One God of all ages."[17]

The most persuasive interpreter of black nationalism during the 1960s was Malcolm X, who proclaimed a challenging critique of Martin King's philosophy of integration, nonviolence, and love. Malcolm X advocated black unity instead of the "beloved community," self-defense in lieu of nonviolence, and self-love in place of turning the other cheek to whites.[18]

Like Turner and Garvey, Malcolm X asserted that God is black; but unlike them he rejected Christianity as the white man's religion. He became a convert initially to Elijah Muhammad's Nation of Islam and later to the worldwide Islamic community. His critique of Christianity and of American society as white was so persuasive that many blacks followed him into the religion of Islam, and others accepted his criticisms even though they did not become Muslims. Malcolm pushed civil rights activists to the left and caused many black Christians to reevaluate their interpretation of Christianity:

> Brothers and sisters, the white man has brainwashed us Black people to fasten our gaze upon a blond-haired, blue-eyed Jesus! We're worshipping a Jesus that doesn't even *look* like us! Now, just think of this. The blond-haired, blue-eyed white man has taught you and me to worship a *white*

---

15. For an excellent introduction to black nationalism, see Alphonso Pinkney, *Red, Black and Green: Black Nationalism in the United States* (Cambridge: Cambridge University Press, 1976). See also John H. Bracey Jr., August Meier, and Elliot Rudwick, eds., *Black Nationalism in America* (Indianapolis: Bobbs-Merrill, 1970).

16. Edwin S. Redkey, ed., *Respect Black: The Writings and Speeches of Henry McNeal Turner* (New York: Arno Press, 1971), 176.

17. Amy Jacques-Garvey, ed., *Philosophy and Opinions of Marcus Garvey,* two volumes in one (New York: Arno Press, 1968), 44.

18. The best introduction to Malcolm X's philosophy is still *The Autobiography of Malcolm X,* with the assistance of Alex Haley (New York: Grove Press, 1965).

Jesus, and to shout and sing and pray to this God that's *his* God, the white man's God. The white man has taught us to shout and sing and pray until we *die,* to wait until *death,* for some dreamy heaven-in-the-hereafter, when we're *dead,* while this white man has his milk and honey in the streets paved with golden dollars right here on *this* earth![19]

During the first half of the 1960s, Martin King's interpretation of justice as equality with whites, liberation as integration, and love as nonviolence dominated the thinking of the black religious community. However, after the riot in Watts (Los Angeles), August 1965, some black clergy began to take another look at Malcolm's philosophy, especially in regard to his criticisms of Christianity and American society. Malcolm X's contention that America was a nightmare and not a dream began to ring true to many black clergy as they watched their communities go up in flames and young blacks shout in jubilation, "burn, baby, burn."

It was during the James Meredith "march against fear" in Mississippi, June 1966, after Malcolm's assassination (February 1965) that some black clergy began to question openly Martin King's philosophy of love, integration, and nonviolence. When Stokely Carmichael proclaimed "black power," it sounded like the voice of Malcolm X. Though committed to the Christian gospel, black clergy found themselves moving slowly from integration to separation, from Martin King to Malcolm X.

The rise of black power created a decisive turning point in black religious thought. Black power forced black clergy to raise the theological question about the relation between black faith and white religion. Although blacks have always recognized the ethical heresy of white Christians, they have not always extended it to Euro-American theology. With its accent on the cultural heritage of Africa and political liberation "by any means necessary," black power shook black clergy out of their theological complacency.

Separating themselves from Martin King's absolute commitment to nonviolence, a small group of black clergy, mostly from the North, addressed the black power movement positively and critically. Like King, and unlike black power advocates, black clergy were determined to remain within the Christian community. This was their dilemma: How could they reconcile Christianity and black power, Martin King and Malcolm X?

Under the influence of Malcolm X and the political philosophy of black power, many black theologians began to advocate the necessity for the development of a black theology, and they rejected the dominant theologies of Europe and North America as heretical. For the first time in the history of black religious thought, black clergy and theologians began to recognize the need for a completely new starting point in theology, and they insisted that it must be defined by people at the bottom and not at the top of the socioeconomic ladder. To

---

19. Ibid., 22.

accomplish this task, black theologians focused on God's liberation of the poor as the central message of the gospel.[20]

To explicate the theological significance of the liberation motif, black theologians began to reread the Bible through the eyes of their slave grandparents and started to speak of God's solidarity with the wretched of the earth. As the political liberation of the poor emerged as the dominant motif, justice, suffering, love, and hope were reinterpreted in its light. For the biblical meaning of liberation, black theologians turned to the Exodus, while the message of the prophets provided the theological content for the theme of justice. The gospel story of the life, death, and resurrection of Jesus served as the biblical foundation for a reinterpretation of love, suffering, and hope in the context of the black struggle for liberation and justice.

As black theologians have reread the Bible in the light of the struggles of the oppressed, the idea of the "suffering God" has become important in our theological perspective. Our theological imagination has been stirred by Jürgen Moltmann's writings about "the Crucified God" as well as Luther's distinction between the "theology of glory" and the "theology of the cross." But it has been the actual suffering of the oppressed in black and other Third World communities that has been decisive in our reflections on the cross of Jesus Christ. As Gustavo Gutiérrez has said: "We cannot speak of the death of Jesus until we speak of the real death of people." For in the deaths of the poor of the world is found the suffering and even the death of God. The political implications of Martin Luther's insight on this point seemed to have been greatly distorted with his unfortunate emphasis on the two kingdoms. Many modern-day Lutheran scholars are often even worse, because they turn the cross of Jesus into a theological idea completely unrelated to the concrete historical struggles of the oppressed for freedom. For many Lutheran scholars, the theology of the cross is a theological concept to be contrasted with philosophical and metaphysical speculations. It is a way of making a distinction between faith and reason, justification by faith through grace and justification by the works of reason.

But when the poor of North America and the Third World read the passion story of the cross, they do not view it as a theological idea but as God's suffering solidarity with the victims of the world. Jesus' cross is God's solidarity with the poor, experiencing their pain and suffering. Black slaves expressed this theological point in the song:

---

20. For an account of the origin of black theology see my *For My People: Black Theology and the Black Church* (Maryknoll, N.Y.: Orbis Books, 1984). See also Gayraud S. Wilmore and James H. Cone, eds., *Black Theology: A Documentary History, 1966–1979* (Maryknoll, N.Y.: Orbis Books, 1979). The best narrative history of black theology by one of its creators is Gayraud S. Wilmore, *Black Religion and Black Radicalism*, rev. ed. (Maryknoll, N.Y.: Orbis Books, 1983). My *Black Religion and Black Power* (New York: Seabury, 1969) and *A Black Theology of Liberation* (Philadelphia: Lippincott, 1970) were the earliest published books on black theology. They were followed by J. Deotis Roberts, *Liberation and Reconciliation: A Black Theology* (Philadelphia: Westminster, 1971), and Major Jones, *Black Awareness: A Theology of Hope* (Nashville: Abingdon, 1971).

They nail my Jesus down,
They put him on the crown of thorns,
O see my Jesus hangin' high!
He look so pale an' bleed so free:
O don't you think it was a shame,
He hung three hours in dreadful pain?

Modern-day black theologians make a similar point when they say that "God is black" and that "Jesus is the Oppressed One." Our rejection of European metaphysical speculations and our acceptance of an apparently crude anthropomorphic way of speaking of God are black theologians' way of concretizing Paul's saying that "God chose what is foolish in the world to shame the wise; God chose what is weak in the world to shame the strong; God chose what is low and despised in the world, things that are not, to reduce to nothing things that are" (1 Cor. 1:27–28).

Another characteristic of black theology is its de-emphasis, though not complete rejection, of the Western theological tradition and its affirmation of black history and culture. If the suffering of God is revealed in the suffering of the oppressed, then it follows that theology cannot achieve its Christian identity apart from a systematic and critical reflection upon the history and culture of the victims of oppression. When this theological insight impressed itself upon our consciousness, we black theologians began to realize that we had been miseducated. In fact, European and North American theologians have stifled the indigenous development of the theological perspectives of blacks by teaching us that our own cultural traditions are not appropriate sources for an interpretation of the Christian gospel. Europeans and white North Americans taught us that the Western theological tradition as defined by Augustine, Aquinas, Luther, Calvin, and Schleiermacher is the essential source for a knowledge of the Christian past. But when black theologians began to concentrate on black culture and history, we realized that our own historical and cultural traditions are far more important for an analysis of the gospel in the struggle of freedom than are the Western traditions that participated in our enslavement. We now know that the people responsible for or indifferent to the oppression of blacks are not likely to provide the theological resources for our liberation. If oppressed peoples are to be liberated, they must themselves create the means for it to happen.

The focus on black culture in the light of the black liberation struggle has led to an emphasis upon praxis as the context out of which Christian theology develops. To know the truth is to do the truth, that is, to make happen in history what is confessed in church. People are not poor by divine decree or by historical accident. They are made poor by the rich and powerful few. This means that to do black liberation theology, one must make a commitment, an option *for* the poor and *against* those who are responsible for their poverty.

Because black theology is to be created only in the struggles of the poor, we have adopted social analysis, especially of racism, and more recently of classism and sexism, as a critical component of its methodology. How can we participate in the liberation of the poor from poverty if we do not know who the poor are and why they live in poverty? Social analysis is a tool that helps us to know why the social, economic, and political orders are arranged as they are. It enables us to know not only who benefits from the present status quo, but what must be done to change it.

In our struggle to make a new start in theology, we discovered, to our surprise and great satisfaction, that theologians in Asia, Africa, and Latin America were making similar efforts in their contexts.[21] The same was true among other ethnic minorities in the United States and among women in all groups.[22] Black theology has been challenged to address the issues of sexism[23] and classism in a global context, and we have challenged them, especially Latin Americans and feminist theologians of the dominant culture, to address racism. The focus on liberation has been reinforced and deepened. What many of us now know is that a turning point has been made in the theologies of black and Third World communities as radical as were the turning points made by Luther, Schleiermacher, and Barth in the sixteenth, nineteenth, and twentieth centuries in Europe. Let us hope that the revolution in liberation theology will change not only how we think about God, but more importantly what we do in this world so that the victims might make a future that is defined by freedom and justice and not slavery and oppression.

---

21. For an account of black theologians' dialogue with theologians in Africa, Asia, and Latin America, see *Black Theology: A Documentary History,* 445–608; *For My People,* 140–56. See also my essays that have been published from the conferences of the Ecumenical Association of Third World Theologians: "A Black American Perspective on the Future of African Theology," in *African Theology en Route*; "A Black American Perspective on the Search for Full Humanity," in Virginia Fabella, ed., *Asia's Struggle for Full Humanity*; "From Geneva to São Paulo: A Dialogue between Black Theology and Latin American Liberation Theology," in Sergio Torres and John Eagleson, eds., *The Challenge of Basic Christian Communities* (Maryknoll, N.Y.: Orbis Books, 1981); "Reflections from the Perspective of U.S. Blacks," in Virginia Fabella and Sergio Torres, eds., *Irruption of the Third World*; "Black Theology: Its Origin, Method and Relation to Third World Theologies," in Sergio Torres and Virginia Fabella, eds., *Doing Theology in a Divided World* (Maryknoll, N.Y.: Orbis Books, 1985).

22. The dialogue between black theology and other ethnic theologies in the U.S. has taken place in the context of Theology in the Americas. For an interpretation of this dialogue, see *For My People,* chapter 7; see also Sergio Torres and John Eagleson, eds., *Theology in the Americas* (Maryknoll, N.Y.: Orbis Books, 1976), and Cornel West, Caridad Guidote, and Margaret Coakely, eds., *Theology in the Americas: Detroit II Conference Papers* (Maryknoll, N.Y.: Orbis-Probe, 1982).

23. See especially, *Black Theology: A Documentary History,* 363–442; Cone, *My Soul Looks Back* (Maryknoll, N.Y.: Orbis Books, 1985); *For My People,* chapter 6.

Chapter 5

An Asian Perspective on the Cross and Suffering

Andreas A. Yewangoe

✝

Asia — A Multifaceted Continent

Asia is not easily viewed as a whole. In fact Asia must be looked at as a continent of great variety, made up of many races, cultures, and religions. The nations of China, Korea, north and south, and Japan all have customs greatly influenced by Chinese culture. On the other hand, the peoples of India, Pakistan, Bangladesh, and Myanmar show influences from the Hindu/Buddhist cultures of India. Indonesia is the meeting place of these two great streams of culture, Chinese and Indian, mixed with the native culture of Indonesian tribes, and then Islam. Out of such a confluence Indonesia has produced its own culture.

Hinduism originated and developed in India, and today the majority of India's population is Hindu. India also gave birth to Buddhism, which at one level can be seen as a reaction to Hinduism, though its rapid growth took place outside India itself. In Thailand, for example, Buddhism has developed extensively, whereas in China, Buddhism has taken shape by assimilation with Confucianism and Taoism. So also in Japan, where Buddhism has been assimilated with Shintoism to produce a Japanese Buddhism. In Korea, indigenous Buddhism is the product of the fertilization of Buddhism with Shamanism. Indonesia had been influenced by both Hinduism and Buddhism before the thirteenth century and the arrival of Islam. However these imported religions have never completely eliminated traces of the indigenous religions of Indonesia. Although Islam is the religion of the majority of its population, in fact it has already accommodated itself to Indonesian culture. In Pakistan, Bangladesh, and Malaysia Islam is also the majority religion. The Philippines is the only country in Asia with a Christian (Roman Catholic) majority among its population. In the light of this, what Aloysius Pieris has said is surely true, namely, that Asia is a continent of multifaceted religiosity.[1]

It is also true to say that Asia is the birthplace of all the major religions we know in the world today. Of course, in other places we do find tribal religions, as in Africa and Oceania, but these tribal religions have never had the widespread and strong influence of the great religions of Asia.

We do not, however, see the distinctiveness of Asia only in the fields of culture and religion. Asia also has a common fate, *suffering*. Suffering is found all over the region, and Asia has been described by Aloysius Pieris as a continent of "overwhelming poverty."[2] This means that suffering as it is seen and realized all over Asia today takes its shape in poverty. In the countries of Asia, humankind struggles with the task of freeing itself from the clutches of poverty. The religions of Asia also have given much thought to the challenge of suffering and to how to gain freedom from it. In the following pages we will try to understand how this struggle has developed.

The Cross and Suffering

The theme with which I will deal is "the cross and suffering." The use of the word "and" here can convey a number of meanings. But what is most evidently conveyed is that the cross is seen as identical with suffering. Or that the suffering of humankind is the cross. This opinion is indeed true, at least if viewed through Christian spectacles. Nevertheless, we must also consider some other points. For instance, in most countries of Asia the cross is certainly not seen as the symbol of suffering but as the symbol of the church's pride and arrogance. The cross is usually identified with the coming of Western European peoples to Asia. The Portuguese in their conquest of Asia used the cross as their symbol. The Dutch used it this way in their conquest of Indonesia. Although Christianity cannot be characterized with things "Western," nevertheless, for Asian peoples the nations of the West are Christian. So it was that in Indonesia Christianity was called the "Dutch religion" for a long time. Only with a concerted effort to understand each other has this opinion gradually been changed.

The cross as something that points us to the suffering of humankind can, in one way, be seen as identical with the cross of Christ. By this I mean that the suffering of humankind is identical with the suffering of Christ in terms of its intensity and the existential experience both represent. On the other hand, it must be acknowledged that the two crosses are not the same. While the cross

---

1. Aloysius Pieris, "Towards an Asian Theology of Liberation: Some Religio-Cultural Guidelines," in Virginia Fabella, *Asia's Struggle for Full Humanity* (Maryknoll, N.Y.: Orbis Books, 1980), 75.

2. Ibid.

humankind bears is something that directs us to humankind's own suffering, the cross of Christ points us to the suffering of Christ as substitute for others.

Hence, using the cross as a symbol for the suffering of humankind must be approached with caution and seen as a Christian interpretation of all the suffering that humankind endures. Using the cross to point out the suffering of humankind has its use, in emphasizing the true nature of that suffering, and as such that it has to be overcome. But the CROSS, in capital letters, cannot be used to authenticate the suffering of humankind, or as an alibi to forget the many crosses that humankind has to bear today. That is to say, we cannot affirm that with the cross of Jesus Christ all the suffering of humankind has been dealt with and is at an end. Often enough people will suggest that this has happened while continuing to cause suffering to their fellow human beings, was the case with the oppression of Indians in Latin America under the control of countries that claimed to bear the "cross."

Asian Religions and Suffering

The religions of Asia have indeed given their attention to the problem of suffering, though with varying degrees of emphasis. This is an indicator that suffering, which is an integral part of the experience of Asian peoples, is not removed from the religious struggles of Asia's religions and their attempt to describe the way of salvation. By noting this, we want to suggest that Asian religions are trying to suggest a way out of suffering for humankind. It must also be agreed, however, that from another aspect religion provides humankind with motivation to continue to live under the burden of suffering. This may cause humankind to become fatalistic in attitude (because God has caused suffering, we need not try to be free from it). Another attitude that may be encouraged is that of "dolorism," whereby humankind can find a kind of freedom through the path of suffering itself.

To provide us with an overview of religious opinions about suffering we will consider them one by one.

Hinduism

According to Hinduism, life is governed by *karma,* a principle that controls all that happens in the world as it develops. So the life of a person is connected to this ongoing process, which does not end and is called *samsara.* Throughout one's life, a person is in a state of becoming; one will continue to undergo incarnation and cannot experience release (*moksha*).[3] As a result of this, the purpose of one's life is to try to free oneself from this process of becoming. This

---

3. J. Bowker, *Problems of Suffering in Religions of the World* (Cambridge, 1980), 195; G. Chemparathy, *God en het Liyden: een Indische Theodicee* (Leiden, 1986), 17. Huston Smith, *The Religions of Man* (New York: Harper & Row, 1958), 13–19.

can be accomplished whenever one achieves a state of unity with *Brahman*. To understand this teaching better, we should consider several key words that arise in the discussion about suffering.

Karma: This word is derived from a verb in the Sanskrit language that means "to do, to act." This verb deals with action. In the beginning, the word was connected with ritual acts but has come to describe all actions, both those that are good (*dharma*) and those which are bad (*adharma*).[4] If *karma* is understood as that which controls the world and its being, it follows that the life of a person is controlled too. This does not, however, mean that one is not responsible for all of one's actions. Indeed one is. If one suffers it is because one has lost control of oneself. Chemparathy has noted that there are two sides to the law of *karma*. First, an action, whether good or bad, cannot be wiped out without first having borne fruit, either in happiness or suffering. Second no one will harvest fruit from actions one did not perform oneself.[5] According to this opinion, the law of reincarnation is immutable; it is an indispensable part of human existence.

Samsara: A literal translation of this word means a continuation of the circle of being, or what is often described as "an endless circle of transmigration."[6] This concept is closely related to *karma* and reincarnation. Whenever one is within that cycle one is in the embrace of *samsara*.

Moksha: Although humankind is fundamentally tied to the chain of reincarnation, i.e., *samsara*, nevertheless there is a way of halting this process of becoming. This occurs whenever someone has achieved the status of *moksha*, which literally means "total release." This status is reached when the human being, in Hinduism called *atman*, realizes that he or she is a manifestation of *Brahman*. *Brahman* is "being itself," existence as such. In a very real way a person is *Brahman*. Suffering then can come about whenever someone is not aware of his or her essential unity with *Brahman*. However, when that realization takes place that person has achieved *moksha*.

Tat-tyam-as, which means "that you are," is the expression used to describe someone who is aware of being now at one with *That* (tat), or in other words with the Most High, *Brahman*.

Buddhism

In Buddhism suffering is described as *dukkha*. This is seen to be caused by desire. Desire gives rise to actions, and these actions have effects, according to the law of cause-and-effect. The life of a person then passes within a circle, as described above, circumscribed by suffering, desire, actions, and results. This reality is called "The Four Noble Truths" and represents the structure of a person's suffering. To be freed from this suffering, a person must be freed

---

4. Chemparathy, *God en het Liyden*, 18.

5. Ibid., 17.

6. H. Zimmer, *Philosophy of India* (Princeton: Princeton University Press, 1969), 53–281; Brian K. Smith, "Samsara," *The Encyclopedia of Religion*, ed. Mircea Eliade (1987), 3:56–57.

from desire, whose root is found in the very existence of humankind. For this reason, the "Noble Eightfold Path" must be followed. This path is made up of right view, right resolve, right speech, right action, right living, right effort, right contemplation, and right concentration. Whoever is successful in following this path achieves the status of *Nirvana*, a state of being that is hard to describe, though in short it can be described as complete freedom from all suffering.[7]

Zen-Buddhism

Zen-Buddhism is in fact one manifestation of Japanese Buddhism. Zen believe that through contemplation and meditation people receive direct enlightenment. According to Zen, essential cosmic unity can be achieved, which undergirds all experiences and happenings in life. One receives this enlightenment through meditation, by which one finds that cosmic unity, i.e., becoming aware that one's own soul and this cosmic reality are one. Those who achieve this status cannot be disturbed whatever disasters and sufferings come their way. Hence, through direct insight persons achieve a mystical experience that gives them direct understanding from "the beyond." In this way Zen-Buddhism opens the way for humankind to be aware of salvation and to free itself from suffering in this world.[8]

Confucianism

Confucianism is better described as a system of ethics than a religion. Suffering, which is considered as one expression of evil, is seen to be unnatural. It is believed that humankind by nature is good. Hence the will of a person is completely free. One is not bound to other persons or to a God. One is lord of one's own life. Thus humankind does not need any help from "outside." In other words the goal of Confucianism is to achieve the status of the ideal human being by considering all that humankind has achieved and can achieve. If suffering represents an obstruction to accomplishing that goal then it must be overcome.[9]

Taoism

Tao is the "ultimate reality" and is the antithesis of Confucianism. *Tao* means "way" or "way out" and also can be seen as that which is not evident, what is

---

7. Bowker, *Problems of Suffering in Religions of the World,* 240, 249; C. J. Bleeker, *Het geheim von de Godsdienst* (Wassenaar, 1973), 47–55; D. E. Harding, *De Wereld en Haar Godiensten* (Wassenaar, 1975), 42–43; G. Appleton, *On the Eight-fold Path* (London, 1961); R. H. Drummond, *Gautama the Buddha: An Essay in Religious Understanding* (Grand Rapids: Eerdmans, 1974).

8. William K. Bunce, *Religion in Japan* (Rutland, 1955).

9. Harding, *De Wereld en Haar Godiensten,* 64–66; Bleeker, *Het geheim von de Godsdienst,* 61–68; James Hastings, *Encyclopedia of Religion and Ethics* (*ERE*), vol. 4 (New York, 1911), 12–15.

not heard and not felt. It is "an absolute transcendental existence beyond all senses." At the same time *tao* is believed to be the essence of all existence. In other words, *tao* is the creative principle that makes everything possible by integrating *yin* and *yang*. These two primordial principles have to be in harmony with each other so that everything can be at peace. In the *Tao Te Ching* it says, "The way is gained by daily loss, loss upon loss, until at last comes rest. By letting go, it all gets done; the world is won by those who let it go! But when you try and try, the world is beyond winning." It continues, "The movement of the way is a return, in weakness lies its strength." Thus, suffering itself can represent "The Way" (*tao*), the ultimate reality.[10]

Islam

Suffering in Islam is understood as the will of Allah, it is Allah's creation. Allah is all-powerful, able to decide and decree all things. There is nothing which is beyond the will of Allah, including suffering. It is clearly stated in the Koran that suffering is the judgment of Allah (Q.IV:80; XLXX:55). Suffering also can be viewed as a test of the faith of a person (Q.II:150–157); XXI:36; III:134–35). Accordingly, the Koran endeavors to harmonize the reality of suffering with the sovereignty of Allah by affirming Allah both as the Great One and the All-loving.[11]

An Indonesian View of Suffering:
Nrimo, Sabar, Ikhlas

I now want to look at and develop Indonesian perspective on suffering, not only because I hail from there and am familiar with its perceptions, but also because this view mirrors the mixture of elements of the indigenous (tribal) religions found in our society, along with Islam.

We want to consider what is customarily called, *"nrimo, sabar,* and *ikhlas."* There are those who say this view is fatalistic, but this is not correct. Several Indonesian experts have weighed this suggestion, i.e., that the attitude of Indonesians is essentially fatalistic. Before we consider this opinion, it must be acknowledged that the idea is influenced greatly by Islam, and so the Islamic background must be looked at first. Only then will an attempt to understand these concepts in a wider Indonesian context be made.

Narimo is usually associated with the Islam understanding of *tawakkul.*[12] This word means "faith in Allah"; to place everything in the hand of Allah.

---

10. Harding, ibid., 72; Bleeker, *Het geheim von de Godsdienst*; Hastings, *ERE*, vol. 12 (1921), 170–202.

11. Bowker, *Problems of Suffering in Religions of the World,* 105, 106, 109; Bleeker, ibid., 29; Harding, ibid., 112–13.

12. Sularso Sopater, *Inti Ajaran Aliran Valentinian dan Inti Ajaran Pangestu* (Jakarta, 1983), 247–48.

But this does not mean that one is discouraged from taking the initiative in one's life. Allah may be affirmed as the only One who looks after humankind, yet humankind is not forbidden from using every means to look after its own life. Even by doing that a person's faith in the sovereign care of Allah is not diminished.

Sabr has several meanings in the Koran. First, it means "patience." (Sura XXXVIII:16; XLVI:34; XXIII:133; XXVIII:54). Second, it also means that someone who is involved in a Holy War will be protected (Sura III:140; VIII:66). Its third meaning is "resignation," especially as used in *Sura Yusuf* (III:18). Finally, *sabr* sometimes means "perseverance" in accomplishing a task in relation to the *"salat,"* the obligatory prayers for a Muslim (Sura II:42, 148).[13] *Ikhlas* represents that inward virtue an Islamic believer possesses. It implies purity that will endure in the works of their religion, worship that is pure and given to Allah alone, devotion that is absolute and offered to Allah and toward those in the fellowship of faith. This purity in the life of the believer and in his witness to the faith is measured by *ikhlas* and *ihsan* (uprightness in good).

Gardet has given three examples of different meanings of the word *ikhlas* arising in the history of Islam:

1. It can be understood as a requirement of faith and a virtue of those who believe including a faith that is complete, the endurance of trials (*sabr*), and openness to Divine decrees, the divine will (*rida*). This view, which is found in the more moderate form of Islam practiced by the Ismailis and deriving from Ikhwan al Safa, understands *ikhlas* as purity and unity of purpose, expressed both in terms of works done before Allah (*Amal*) and answers rendered to Allah (*du'a*).

2. It can be understood as the secret of the heart that is brought close to Allah through the mediation of great works (*al-takkarub bi-l-nawafil*), especially during the time of fasting for forty days and the "retreat." This emphasis is felt most in the meditations of the Sufi.

3. It can be understood as proclaiming values with respect to an outside judicial agent and obedience in all actions to the law of their religion. This perspective, which is met in Ibn Taymiyya, who was influenced by Abu Talid al-Makki dan Al-Ghazali, emphasizes the idea of devotion to Allah, to the prophet, and to the fellowship. If someone wants to add "deeds in the way of Allah," then he will widen in the world the "rights of God and man," and so make *djihad* the highest form of *ikhlas* toward Allah. Worship that is pure and devotion that is unconditional can then be seen as the "most profound attitude" expected from every person who believes.[14]

From what we have considered above, we can say that it is too easy and simplistic to view these perceptions as having a fatalistic attitude.

---

13. A. J. Wensinck, "Sabr," *Enzyklopaedie des Islam,* Houtsma and Wensinck, eds. (Leiden, 1934), 26–28; Bowker, *Problems of Suffering in Religions of the World,* 116.

14. L. Gardet, "Ikhlas," *The Encyclopedia of Islam,* 2d ed. B. Lewis, ed. (London, 1971), 3:1059–60.

We turn now to look at how Indonesian people themselves judge these matters. Sumantri Hardjoprakoso, in his dissertation entitled "Indonesisch Mensbeeld als Basis Ener Psycho-Therapie" (Indonesian Concept of the Human Being as a Basis for Psycho-therapy)[15] explains that *narimo* must be understood as a soul balance. Thus what happens is a matter of persons receiving what comes their way in life. *Narimo* is an attitude of not wanting things or the possessions of someone else. It can even be said that *narimo* is richness, richness that has no limits.

Sabr is one of those prime virtues humankind possesses. Although *sabr* is resignation, it does not mean surrender. On the other hand, through *sabr* a person has the ability to withstand suffering. By possessing *sabr* one can widen one's insight.

Ikhlas (openness, or *rila*) is a state of mind that allows a person not to be tied or restricted to something transitory, and this because everything depends on the sovereign *Suksma Kawekas,* "the First and the Highest Facet," which is considered the Source of all that lives, without limitation (and often symbolized as the ocean and rest). *Rila* is then the act of differentiating between "I" and everything that is transitory. This does not, however, mean that one can set aside one's responsibilities. Those who achieve "openness" are increasingly freed from "I" (self) in relation to material things. Hence, *rila* is a sign of maturity in faith.

By understanding these key words we may grasp how Indonesians view suffering. It is true that these words are focused on the inward state of human beings. It cannot be imagined that the person who has *sabr* (is patient) will cause a riot. Nevertheless, it does not mean that Indonesians do not know what it is to resist! They certainly know how to express themselves. In many parts of Indonesia, and indeed in most parts of Asia, there is an interest in Messianism.[16] The hope is that someone will appear to lead humankind out of a critical situation. That personage can be viewed as an incarnation of a god, as in the phenomenon of *Avatara* in India, or as a person of great spiritual power who can thereby influence the population at large.

In Indonesia we meet this phenomenon in the person of the *Ratu Adil.* Literally this means "the king who brings justice," and the expectation for the coming of this king is based on the *Treatise on the Predictions of Djajabava.* According to this treatise, a time will come, called the age of madness, when there will no longer be law or principle, or even morality, so the Righteous King will arise on the stage of world history. This *Ratu Adil* is Raja Erutjahra.

This belief is found in the hearts of many Indonesians, so that whenever natural disaster threatens, people immediately start to look for the coming of the

---

15. Leiden, 1956.

16. J. M. van der Kroef, "Messianic Movements in the Celebes, Sumatra and Borneo," in *Comparative Studies in Society and History,* supplement 2 (New York, 1962), 80–121; A. Kruyt-Adriani, "De Godsdienst Politieke Bewegung 'Mejapi' op Celebes," *BKI* (The Hague, 1986); Sartono Kartodirdjo, *Tjatatan tentang segi-segi Messianistis delam sejarah Indonesia* (Yogyakarta, 1959).

Righteous King. Just such a thing happened with the case of Sawito in 1977. Sawito was an Indonesian who came from Bogor in West Java. He was sure that he possessed *wangsit,* a direct revelation from God. This insight compelled him to help his nation in its struggle with injustice. In his opinion President Suharto was not fit to lead Indonesia and so should have handed over the reigns of power to ex-Vice-President Hatta. Of course Sawito fell afoul of the law because of this opinion. This was an instance of the belief in a Messiah found in the hearts of suffering Indonesians giving rise to the expectation of *Ratu Adil's* coming.

This is but a short treatment of the views on suffering held by the major religions in Asia and how they seek a way out of that suffering. What is clear is that suffering is indeed a reality and of the essence of humankind. Whatever religion people follow, suffering is something that unites. Because of that we can say at least in theory that unity among the peoples of the world can be envisaged in their common fight against suffering. It is sadly true that historically humankind has seldom come together to confront suffering. Rather, followers of one religion often have visited suffering on those of another. In cases like this we can imagine the true values of a religion being turned around or manipulated to achieve singular ends.

The Church and Suffering

The Christian church in Asia is in the minority (only 2 percent of the total population). In many nations of Asia the Christian population has not been given the freedom to develop itself, in Myanmar, for example. The lot of Christians is one of suffering, and for that reason much thought has been given to the question. Its focus, though, has not been only on the suffering of Christians. Instead, the feeling of solidarity with people facing suffering has given rise to these reflections. What Kazoh Kitamori wrote in his book, *Theology of the Pain of God,*[17] is a case in point.

Kitamori begins with the anguish of the Japanese people after the atomic bombs exploded over Nagasaki and Hiroshima and tries to contextualize the gospel in the living situation prevailing in Japan. We cannot consider this book too deeply here, but what we can draw from it is the focus on God's awareness, even God's suffering in this context. For Kitamori suffering is the essence of God's being. Hence God in God's essence can feel and take up our suffering. Jesus Christ is the Lord who takes up our suffering. According to Kitamori, the cross of Christ is the realization of God's suffering in history. On the cross, God's suffering can be understood, though it must be sought through a knowledge of Jesus in history. The suffering and death of Jesus then are the revelation or expression of the suffering of God in the midst of history. In that case what do we say of the suffering of humankind? For Kitamori, human suffering is not

---

17. London, 1966.

lost or without meaning because of a person's perspective on God's suffering; instead it is seen as a symbol of the suffering of God (*analogia dolores*).

Another example in which the suffering of a nation has caused the local church to wrestle with this problem is in Korea. Recently in Korea, *minjung* theology has come to the fore.[18] *Minjung* is a Korean word that means "people." The *minjung* are those who resist in a situation where they are oppressed, those who do not lie down under their fate. Their every effort is to free themselves from the burden of oppression, even though the immediate results are even greater dangers than they faced before. Against such a background, *minjung* theologians have developed their own theology. In fact it is an accumulation and articulation of theological reflections on the experiences of Korea in the 1970s.

According to these theologians the *minjung* are those who reflect upon their history in which they are not in control of their destiny. History is normally written from the perspective of those who have power and reflects that power and those who govern with it. *Minjung* theology encourages a change in that situation. The writing of history must begin with the *minjung,* with the result that the *minjung* will themselves become aware of their own destiny as a vital part of that history. To affirm this reality, the Exodus event becomes a paradigm to be appreciated. Just as the people of Israel were freed from Egypt, so also the *minjung* will be released from all their burdens. Jesus then is seen as the One who sets free. According to the *minjung,* Jesus takes sides with them. This means that the cross becomes vitally important for them, as it is seen as a sign of the most intense suffering. And the suffering Jesus had to undergo when crucified is intimately related to the suffering of the *minjung* themselves, especially under Japanese occupation. Humankind identifies itself completely with the suffering of Jesus on the cross, and that cross becomes a symbol of its own crosses. This theological perspective, as we have seen above, is drawn directly from the suffering of the nation.

In many nations of Asia the problems of poverty, justice, and truth are real issues. This is then reflected in the theological developments we see in these places. In the Philippines we meet a kind of liberation theology, similar to that which has arisen in Latin America. For a long time the Philippines had been under the colonial control of the Spanish, and a large number of their population are Catholic. The problem they faced during the years of the Marcos regime was how to become free from that dictatorship. Since that time the challenge has been to find a way to rebuild the Philippines from the ruins of a mismanaged economy. Hence development has become the main subject for theological debate, not only in the Philippines, but in many other parts of Asia also. These reflections have as their goal the establishment of a firm foundation for Christian involvement in development. In Indonesia since the time of the Seventh

---

18. The Commission on Theological Concerns of the Christian Conference of Asia, ed., *Minjung Theology: People as Subjects of History* (Maryknoll, N.Y.: Orbis Books, 1981).

Synod of the Indonesian Council of Churches (DGI) in Pematang Siantar, constant reflection has gone on about the meaning of the Christian commission, being sent into the world. Each Christian is charged to bear the good news that sets free. In this case the gospel is understood as the news of freedom for all who are oppressed. "The church is sent into the world to proclaim the gospel of Jesus Christ. The gospel is Good News of repentance and renewal provided for humankind, and of the freedom, justice, righteousness, truth, and welfare that the Lord wills for the whole world."[19] The churches in Indonesia have tried to reformulate their understanding of the gospel so that they can articulate more clearly their mission to the world, and especially to the nation of Indonesia, preoccupied as it is with the challenge of development.

This enterprise is seen as a participation in the work of God, already begun in the past, continuing today, and stretching out into the future of Indonesia and its people. The churches have already taken practical steps to realize this goal. Several "development centers" have been established both in Jakarta, the capital, and in regional centers also. Through these centers, people are trained to take their part in the planning and realization of development. What they receive is not just skills training but training in how to motivate others to become involved as they to understand the meaning and goals of development. In this way the people of Indonesia hope that the people will not be seen as merely tools used to produce the fruits of development; rather all development activity will be directed toward what upbuilds humankind itself.

The theological principles that were accepted at Pematang Siantar, based on a reexamination of the gospel with very real implications for the churches in their struggle with suffering and for freedom, have become a clear guide for the churches on the road ahead. In many subsequent meetings of the churches and in practical projects undertaken, these issues of freedom and suffering have been prioritized. As Indonesia enjoys economic growth at an increasingly rapid rate, the churches in turn have played their part in highlighting the dangers of social inequality. As some get richer, many get poorer — a clear question of social injustice. If this is the reality today, the threat to social order and the well-being of the nation is all too obvious. In a situation such as this the churches stand alongside the poor.

Clearly *poverty* has become the biggest challenge for the churches in Indonesia. At the Tenth Synod of the DGI in Ambom in 1984, the churches affirmed their concern. In a period of service (e.g., 1984–89), when poverty and other social suffering are the main problem in national development, preaching the gospel of Jesus Christ, who "for your sakes ... became poor ..." (2 Cor. 8:9), means giving special attention to the poor and oppressed. Preaching the gospel to the whole of creation (Mark 16:15) means proclaiming good news to the poor, proclaiming liberation to the captives, giving sight to the blind, and announcing

---

19. D. G. I., *Diutus Kedalam Dunia* (Jakarta, 1972).

the year of God's mercy (Luke 4:18–19). This is the sign of the coming of a new age, beginning in Christ (Luke 4:20–21).[20]

At the Eleventh General Assembly of Surabaya, 1989, this goal was pursued further, as the assembly met under the theme, "The Holy Spirit empowers us to become witnesses," and the subtheme, "Together tackling poverty through national development as bringing into practice Pancasila."[21] This subtheme shows clearly the reality of life in Indonesia. Indeed there is progress, but the price of that progress is that a greater part of Indonesia's people face real poverty. The church feels it is called to address this problem of suffering. To overcome it, however, requires not only the participation of the church alone, but of all parties working together. "Together" is the key word in this process. Although Indonesians as followers of different religions have different perceptions about who God is, nevertheless this one thing unites them — their common struggle to overcome the effects of suffering, poverty, injustice, and untruth. In this "arena" all people can come together, because we are facing problems that are common to our humanity.

The church has also been called on to play an important role in the field of advocacy. What I mean is that the church must be courageous enough to stand alongside those who are weak and defend their cause. It is not a secret that in the process of national development in Indonesia many people have been moved from their land. In each case there is a compensation payment made, but that payment is not commensurate with the true value of the land. Those who have had to move cannot now buy land to replace what they have lost, which in turn means they in time fall prey to poverty. Even more distressing is that in such a situation they cannot defend themselves before the law because they do not understand it. Here the church exercises an essential ministry, providing them with a defense before the courts, but also, and more importantly, raising a prophetic voice and bringing a constant note of warning about injustice. Not only that, the church also provides through prayer and action a ministry of restoration, seeking to build up and causing none to suffer loss.

Of course, I am not suggesting that this is an easy task. While it is hard to give precise figures, there is no doubt that Christians are a small minority in Indonesia and as such do not find it easy to raise their prophetic voice. For that reason the church's task is accomplished in partnership in society. Certainly we do find points of agreement when we are considering together the suffering of our common humanity. This suffering knows no limits and is not bound by religion or race.

To conclude this section I want to raise one further point concerning the recent discussion in Asia of liberation theology, or a theology of development. As we know, Latin American theologians are more inclined to speak of "libera-

---

20. D. G. I., *Pokok-Pokok Tugas Panggilan Bersama* (PTPB) 1984–88, 21.

21. *Pancasila,* or the five pillars, on which the Indonesian Republic is established, consists of belief in God, Humanity, Nationalism, Democracy, and Social Justice.

tion," as opposed to "development." Development, according to them, does not adequately address the problem faced in Latin America where people are not able to fulfill their potential as human beings. Instead of freeing humankind, development only brings advantage to those capitalist nations (read: U.S.A.) along with those who act for them, those in power in their own countries in Latin America.[22] This may well be true. In Asia, however, the tendency is to stress a theology of development; one theologian who has articulated this view in a systematic way is C. G. Arevalo.[23]

According to Arevalo, development in Latin America truly has not set people free, but in other parts of the Third World it has. For Arevalo, this is related to the Christian understanding of what the true church is and our perception of Christ as the touchstone of all humankind's endeavors for truth, the preservation of good human values, human culture that is genuine, and true human development. The Christian vision of development then is something that can set free, because it is not imperialistic. Also, this vision of development is optimistic, because we believe that through Christ, who has been crucified and raised to life again, we are freed from the power of sin, and redeemed humanity has entered a new life. According to Arevalo, this vision is one that brings great joy, as humankind is able to truly find itself.

Arevalo describes a theology of development that has a christological foundation. This foundation is firm because Christ is the root and foundation of all being, the archetype and prototype, the light and power, the meaning and value, the support and goal of all creation (Col. 1:15–20). More than that, Christ is the image of God, the first-born of all creation; he is the fullest revelation of all the divine wisdom. So to try to understand the world is in essence an attempt to understand the wisdom of God.

Finally, our involvement in the process of development is to be caught up in the three great moments of God's involvement in this world: creation, reconciliation, and fulfilling God's purposes toward humankind. Our involvement is an affirmation about Christ in the world of matter and the world of human beings, in the world of power, technology, politics, and relationships; about the unity of humankind in the struggle for justice and peace. This in short is the perspective of Arevalo.

Summary

I will try to summarize. First of all we must acknowledge that to talk of "an Asian perspective" on suffering is not easy. It is often better to consider the many different perspectives that arise from the many countries of Asia, each with its own background, religion, and culture.

---

22. See Gustavo Gutiérrez, *A Theology of Liberation* (Maryknoll, N.Y.: Orbis Books, 1988).

23. C. G. Arevalo, "Notes for a Theology of Development," in D. J. Elwood, ed., *What Asian Christian Are Thinking* (Quezon City: New Day Publishers, 1976), 398–424.

Suffering is a common thread binding together all the religions of this region. So also is the common struggle to overcome it. At different times and in different places suffering will show itself in different ways. Today suffering is most keenly felt through the blight of poverty.

Although people may differ in their perspectives about suffering there is something essentially the same about all suffering, namely, that it threatens people's very existence. If humankind is aware of this threat, it will do all in its power to overcome it. Perhaps in its endeavors to overcome suffering humankind will be able to achieve a kind of unity. After all, isn't suffering a problem of being human and of human dignity?

Is the cross identical with suffering? Or is suffering identical with the cross? We only begin to answer these questions as Christians as we struggle with the true meaning of both the cross and of suffering. We must remember that the cross has at times also been a symbol of pride in the church.

Churches have never ceased in their task of proclaiming the news of freedom, even freedom from suffering. But the source of that suffering is found in the sin of humankind, and in this modern age the notion of sin does not stir the heart of humankind. Perhaps therein lies the problem: when we suppose we are already free, we are inclined to fall prey to egoism and self-importance. The meaning of the cross of Christ is found precisely here, where all sin is dealt with. That is the meaning of redemption.

Chapter 6

A Latin American Perspective on the Cross and Suffering

Walter Altmann

America, Amerindia,
still in Passion:
one day your death
will be Resurrection!

This is a quotation from a poem by Dom Pedro Casaldáliga and Pedro Tierra, taken from the "Mass of the Earth without Evils,"[1] a musical mass that celebrates the suffering and the faith of the native peoples of the Americas. The non-natives, who in this mass unite themselves with the native peoples, join themselves in the memory of the pain, repent for the historical crimes committed against the indigenous peoples, and celebrate a new commitment supporting an earth without evils. In Latin America we have learned to link the people's suffering deeply with Jesus' suffering on the cross. Aware of his uncompromising solidarity with all those who suffer, we perceive in the people's suffering the continuous presence of Jesus Christ on our continent. As in the gospels, so also in Latin America, Jesus suffers a long, intense, and unbearable passion. We confess as well that, as in the gospels, resurrection and liberation break forth from the depth of the suffering in the midst of this passion.

Of course, disbelief is always possible. The crude facts seem to contradict the faith, and those who are indifferent, skeptical, or unbelieving will find much more meaning in mockery than in hope. This was already the reaction of those persons who passed in front of the cross of Jesus at Golgotha: "Aha! You who

---

1. D. Pedro Casaldáliga et al., *Missa da Terra sem Males* (Rio de Janeiro: Tempo e Presença, 1980), 67.

would destroy the temple and build it in three days, save yourself, and come down from the cross!" (Mark 15:29, 30). Without a doubt they were very sensible people facing that failed and radical utopian. There will also be those powerful ones who will take the opportunity to celebrate the misery of Latin America, just as in that time the priests and scribes did in relation with Jesus: "He saved others; he cannot save himself. Let the Messiah, the King of Israel, come down from the cross now, so that we may see and believe" (Mark 15:31ff.). Come down now. . . . Power does not know hope, only crude facts. The realities of the present seem to indicate that the powerful are right.

In contrast, the text which I quoted in the beginning is a devotional text. It comes from communities that gather together to celebrate their faith, remember their history, confess their guilt, strengthen themselves with a word of God and the sacraments, give praise with new songs, intercede for those who suffer, take on a renewed commitment of struggle and love. The community reading of the Bible, the freedom of prayer, the fervor of new songs, the groan of pain, the cry for help, but also the silence for reflection, the hug between brothers and sisters, the caring gesture, the sharing of life, the commitment to the poor and the wronged — all this is greater than and comes before any theology. Liberation theology is preceded by the spirituality of liberation, and only through the former's close connection with the latter can it be relevant as theology.

With these premises I will develop my theme in three steps: the suffering of the peoples, the images of Christ, our challenge.

The Suffering of the Peoples

When, at the end of the fifteenth and the beginning of the sixteenth centuries, the Spanish and Portuguese came to the American continent, they found it inhabited. Many millions of native people, in innumerable nations, occupied the continent as their living space. Even so, this arrival of the white people, so tragic in its consequences for the native population, was classified by the Spanish and the Portuguese as the "discovery" of America. The schoolbooks of today invariably continue to classify it so. However, the continent had already been discovered many centuries before by those who were then occupying it. Pronouncing this new arrival as a discovery masks the reality. In truth it was an invasion and a conquest, motivated by uncontrolled colonial interests and by the insatiable greed of the conquerors. The native populations, which almost always received the intruders peacefully, began suffering a long history of horror, slavery, and extermination. Ninety million American Indians died violently. Is there another continent so deeply impregnated with blood? The "white" sword is so viscerally grounded in American soil that it will be impossible to ever yank it out again. The name "America," itself, which is the name given by the conquerors, betrays the fact that conquest led to domination. Today, other populations definitively occupy almost all the space. On the present Brazilian

territory, which, at the time of the so-called discovery was occupied by an es-
timated 2 to 5 million natives, there exists today a population of 150 million
inhabitants, of which only some 220,000 are native Brazilians, and these find
themselves threatened by the final assault of the white people on their lands,
forests, and remaining mineral wealth.

However, it is not only the sword that is grounded in the fertile soil of this
continent, but at its side, grounded equally firmly, is the cross, the fundamental symbol of Christianity. The sword and the cross — today we know that
fortunately, throughout all of our history, there were those who prophetically
recognized and denounced the total contradiction between the two of them.
Both are symbols of death. The sword reminds us of the bloody white hand
that grasped it. The cross, although a Roman instrument of execution, evokes
the One who because of his justice suffered on it. To remember it again, in our
history there were also those who denounced the profound contradiction, placed
themselves at the side of the indigenous populations in their defense, and eventually paid for their audacious witness with their own lives. These were those
killed because of this Christian witness from the sixteenth century on until our
own days. The blood of martyrs of all these centuries was added to that of the
native and the black peoples.

However, for the great majority of the Portuguese and the Spanish there was
no contradiction between the sword and the cross: both cooperated in spreading
Christianity. The conquerors understood themselves as servants of the crown
and God. They took the true faith, with steel and fire if necessary, to the
unchurched and "barbarian" nations — this is how they classified the dominated ones. It is a tragic story not only because of the unequal confrontation
of weapons but also because of the cultural and religious imposition. The conquerors understood themselves as representatives of a culture that was not only
superior but also all-encompassing, into which they sought to incorporate, by
any means possible, the dominated culture. They were confronted with the native culture, which was markedly open and receptive. The native perception of
the world reserved a space for the "other," for the "different," for the "new."
Their open space, however, was invaded by another culture, the European,
which was closed and absolute and did not know tolerance, only imposition.
They carried the so-called true faith as the greatest value, to which all had to
adhere voluntarily or, if necessary, compulsorily. The conqueror had a sense of
mission and was carrying out what was called the "project of Christendom,"
which would be complete only when it had spread throughout the whole world.

There is a story from the sixteenth century that illustrates in a simultaneously
beautiful and painful way this reality. It is a text by an anonymous person from
Yucay (the present territory of Peru) who wished to protest against the preaching
of the priest and bishop of Chiapa, which in his view was false. The bishop's
preaching stated that the riches of the Incas should not be taken from them and
that the Incas should hide their gold and silver for their own protection and
survival. Now, the anonymous person, who criticized the bishop, was convinced

that the gold and silver of the natives constituted their "means of predestination and salvation," since the gospel goes to where there are riches and inversely the "Gospel will never come to where there are no riches because there will be no soldier nor captain nor even minister of the Gospel who will want to come." Thus God gave them riches so that in exchange for these riches they might receive the faith, Christianity, and salvation. Only the devil could be suggesting to them that they should hide their wealth so that they would be blocked from reaching heaven. The anonymous person from Yucay exemplified this with an impressive and sadly significant story:

> God has dealt with these miserable Gentiles and with us as a King who has two daughters: one of them is very beautiful, very discreet, graceful, and charming; the other one is very ugly, capricious, stupid, and crude. It is not necessary to give the first one a dowry to marry her off. It is sufficient to place her in the palace and there will be competition to see who will marry her. As to the ugly, apathetic, lazy, and disgraceful one, this will not be sufficient. It will be necessary to give her a very large dowry, many jewels, rich clothes, and luxurious houses.... So God has done with these Indians and with us. All of us were unfaithful — also in Europe and Asia — but by nature we had great charm, many sciences, discretion; little was needed for the apostles and the apostolic men to betroth these souls with Jesus Christ through the faith of baptism. As to these (other) nations, however, they were creatures of God destined to heavenly bliss, capable of this matrimony with Jesus Christ, but they were ugly, rustic, stupid, incapable, capricious....[2] A great dowry was necessary. And so (God) gave them even mountains of gold and silver, fertile and delightful lands so that in being attracted to this sweet smell there would be people for God's sake who would want to come and proclaim the gospel and baptize them so that these souls could become spouses of Jesus Christ.[3]

It would be hardly possible to imagine a story that would combine the missiological sense with the conviction of superiority and the economic greed as well as this one does. However it may be, where there were riches — and this continent was full of riches — that is where the soldiers and religious ministers headed. It is therefore not surprising that the sword and the cross are thus grounded side by side in this land.

I chose as an example this issue of the native peoples in the Americas because it is in fact the native peoples who are the greatest victims and the most

---

2. Let me introduce here a brief commentary of my own: this author at least still remembered the times of paganism in Europe itself and, conversely, is convinced that the natives were created by God as human beings. We remember that for a long time there had been a discussion about whether or not the so-called Indians had souls, that means ultimately whether they were human or not.

3. This account was discovered by Gustavo Gutiérrez and I obtained it from Felipe Adolf, general secretary of the Latin American Council of Churches.

defenseless in this tragic process of conquest and exploitation of the natural wealth of this continent. However, this is by no means a unique case, unfortunately; to the contrary, it is only an example. I could well have developed the issue of the suffering of women in Latin America under the prejudices and oppressive practices of traditional Latin American *machismo.*

Let me mention briefly the racial domination of the blacks. By the millions they were hunted down in African territory and piled onto infested slave ships. The survivors of the oceanic crossing were commercialized as merchandise in the market places of the "New World," maintained in slavery and ill treated, violently separated from their lands, their families, their culture, their language, their religion. At the time of the independence of Brazil, in 1822, for example, no less than two-thirds of the population of four million inhabitants were African. And — once again — the sword and the cross: Many times they were baptized by force before embarking on the slave ships so that if they died during the crossing they would not die as pagans. History has even registered cases where they were branded like cattle with the sign of the cross!

Another example is the issue of the land structure that was established on this continent: a structure of feudal characteristics where owners of giant tracts of land — today also including foreign citizens and companies — contrast on the one side with millions and millions of rural workers with no access to land ownership on the other side. Referring to my own ethnic background, I could also tell stories of German descendants. People whose survival was threatened in the last century by the European process of industrialization and urbanization followed by excess population in rural areas and their consequent impoverishment, they came to settle in the promised land in southern Brazil. (Naturally, there still were natives there, but what difference did that really make?) Subsequent generations of these immigrants were forced many times to migrate from place to place, always in the direction of north and west, and today they can be found together with other Brazilians and people of other ethnic origins cultivating the Amazon forest, the last available outpost, which is already being threatened. Behind them come the powerful, who once again appropriate the land and the wealth.

Finally, we could describe the process of industrialization, which in recent decades has been linked with international capitalist interests, and how this industrial expansion has taken place at the cost of the degradation of salaries and living conditions of the Latin American workers. For example, in Brazil there was an impressive leap in industrial growth, and the nation came to be the eighth-largest capitalist economy in the world. However, the minimum salary, which was instituted in 1941 to meet the basic needs of the worker, already does not stretch to buy even one-sixth of the goods deemed essential in the pertinent legislation. Today this process is aggravated by the necessity of paying back the huge international debt, caused — not only, but decisively — by an extortionate, unilaterally decided increase of interest rates in the 1980s. All this means that in Brazil, as a dependent country, economic progress took place at the cost of impoverishment of the population. One has to do with the other. This model, which is advantageous for the multinational interests and for the national rich minority but tragic for the workers, was imposed only a little more than a decade ago by the armed forces in almost all Latin American countries. Those successive military coups, which many times were carried out with external support and claimed to be in the name of "God" and "Western Christianity," more recall the disgraceful connection between the sword and the cross.

The Images of Christ

If such has been the suffering of the people of Latin America and if this suffering was imposed by the alliance between the cross and the sword, can one talk of experiencing liberation *in* Christ? Inversely, would not a liberation *from* Christ be necessary?

In fact, there is no easy answer to this crucial question. Many will not know how to escape an anguishing silence in the face of it. Dietrich Bonhoeffer reflected about the mission of the church while he was in prison, and he wrote the following for the baptism of his nephew and godchild: the church has been more interested in its self-preservation than in justice and doing good. Because of this sin, the church "lost its chance to speak a word of reconciliation to mankind and the world at large."[4] Because of this it must become silent, and "our Christianity today will be confined to praying for and doing right by our fellowmen. Christian thinking, speaking and organization must be reborn out of this praying and this action."[5]

It seems to me that each one of us should ask ourselves whether we have reasons to speak or whether, maybe, we should not adopt Dietrich Bonhoeffer's counsel and be silent. Have we already prayed intensely enough and been heard by God, whom we have offended so much? Have we delved into the practice of justice sufficiently to once more give credit to our word? Would not our talk be premature and, who knows, an excuse for our unbelief and laziness in prayer and for our insufficiently committed action in relation to the necessities of the poor and oppressed?

Nevertheless, we cannot cease to reflect on our historical situation, our experience, and our faith. What was the historical process that brought us to the present situation? What are the perspectives that our future history opens for us? What forces and interests were and are at stake? Or, more concretely, what are the powers and structures that over the course of our history have victimized so very many people? What caused and what is still causing such suffering? How have the poor and oppressed resisted and how do they open up a way for a society without exploited and without exploiters? What is the responsibility and the

---

4. Dietrich Bonhoeffer, *The Cost of Discipleship* (New York: Macmillan Co., 1963), 149.
5. Dietrich Bonhoeffer, *Letters and Papers from Prison* (New York: Macmillan Co., 1971), 140.

guilt of the churches? How does one commit oneself concretely to the poor and the wronged? What is the hope that puts life into our practice? To what extent is our practice molded by the Reign of God? We take in the gospel of Christ as pardon, but do we also let it be an impulse to new life? Do we let ourselves be motivated by our faith? Where do we see the presence of Jesus Christ on our continent? Are we following his path and are we in his discipleship? These are examples of questions that we cannot refrain from asking, and therefore we also have to dare to formulate answers — hopefully not empty words. However it may be, Latin American theology — in particular liberation theology — should be seen in this context: it intends to be above all else a theology of repentance and conversion and a theology committed to seeking liberation from those evils for which Christianity itself is co-responsible and for which it expresses repentance. Whenever liberation theology is not understood as a penitential theology, it will not have been understood at all.

After this rather extensive digression, let us reflect more directly about Christ on the Latin American continent. Throughout the history of the colonization of this continent, two christological images became crystallized above the others: a dead Jesus and Jesus as celestial monarch.[6] Both of these images have their origins, that is, their historical experience on the Iberian Peninsula. But they were transplanted to Latin America and there obtained a special form in accordance with the historical experience of that continent. The image of the dead Jesus comes especially from southern Spain and reflects the people's experience under the centuries-long domination by Arabs and Muslims. Jesus suffered for the people, but is defenseless, impotent, and defeated. In Latin America this same image of a dead Christ serves as an element of identification for the suffering people, the massacred natives, the enslaved blacks, the despoiled poor. All of these recognize this: Jesus suffered as we are suffering. The sculptured images of the dead Christ show him laid out, totally defeated and impotent, bleeding and with an expression of unspeakable suffering. These images remain in the crypts of the churches throughout the year, exposed to the devotion of the people. During Holy Week they are carried out in procession and the people repeat the stations of the cross along the *via sacra.*

It has not been difficult to recognize in this image the impotence of the people and perceive in it an essential factor responsible for the frequent apathy in facing the events of their lives, the conformity with suffering, and a lethargy in search of social transformation. It has not been difficult for critical reflection to detect in this image and in the devotion toward it an alienating role: the people identify themselves with the suffering of Christ and his spilled blood, but they are not mobilized to transform their situation of suffering.

Let us look at the other image: the one of Christ as a celestial monarch. That is, Jesus is seen in the image of the king (of Spain or Portugal). His glory and

---

6. See José Míguez Bonino, ed., *Faces of Jesus: Latin American Christologies* (Maryknoll, N.Y.: Orbis Books, 1983).

power are transferred to heaven. Like the king on earth, Jesus is the monarch in the sky. In fact, the paintings and sculptures of Jesus in heaven at that time represent him as an Iberian king: seated on a throne, luxuriously dressed, and ornamented with a golden crown. It is clear: the power and glory of this Jesus are not instruments of change nor agents of limitation for the terrestrial powers, but are quality attributes that Jesus saves for himself. The power that is actually exercised remains in the hands of the terrestrial kings.

It has been even easier to recognize in this image its use in favor of the powerful. Just as it served to legitimize the kings, it serves equally to sacramentalize the whole system of conquest and colonization. How could the cross not be united to the sword since the kings on earth are equal to Christ in heaven?

In fact, the conjunction of the two images, even more than each one alone, has played a particularly tragic role throughout the history of Latin America. When, on the one side, the power of Christ is transferred to heaven in the image of the effective terrestrial power of the king and, on the other side, a defeated Jesus is left for identification with and devotion of the people, systems of domination are obviously being supported.

However, there still remains the task of what we could call a revolutionary rescue in the light of the biblical message of the themes focused on in the images: the authority and the cross of Jesus. On the one hand, the image of Jesus as celestial monarch radically perverts the legitimate and indispensable remembrance of the authority of Christ, this authority that is above all powers and therefore is a limitation and judgment on those powers. So we read in the song of Mary, the exaltation of the power of God: "He has brought down the powerful from their thrones, and lifted up the lowly" (Luke 1:52). As for the dead Jesus, it cannot escape us that in centuries of oppression, many times without an immediate possible way out, the image of the dead Christ has been an important tool for the survival of a critical consciousness. Native peoples being exterminated, black populations being maintained in the severest slavery, millions and millions of people exploited to death by the most unmerciful systems of exploitation: what does it mean to them that Jesus also — as much as they — was victimized by evil and injustice? Thus the devotion to a dead Christ has also been throughout the centuries an important instrument for the survival of critical awareness. We are dealing with a passive resistance in the most literal meaning of the term. It could be indispensable in order to get through periods of captivity that seem endless.

What does it mean that Jesus was born marginalized, in a stable, and laid in a manger used exclusively to feed the animals? What does it mean that Jesus had no place to lay his head? What does it mean that he sweat blood before his imminent death? What does it mean that he was executed? What does it mean on the other hand that he said, "Blessed are you who are poor, for yours is the kingdom of God" (Luke 6:20b) and conversely, "Woe to you who are rich, for you have received your consolation" (Luke 6:24)? Jesus never said the opposite, even when he visited the rich in their houses. To the contrary, he tried to open their eyes and hearts to their sin and to the necessities of the poor. What does it mean that in one of his parables Jesus identified himself so clearly with the needy and the marginalized: those who are hungry and thirsty, those who are naked, sick, and in prison (Matt. 25:31–46)? All of these texts and many others may have often been spiritualized, but among the poor they have been recognized as effective images of their own history. The biblical text has thus ceased to be a historical account referring to the past, nor is it an intellectual message, but has rather come alive and current, in experience, practice, and history.

The processions of the cross, typical for Catholic religiosity, when celebrated by communities who have made this rediscovery, are no longer limited to intimate meditation nor do they finish with the importance of death. On the contrary, they are concretely connected with the experience of the people and culminate with the resurrection.[7] Thus, for example, a community of rural workers can combine devotion and meditation on the lands of a big plantation, reflecting at each station of the cross on the real situation of suffering of the workers and their family, of the women from the rural area and the children, who know of a real instance of expulsion from the land, of the burning of these farms, of the assassination of a companion carried out by order of the big land-owner. But it will end with the live hope that God does not abandon those who fear God, and their ardent expectation of the kingdom can take shape now in concrete actions in the struggle for the indispensable and urgent agrarian reform.

Even if the turn of events in Central America may have overshadowed much of its impact, we still may register how vigorous this rediscovery of the gospel sounds in this poem by Carlos Mejía Godoy, from the Nicaraguan Rural Mass. It is part of the Creed, the confession of faith in Christ:

> I believe in you, worker Christ,
> light of light and truly the only One of God,
> who, to save the world,
> in the humble and pure womb of Mary became incarnate.
> I believe you were beaten, scornfully tortured,
> martyred on the cross
> when Pilate was governor: the Roman imperialist,
> shameless and soul-less, who by washing his hands
> wanted to erase the mistake.
> I believe in you, companion,
> human Christ, worker Christ,
> conqueror of death,
> with your immense sacrifice
> you begot the new person
> for liberation.

---

7. See for example Leonardo Boff's exercises in spirituality in *Via-Sacra da Ressureição: A paixão, a morte e a ressureição navida de cada pessoa* (Petrópolis: Vozes, 1993).

You are resurrecting in every arm that rises up
to defend the people from exploiting domination:
because you are alive on the farm,
in the factory, in the school.
I believe in your struggle without truce,
I believe in your resurrection.

Our Challenge

In recent years there has been a new and dramatic shift in the life experience of the Latin American peoples characterized by loss of hope for the future. Today, the Latin American people as well as millions of their counterparts in the rest of the Third World have succumbed to an overwhelming sense of hopelessness. They are being attacked on all sides: through the drastic decline of their already low living standard, by harsh economic measures and unemployment, through the breakdown of essential public services like health and education. During the time of military dictatorships, the light of democratic government that appeared at the end of the tunnel inspired the hopes of the people. Memorable street demonstrations sparked the disappearance of the military regimes. Hope took wings and flew freely and happily. But where do we look now that hope has been wounded to its very soul as it flew?

At this moment, those who want to work with the common people in Third World countries are faced with a very dramatic challenge: how to struggle with people who have been discarded as useless articles? How to work with those who have been deceived and trampled on so many times that they no longer hope for anything? For the churches also it will be essential to work on the issue of how to stimulate credibly the rebirth of hope and the will to struggle.

I come to a close — certainly not a conclusion. In these concerns, there can be no conclusion. Indeed, this isn't even a beginning. I have mentioned the tribulation of the people of the Third World. I have talked about their sense of hopelessness. Nevertheless, as Christians, "we are afflicted in every way, but not crushed; perplexed, but not driven to despair; persecuted, but not forsaken; struck down, but not destroyed, always carrying in the body the death of Jesus, so that the life of Jesus may also be made visible in our bodies" (2 Cor. 4:8–10). Surely, one of the main tasks of a Christian community in solidarity with the impoverished and with those who have been plundered and marginated is to contribute to the rebirth of sensitivity to suffering, of hope in the midst of hopelessness, frustration, and discouragement. It will do so through its proclamation of the Good News of God's undeserved but abundant love, its celebration of worship, and its social involvement.

"Hope is the last thing that dies," is a Brazilian saying. It would seem that we have approached the final stage. The apostle Paul was so bold as to distinguish between something we would classify as "hope that leads to death" and "hope that leads to life." Like Abraham, he believed in a "hope against hope" (Rom. 4:18). Even so, can we have hope? Is not reality too cruel? Should we not despair? Does not death have the last word? Indeed, of all the powers that threaten human beings, Paul saw death as the last and greatest enemy.

However, when remembering Abraham, Paul detects in his faith the "justice" and with it the strength to overcome death, in a situation that was apparently without solution and without hope of descendants. God is then called someone who "gives life to the dead and calls into existence the things that do not exist" (v. 17). Furthermore it says that Abraham "grew strong in his faith" (v. 20). He and Sarah became the source of life that overcomes imminent death and extinction. Thus, Paul can no longer attribute the final word to death, so sure was he of Christ's resurrection (1 Cor. 15:19, cf. 15:1–28). And, as we know, according to Paul, this hope surges from our faith and leads to love. It has a definite source and a just as definite a goal. "And now faith, hope, and love abide, these three: and the greatest of these is love" (1 Cor. 13:13).

The date of the quincentennial of the so-called discovery of America was October 12, 1992. The churches, especially the Catholic Church, prepared themselves to celebrate the occasion. In what spirit was it done? There is the risk of an official celebration, commemorating colonization as the salutary Christianizing of the continent. This would be the celebration of the cross grounded at the side of the sword in American soil. It would be the celebration of the dominators. On the other hand the poor celebrated the date in penitence and as an expression of a liberating commitment. Yes, they recognize once more, more profoundly, that in fact Jesus Christ is in their midst as crucified — not at the side of the sword but stabbed by it.

In expressing the necessity of contributing to the rebirth of people's hope in the midst of widespread and intense hopelessness and in the face of the power of death, I come to an end by recalling a song composed in Brazil under the theme of "Jesus Christ, hope for the world" for the assembly of the Lutheran World Federation in Budapest in 1984. Since then it has been sung in very many services. The poetic text of my colleague, Sílvio Meincke, expresses the faith, hope, and love of the Christians of this land of suffering. The text affirms in the third verse:

> Yearning for a land without evils,
> for the Eden of plumes and flowers
> for peace and justice joined together
> in a world without hate nor pains.

> Yearning for a world without wars,
> craving desire for peace and innocence:
> for bodies and hands that meet,
> without weapons, without death or violence.

Yearning for a world without owners:
without strong or weak,
overthrow of all systems
that create palaces and shacks.

We already have a precious seed,
a pledge of your Kingdom, now.
The future lights up the present;
you are coming and will come without delay.

The hopeful and jubilant refrain says:

Oh, may your Kingdom come, Lord!
The feast of life to recreate!
Our hope and passion
transform into full joy!

Chapter 7

Is There a Feminist Theology of the Cross?

Elisabeth Moltmann-Wendel

Nowadays the cross, the most important symbol in Christianity, has become a problem for many women. The tortured body of Christ on the cross and his death — interpreted as an atoning death — no longer give them any strength. A Swiss woman theological student made a brief, ironic comment on the Christian cross: "I am not hanging any guillotine round my neck!" A woman suffering from cancer expressed what many people feel: "The crucified Christ no longer says anything to me, but the picture of Mary with the child radiates comfort and security for me."

The cross as it is often preached has often had fatal consequences for women. "Taking up one's cross" could mean patiently tolerating a violent husband, social injustice, and other wrongs that need to be remedied. Such preaching of the cross could contribute to keeping women down and oppressing them. "Crucifying the flesh" has usually been understood as the renunciation of pleasure and joy and as crucifying the desires.

Can a history of the cross with such effects be rescued? What significance can the story of the crucifixion of Jesus and the cross as a symbol have for women? These questions have bothered me for a long time in the face of a feminist theology that is again outraged at the theology of the cross. This outrage is reinforced by the antipathy to a necrophilic symbol expressed by other psychological and religious camps. It receives support from Jewish Christian groups who do not see the crucifixion of Jesus as anything special, but rather as an instance of a capital punishment that was often inflicted in the Roman Empire, thereby putting in question the Christian claim to the uniqueness of Jesus and the significance of the crucifixion. So we have a massive criticism of the central symbol of Christianity, not only among women in general, but above all among a group of women that has hitherto been silent in the church, that has a new psychological and social understanding of itself. The criticism — and this seems to me to be important — is a religious criticism that is at the same time a criticism of patriarchal thought patterns. Will feminist theology become a theology without the cross? What presuppositions underlie this? What repudiation of patriarchal notions is justified? And what content remains?

Approach of Feminist Theology

First I would like to say something about the approach of feminist theology in contrast to that of traditional theology.

Feminist theology begins from experiences and not from the revelation event. It begins especially from the social experiences of women, the discrimination against them and their invisibility in male-dominated societies and churches. It points out that women and men are shaped by different psychological and social presuppositions, which then in turn also shape their images of themselves, the world, and God. In the meantime, as a result of the works of Carol Gilligan and Anne Wilson Schaef,[1] we have come to know the difference between masculine and feminine thought patterns. However, we should not in any way understand these different thought-patterns as eternal modes of being, but regard them as being above all socially conditioned. Most of our current theological ideas are strongly stamped by masculine patterns of thought and life. When women understand this, they find it easier to see traditional theology as an expression of such a view of self and the world, rather than accusing it of being destructive or necrophilic. Such psychological and social analyses seem to me to be the only chance of entering into a critical dialogue. From this point, I want to attempt to get closer to the conflicts over the theology of the cross.

The theology of the cross as it has now fallen into disrepute contains some typical elements of the Male picture of man and the world. I can only make a few points here in a brief and oversimplified way. In leaving the sphere of the mother, the feminine, the world of the feelings and an initial security, to enter a male society and to have to assert himself in this society through achievements, a man may perhaps be in conflict all his life: guilty at having abandoned his origins and having — with hubris — to attain high ideals, e.g. equality with God. This is the sin that Kierkegaard describes as despair at wanting to be oneself.[2] These primal experiences are matched in theology. The Abrahamic religions, with their approach from the need to depart from the father's house, have legitimized the secret contempt for origins and the forward pressure toward future

---

1. Carol Gilligan, *In a Different Voice: Psychological Theory and Women's Development* (Cambridge, Mass.: Harvard University Press, 1982); Anne Wilson Schaef, *Women's Reality: An Emerging Female System in a White Male Society* (New York: Harper & Row, 1985).

2. Søren Kierkegaard, *The Sickness unto Death* (New York: Penguin, 1989).

fulfillment. To become a man, it is necessary to leave one's origins, but that brings a feeling of guilt; it can be experienced as godlessness, since the goal is unattainable. As Anne Wilson Schaef sees it, "In the White Male System, living in tune with God means getting in tune with something outside the self. . . . In order to be attuned to God, then, one must learn to deny or transcend the self. One must strive to be what one is not."[3]

In my view, sin as an expression of distance from God thus has its central place in the male system, as the experience of incompetence and helplessness, the fundamental alienation from God and other human beings. The one who is God-less is a frequent theme of theology and the starting point for the theology of the cross.

In the female system, by contrast, Wilson Schaef argues, "Living in tune with God means being in tune with what one already is." Anyone who is in harmony with her own process is also in harmony with God. "And God is not just our process and yet God is our process. . . . When we are out of tune with our internal process, though, we distort ourselves and are often destructive to others. That is the real nature of sin."[4] One does not despair of wanting to be oneself — Kierkegaard's other sin is more in accord with women's experience. The themes of feminist theology — the search for Goddess as the principle that is friendly to life, for a feminine God-ness, the motherly God or process theology — are an expression of this feminine system, this distinctive way to theological self-determination.

If we make a list of the conceptions of God in the two systems, we get the following result: in the male system God is above all a person and a secret pattern for identification. He is thought of as being outside this world and as the goal of one's being. By contrast, in the feminine system God is seen above all as a power of life, less personal and more transpersonal, and as a power of relationship. God/Goddess is named and experienced within the world and is an experience of origin and permanent power of relationship — like life itself. At present, the two systems stand over against each other as absolutes, and the reciprocal attacks end up in suspicions of a "Fascist religion of origins" or a "necrophilic religion."

This rough list helps me to understand male and also female theological approaches better, and at the same time also to see them critically. Where has masculine theology distorted the passion stories with its principle of sins? Where does women's theology attempt to trap God/Goddess in an immanent system and to skirt the fringes of the passion?

I want to go on from here in the second part to give an account of the feminist critiques of the theology of the cross and at the same time of my own criticism of the feminist critiques of the cross. In the third part I shall outline the possibilities for a feminist theology of the cross.

---

3. Schaef, *Women's Reality,* 168.
4. Ibid.

A Criticism of Critiques of the Cross

So far, the charges against the theology of the cross are unresolved. I want to see them in their context of male thought and at the same time ask how far they are justified.

Sado-masochism

Obviously God as person and also as a secret figure with whom to identify stands at the center of the masculine theology of the cross. This image of God has been attacked by women. Feminist theology seems no longer able to tolerate a God who according to Paul's testimony in the Bible has given up his Son (Rom. 8:32). Comparisons are made with Himmler. Women have said that this attitude of God's and of the men who interpret it is sado-masochism. At the same time, however, what they have proclaimed as "men's theology" is also a defamatory distortion. For example, Elga Sorge presents Gollwitzer as having said that God has his Son "murdered" instead of "killed." She then concludes from this: "The traditional image of God encourages an attitude of faith that is orientated more toward suffering, torture, and violence than toward love, pleasure, and joy," without perceiving the mysterious surrender, God's allowing or permitting, which is Gollwitzer's point.[5]

This surrender plays a central role in both the New Testament and the theological tradition. It is Passion terminology, for two thousand years burdened with and trapped in male experiences of themselves and the world, above all with experiences of helplessness. The notion surfaces in the New Testament. In the gospels it is Judas, the one who betrays Jesus, who handed him over. But in Paul, God himself already seems to have become the agent. This interpretation is then developed fully in Christian piety, for example, in hymns. God can appear as an incomprehensible, cruel Father who needs satisfaction for insults caused by human alienation. Unfortunately the Pauline version won out over the synoptic version. But strictly speaking, *paradidonai* contains something of the enigmatic character of this event: a human being, Judas, was the agent, but if God has all the power in his hands, then in an enigmatic way, God is also involved.

We should detect in the protest of women that the theology of the cross should not just be coupled to a personal image of God that can give the impression of a God who acts in a sadistic way. It should allow the *paradidonai* to stand or return to the statements of the gospels that a human being handed Jesus over.

In connection with reflections on Auschwitz in recent years, images of the pain of God have been rediscovered. They protect male theology from coming

---

5. Elga Sorge, *Religion und Frau* (Stuttgart, 1985), 43ff.

to grips with the enigma of God. They teach us to maintain it and not to resolve it in an easy way.

However, a God who is only pleasure, love and joy, and the promise of a Jesus-like happiness arouses in me the suspicion that Barbara Sichtermann once critically noted in connection with feminist notions of sexuality that she called "cup-a-soup sexuality": an all-too-easy agreement of bodies in an exchange of affirmations. Is there not in normal sexuality, she asked, some sado-masochism, the giving and enduring of pain, an element from the figure of the dance, initially independent of gender and only by cultural definitions split into feminine here and masculine there? In every pleasure there is a pain, a little death. Without passion there is no ecstasy.[6]

A kind of "cup-a-soup" God keeps cropping up in the quest of feminist theology for life. This God cannot do justice to us as whole persons and forces us into niches that no longer match reality. I can also rediscover the figures of the dance, of which Barbara Sichtermann speaks, in the old ideas of the perichoretic dance in the Trinity and the new ones that have been discovered today.

The Cross as a Legitimate Force

Women have sometimes replaced the unpopular theology of the cross with a Jesus who has been domesticated in line with their own ideas. They have de-crucified Jesus. In contrast to the theology of the cross, Maria Kassel, for example, develops her own conception of death and resurrection from a feminine context, using the myth of Inanna's journey into the underworld. In it she discovers a "creative, birthing feminine death, the goddess death." The message of the myth is then: "The suffering of birth and the blood that is naturally poured out with it redeems life from death. . . . The fate of the dead goddess of life hanging on the tree who at the same time gives birth as the goddess of death 'needs' no justification from a theology of 'sins.' "[7] For many women — including myself — this image is very attractive in that it depicts the process of human life, letting go and becoming new, takes the experience of death into life, interprets death existentially, and frees us from rigid patriarchal patterns of life.

However, the critical comment has to be made that this is a mythological image that has hardly any connection with the notion of the cross. Two essential elements of the story of the cross as it is told in the New Testament are missing. Maria Kassel has quite deliberately overlooked one of them, namely, the violence of the death of Jesus. Kassel wants the Christian theology of the cross "for the salvation of human beings and the world" once again to take up the symbols of nonviolent suffering and dying. Here, however, she has failed to note an important cornerstone in the theology of the cross: the brutal power

---

6. Barbara Sichtermann, "Vergewaltigung und Sexualität," in Marielouise Janssen-Jurreit, ed., *Frauen und Sexmoral* (Frankfurt, 1986), 382ff.

7. Maria Kassel, "Tod und Auferstehung," *Feministische Theologie: Perspektiven zur Orientierung* (Stuttgart, 1988), 212.

of the state that destroyed Jesus as an enemy of the state. Without this aspect, a theology of the cross is a help only to individual living and dying. In such a mythological reinterpretation of the cross — helpful though it may be in coping with existence — the personal and political significance of the story of Jesus can no longer be recognized.

The second forgotten element is just as important: the dereliction of Jesus expressed in the cry "My God, why have you forsaken me?" I find it striking that this cry hardly ever appears in women's accounts. For example, Carter Heyward cannot imagine the anger of Jesus as anger against God. She talks of an "exception."[8] In this cry it becomes clear to her that Jesus finally and fully recognized "the price of relationship." "The wrath of Jesus was not diffuse or unconcentrated. The wrath of Jesus had a particular focus: ... the non-relationship, the broken relationship, the violated relationship, the destruction of God in the world. ... " This interpretation seems to me to be mistaken, since there is in it no insight into this cry of dereliction from Jesus! It is an expression of the most helpless dereliction. It is an elemental cry without purpose and aim. The question is, may there no longer be any despair in feminist theology? Has a harmonious feminine religious solution done away with all anxieties?

I find a similar reinterpretation, which takes the edge off this dereliction, in Rita Nakashima Brock when she writes: "Jesus does not die totally abandoned, though he is described as feeling godforsaken. The divine erotic power illuminated through Christa/Community in Galilee and the woman at Bethany is sustained through Jesus' death by those who watch him die and mark his burial site."[9] But the New Testament makes a distinction between godforsakenness and being forsaken by human beings. It describes the presence of the women, but this cannot remove the godforsakenness. The godforsakenness of Jesus remains the riddle that I simply cannot reinterpret. There is godforsakenness that cannot be done away with by any erotic power or power of relationship. We cannot simply reduce experiences of God to human experiences. "Where 'God' is only a title of the event of interpersonal love, what could be said to the one who is abandoned by all people and all love? The tautology between God and the event of interpersonal love is done away with by the gospel of God's love."[10]

The Cross as the Cause of an Ethic of Subjection

In the meantime, critiques of the cross have been extended to questions of soteriology, ethics, and exegesis and now culminate in the question put by a Swiss theologian, Regula Strobel:

---

8. Carter Heyward, *Our Passion for Justice: Images of Power, Sexuality and Liberation* (New York: Pilgrim Press, 1984), 105.

9. Rita Nakashima Brock, *Journeys by Heart: A Christology of Erotic Power* (New York: Crossroad, 1988), 98.

10. Helmut Gollwitzer, *Von der Stellvertretung Gottes: Christlicher Glaube in der Erfahrung der Verborgenheit Gottes* (Munich, 1967), 147.

How can we think of the act of violence, the judicial murder of Jesus, in connection with the theological concept of redemption? On the basis of what experience are we to see our redemption specifically in the crucifixion of Jesus?...Can such a repressive bloody act ever bring redemption, salvation, and blessing?[11]

Strobel's presuppositions for the traditional theology of the cross are (1) the general sinfulness of human beings; (2) God and human beings as counterparts; *and* (3) human impotence to do good. Therefore a bloody human sacrifice has to be justified, which, for her, has catastrophic consequences in ethics, both old and new: looking for scapegoats for social disasters (persecution of witches and Jews, for example); human injustice (such as bombing in El Salvador) in order to imitate the saving action of God. An ethic of obedience and subjection then amounts to following the attitude of Jesus. The values mediated through the cross and the theology of the cross have thus stabilized oppression.

The conclusion from these general considerations that can be derived above all from the history of the effect of the cross is that Jesus redeems by his life and action and not by his death. People should again rely on just action in solidarity, restraint, and love, the development and requirement of which could be our redemption and the redemption of the world. Redemption does not take place through an objective act of salvation — what happens on the cross — but in the continuation of the healing activity of Jesus in human mutuality. The presupposition of this concept is the immediacy of God and human beings as it is expressed in the experience of women: to be oneself is to be with God. To interpret the cross only as an atoning sacrifice is to restrict theology. Here feminist theology is right. There is a need to give a new theological foundation to an ethic of reciprocity. The question remains whether this is possible only in the limited form of the life of Jesus and whether human redemptive action is already redemption. From this perspective, Christian theology is reduced to a moral action with the highest claims; redemptive action is put in the hands of human beings themselves.

To sum up, it has to be said that all three theological outlines presented here are reactions to violence suffered personally and socially. They attempt to develop a gentle theology of nonviolence and a utopia of feasible, achievable happiness. They attempt to grasp God in immanence, in the process of life, and in an ethic of reciprocity. Men and women are activated, ethics replaces dogmatics. The problem is whether as a result a religion of the nearness of God without the terror of God is dreamed up, a human picture of strength, will, and divine immanence that passes over our abysses and God's riddles. I think that even the power of relationship can break. Even Jesus broke on it. Even this Godhead/ Goddess can die. God is not just in our forces, open and hidden, nor just in our solidarity, nor just in our will to life or our lifeblood. God is also there. But

---

11. Regula Strobel, "Wollte Gott uns durch Blut erlösen?" Stuttgart lecture, March 12, 1990.

God is not only there. The women's concept of an absolutely nonviolent religion must ask itself whether it is overlooking reality in its dreams and taking refuge in a life-of-Jesus-religion without perceiving the death of Jesus, and whether, remote from all criticism of religion, it is creating a transpersonal image of God as a power of life that no longer allows any paradox.

However, in view of this massive feminist critique we must ask whether the violence experienced in male socialization (detachment from the mother, from the origin, from the feminine sphere) does not perhaps make it too natural to accept and to integrate violence. To what degree does the theology of the cross reflect a degree of male individuation that many women have also had to copy? And has not Adorno grasped something of this "cross" when he writes: "Humanity has had to do fearful things to itself in order that the self, the identical, purpose-orientated, male man, the male character of man, should be created, and something of that is still repeated in every childhood"?[12] Traditional theology has to ask itself whether its one-sided personal image of God has not sanctioned God as the agent in world history who is responsible for everything and therefore cruel, even to the extent of a personal experience of violence.

A Feminist Theology of the Cross

How can the passion for immanence that arises among women from so much suffering be preserved without bracketing out the passion story? Is there now a feminist theology of the cross? I think that there is, but it must be embedded in a christology and an account of Jesus in which it is not just Jesus' "work" — in parallel to the male's life work — that makes up salvation history, as is the case with so many traditional outlines from Paul to the present, but rather his whole life. In the masculine self-understanding, person and work are important, but in the feminine understanding so too is the network of relationships, the effect of people. So there is a need to look at this network of relationships from which Jesus lived and which make up his life work, as well as at his death and resurrection.[13] For example, the healing stories in which he healed and was healed are as much part of this work as his political murder. However, the cross may no longer overshadow the healings. When that happens, the "for me," "for us" can turn into a historical and spatial "before me": I can live in his history and the protection it provides.

I can see three feminist dimensions of the cross that do not reduce the cross to the principle of the forgiveness of sins and in which women can involve themselves existentially.

12. Max Horkheimer and Theodore W. Adorno, *Dialectic of Englightenment*, trans. John Cumming (New York: Continuum, 1974).

13. There is more on this in Elisabeth Moltmann-Wendel, *Weiblichkeit in der Theologie: Verdrängung und Wiederkehr* (Gütersloh: Gütersloher Verlagshaus, 1988), 23f.

The Cross as Solidarity in Suffering

The New Testament story of the cross has two sides. On the one hand is the story of the guilt of the disciples who fled. On the other is the story of the solidarity of the women who remained under the cross. The latter has so far usually been overlooked. Two or three women remained under the cross who — unlike the disciples — had not fled. Despite the danger to life and limb, they remained at the place of execution, were present at the death and burial of Jesus, and became the first witnesses to the resurrection. They stayed under the cross out of solidarity and compassion. In contrast to the disciples, for whom the betrayal and guilt, the feeling of having abandoned Jesus, was the starting point of their experiences of God, for the women the cross is the place of communion with their friend in his sufferings. At the same time it represents detachment from family, custom, and social status. It amounts to social death, and brings them the danger of physical death. For them the cross is not the contradiction of their images of God and their expectations of life. Their own experiences of helplessness are reflected here, their own knowledge of the meaning and the power of solidarity. I regard this tacit counter-theology from the gospels as a theology of the cross that we should develop further. Elisabeth Schüssler-Fiorenza has pointed out that the statements about these women at the cross, that they followed Jesus, served him, and went up to Jerusalem with him, mark them out as the real disciples. They serve, as Jesus himself came to serve and to give his life. This statement is never made about the disciples who were in love with success.[14]

Here the feminist theology of the cross meets up with the last thoughts of Bonhoeffer from his cell. For him, what is now important is not the individual in search of freedom, nor the Christian come of age, nor the "religious act," but "participation in the suffering of God" in the life of the world or "participation in the suffering of God in Christ."[15] The New Testament instances of this that he cites also include the women in the passion story. For him the question of Jesus in Gethsemane, "Could you not watch with me one hour?," becomes important as the "reversal of all that the religious person expects of God." But the biblical answer is really only that watching is impossible. Bonhoeffer has not yet realized that in the story of the women, the image of the women who watch with Jesus in Gethsemane, there is a starting point for the tradition of the women in the passion stories. It was not seen at that time that there are subversive traditions with other answers than the reaction of the disciples — sleep.[16]

The individual male experience and knowledge behind such statements about participation in the suffering of God are perhaps different from those of women. Whereas Bonhoeffer says, "Christians stand by God in his suffering," it is more

---

14. Elisabeth Schüssler-Fiorenza, "The Twelve," in Leonard and Arlene Swidler, *Women Priests* (New York: Paulist Press, 1977), 117f.

15. Dietrich Bonhoeffer, *Letters and Papers from Prison*, enlarged ed. (New York: Macmillan, 1972), 370.

16. Elisabeth Moltmann-Wendel, *The Women around Jesus* (New York: Crossroad, 1982), 73f.

natural for women today to say, "Where people suffer, Christ suffers with them." Here I see differences that are specific to tradition and sex, but that for me are not opposites. They are two sides of the same coin, pointing to different expressions of theological culture that are not just gender-specific. They should not separate us, but invite us to dialogue.

The Cross as Suffering from Structural Sin

Alongside the tradition of the cross as solidarity with those who suffer there is another women's tradition down through the centuries: the image of the cruci-fied women. This type of image comes from the saga of the father who wanted to marry his daughter to a pagan; when she refused, in his fury he had her cru-cified. At the present time, pictures of crucified women have appeared in many countries and cultures as a reflection of women's reality. They can shock both women, who find in them only a reflection of their own humiliation, without drawing strength and identity from them, and men, who see them as blasphemy. I lectured to women theologians in a church in Korea under the giant picture of a crucified Asian woman. For a long time a crucified "Christa" by Edwina Sandys, a British artist, was in the Women's Center in Berkeley and provoked a wealth of reflections and reactions. In its vulnerability and nakedness, women saw themselves as objects of forbidden pleasure, as anorexic and self-scorning, as those who could no longer develop any creativity and spirituality from them-selves and their bodies. Men saw their Jewish mothers weeping over Auschwitz. They also saw their own feminine aspects crucified and destroyed. Remarkably, here this image of the crucifixion was not felt to be destructive, but a way from death to life. In her book *Transforming Grace,* the American feminist theologian Anne Carr has called the cross "a central Christian symbol and an important one for Christian women who experience the pain of exclusion and denigration in their own religious heritage."[17]

The Cross as a Paradoxical Symbol of Life

If many women always reject the cross as a symbol of the forgiveness of sins, the question remains, is this a women's sin? In what feminine context of life is it represented? And is there a healing (forgiving) symbolism for it? For me, the passion stories have always been a help in recognizing in our theological thought patterns gender-specific situations and modes of behavior from which gender-specific ideas then arise. The end of the Gospel of Mark illustrates this problem for me. Whereas the disciples fled on the arrest of Jesus, the women fled full of terror at the message of the resurrection (Mark 16:8). Whereas the disciples fled in fear of losing their life and disappointed at the failure of their

---

17. Anne Carr, *Transforming Grace: Christian Tradition and Women's Experience* (New York: Harper & Row, 1988).

aims, the women fled when their world shattered, as the result of an invasion from outside, when their network of relationships was torn apart and they no longer had the dead person as the object of their concern and love. They fled when their immanence had holes made in it through the experience of transcendence, when their "power of relationship" was put in question. "They have taken away my Lord, and I do not know where they have laid him" is Mary Magdalene's lament in the Gospel of John (20:13). "Why do you look for the living among the dead?" is the question of the angels to the women in Luke (24:5).

There are two strident statements in the New Testament, in Mark, which are already harmonized in the later gospels: Jesus' cry of dereliction on the cross and the flight of the women on Easter morning. They belong in the earliest Christian history. They cannot be harmonized, and they give us a glimpse into abysses. They cannot be removed morally. They belong to the dark side of God and the dark night of the soul, without which the Christian religion, including feminist theology, is in danger of descending to a program of psychological health or plans to change the world.

In this story of the flight of the women I see parallels to the experiences of many women: they despair when their networks of relationships are torn apart. They can give up everything, but this world of surrender, of work to do, must hold. They can remain trapped in the helper syndrome, even the syndrome of helping God. Not to be able to bear the loss of love — that is godforsakenness that prevents people from entering into new spheres independently, upright and alone. Perhaps there is a human quest for love and life that does not come to grief on the solidarity of the cross but on the capacity for resurrection. Perhaps the search for symbols of resurrection is also a problem for humanity that we are learning to express today.

If Western theology is fixed on the cross as its real field of conflict, the unbelievable resurrection, the incursion of another world into a network of feminine relationships that is apparently so intact, seems to be women's real field of conflict. Women can come to grief on the resurrection, just as the disciples came to grief on the cross. But they can also experience resurrection: by growing out of their narrow, comprehensible, limited world; by letting go of traditional feminine patterns of life; by coming out of themselves and entering into an experience of transcendence that at the same time is immanent, that extends from the narrow feminine sphere into a cosmic and social sphere. This is the message that John's Mary Magdalene experiences in her encounter with the risen Christ: "Do not hold on to me" (20:17). She must and may be herself. The resurrection brings the pain and grief of becoming a self and entering into new relationships with the world.

Feminist theology, which starts not from a general but from a differentiated understanding of sin, can no longer see the cross in isolation nor just as the symbol of the forgiveness of sins. The cross and the history of the cross can be interpreted in different ways. However, they must no longer just be fixed on a Western patriarchal context, but be extended to new conceptions of life in which the crosses of the world become oppressive. Women nowadays are pointing out how deadly and paralyzing a wrong understanding of the cross can be, and with their protest they are calling attention to long-forgotten dimensions of the cross.

In the last resort, the cross is a paradoxical symbol. This insight is strengthened by research into symbols: the cross is not just the guillotine or the gallows. Subconsciously it is also the symbol of totality and life and probably was able to survive as the central Christian symbol only with what was at the same time a subconscious significance. Remnants of it are still preserved in the Celtic cross, the old symbol of life; in depictions of the cross that at the same time portray the tree of life; and in the symbol of Lutheran theology, the rose in the cross of the present.

Perhaps we shall again be able to see the paradox of this symbol one day when the cross is liberated from one-dimensional male experience and is understood anew from the experiences of many people, above all women, experiences that are then not just gender-specific as society changes. Perhaps then we shall see the cross as a symbol of solidarity, as the representation of human suffering, new dimensions of which can always be uncovered, and a sign of salvation that we can erect out of death and nothingness and transplant into new spheres.

Chapter 8

Contextualizing Luther's Theology of the Cross

Theo Sundermeier

✝

20. He deserves to be called a theologian, however, who comprehends the visible and manifest things of God seen through suffering and the cross.

21. A theology of glory calls evil good and good evil. A theology of the cross calls the thing what it actually is.

24. Yet that wisdom is not of itself evil, nor is the law to be evaded; but without the theology of the cross man misuses the best in the worst manner.

—From Luther's Theses for Heidelberg Disputation

I

Let me start by posing the question of whether Martin Luther's theology of the cross can be universalized as a contextual theology. This is exactly what has happened with Luther's theology. It was cast into the shape of a confession and thereby reached worldwide significance and had a determinant influence on the confessions of churches throughout the world. It was adopted all over the world. Nowadays various theologies and churches have named themselves after it. Nevertheless the question as to what extent it is also bound in a contextual and local sense has remained open.

In the following I will go into the matter of contextuality and universality by presenting Luther's *theologia crucis* on the basis of his Heidelberg disputation of 1518. In this disputation, which took place at the invitation of Johannes von Staupitz, Luther for the first time presented his theology in public; he did not appear at the assembly of the Augustinian congregation at Heidelberg, but instead he put it forward for public discussion at the university. By using the notion *theologia crucis* Luther reduces his theology to the denominator which, according to McGrath, is considered to be "one of the most powerful and radical understandings of the nature of Christian theology which the church has ever known."[1]

In many respects Luther's theology was determined by his context: biographically by his life as a monk; pastorally by his ministry as a confessor and preacher; ethically by the challenges within church and society; and philosophico-theologically by his teaching activities at the university in Wittenberg.

Luther was a monk. Whatever interpretation we may find for his sudden decision to give up his studies of law in order to become a monk, it definitely determined his further development, even though it did not solve all of his spiritual problems. It was only the encounter with mystical theology that made him experience a ray of light and hope. Temporarily his growing love for Jesus even managed to overcome his fear of the Supreme Eternal Judge in front of whose bench he feared not to be able to justify himself, in spite of his intense spiritual exercise and his self-imposed punishments, which by far exceeded the average standard of obedience required. He searched for redemption and approached Christ more and more while simultaneously withdrawing from the other ways of access to God that were offered by the church in the form of its saints.

The actual trigger for his reformatory act was not so much biographically as pastorally conditioned. The monk's cell and especially the confessional box were where reformation was born. Such small, almost private, places saw the beginning of the awakenings that were to change the world. It could hardly have been more personal, yes, almost intimate.

Luther simply noticed that his sermons calling to repentance and his rules of confession were no longer taken seriously and, finally, the people even neglected confession. The indulgence, originally a pastoral institution that was supposed to take away the people's dreadful fear of purgatory, had turned into a business for many institutions, for leaders of churches, for secular and ecclesiastical rulers and finally even for the pope himself — and of course for the bankers.

Due to the great amount of indulgence money, the Fugger family of bankers, for instance, felt obliged to establish its own office in Rome. Rome's greed was enormous. Money was taken for past and future sins. One was able to be redeemed from minor sins in advance. Thereby the system of penance had been turned upside down. The poor became poorer and poorer, since the drain of money proved fatal for towns and principalities. To take steps against this, more new relics were imported so that the people left more and more indul-

---

1. See A. E. McGrath, *Luther's Theology of the Cross* (Oxford: Basil Blackwell, 1980), 1, for further information.

gence money with certain churches, as for example with the castle church of Wittenberg. The sovereigns were dependent on this revenue.

Luther does not only attack the prince bishops but also his own prince and advises him to deal with secular matters instead of the accumulation of new relics in the castle church. Pastoral problems interfered with social ones and were closely interlinked.

As a doctor of theology and lecturer at the university, Luther was never able to approach a problem without at the same time getting to its theological basis. In his opinion problems of social life were theological, and the basic theological issues deeply touched the social life of human beings — as he knew from his own experience.

In Luther's way of thinking it is the individual who is at the center of consideration because each individual leads his or her life before the eyes of God. Whatever we nowadays may consider an individualistic imitation of outlook was a break away from a society with a strict estate system in those days, in which the individual did not count. Nonetheless, Luther's approach was not completely new. As has been pointed out, Luther had been trained in the Ockhamist way of thought (also known as nominalism), which had a tendency to see a degree of tension between philosophy and theology.[2] Luther was also influenced by humanism, which served as a fertile ground for rethinking intellectual and philosophical "givens."

In his critique of Aristotle, Luther was affected by the spirit of the age. He took the critique over from his teachers. One could say that it was in the air. Luther, however, radicalized it in a hitherto unknown way and broke away completely from Aristotelian ontology. The reason he refers to Augustine in this context is certainly because he belonged to an Augustinian order. We must not underestimate these specific concrete influences.[3]

I begin with Luther's disputation concerning Aristotelian ontology by looking at the final thesis (28) of the Heidelberg disputation, which forms its highpoint. Aristotle's argument is the following: Human beings love what is good. Since they love the good they do the good and strive for the good. Only by continuously doing good works may they achieve and love what is perfect. The most perfect is God. The aspiration to the good leads to the recognition of the absolute good, that is, God.

Luther completely abandons this approach. It does not correspond with reality, and we all fail according to this pattern. A rotten tree cannot yield good fruit. Since the fall of humankind all of us are totally rotten trees. Good works are a

---

2. Gerhard Ebeling, *Luther: An Introduction to His Thought* (Philadelphia: Fortress Press, 1972), 86.

3. On Luther's argument with the scholasticism and Aristotelianism of the Middle Ages, see, among others, McGrath, ibid.; K.-H. zur Mühlen, "Luthers Kritik am scholastischen Arestotelismus in der 25. These der 'Heidelberger Disputation' von 1518," *Luther Jahrbuch* (1981), 54–79; R. Söderlund, "Der Meritum-Begriff der 'Heidelberger Disputation' zum Verhältnis zur mittelalterlichen und zur späteren reformatorischen Theologie," *Luther Jahrbuch* (1981), 44–53.

disguise, make-believe, a perfume to cover up our filth. The world is full of our corruption, but has God no share in this world of degeneracy, evil, and filth?

This is the crucial question of Luther's anthropology. In his twenty-eighth thesis, which together with the first represents the theological frame of the disputation, all this is reduced to the following: "The love of man comes into being through that which is pleasing to it." For example, a man loves a woman because she is pretty. The young woman feels attracted to a handsome man. A woman wants to buy a dress because it is nice. A car needs to shine, to serve as a status symbol if it wants to lure a buyer. The entire economy and all advertising campaigns are based on this principle: "Love comes into being through its object."

Luther is familiar with this principle from metaphysics. If we love God we have to think of God as good, pleasing, strong, and mighty. In this way we create an idol of God according to our own wishes, at our own discretion. People twist the works of creation and adore them. But in this way it is not God whom they worship but their self-created idols. Thesis 17 of the Disputation against scholastic theology of 1517 says: "Man is by nature unable to want God to be God. Indeed, he himself wants to be God, and does not want God to be God."[4] Thus the yearning for the always better is not satisfied. Idolatry produces further idols, just as "the love of money grows in proportion to the increase of money itself" (Thesis 22). And Luther refers to this as "dropsy [*Wassersucht*] of the soul" and comes to the following (almost Buddhist) conclusion: the remedy for curing desire "does not lie in satisfying it, but in extinguishing it."

Let us look at the opposite perspective: If God acted this way and loved us in such a human way, God could no longer love us. God sees through our disguises and realizes the misery, egoism, and greed behind the deceptive facade. We are not lovable. We are thoroughly miserable sinners.

The love of God differs from the love of human beings. It flows forth, takes effect, and transforms its object through the love. That is the secret: "God 'loves' what is sinful, foolish, and weak" (Thesis 28). This love changes human beings, it makes them "righteous, good, wise, and strong." That is the paradox from which all other paradoxes follow — and the Heidelberg disputation is full of them. But where is the proof for the thesis that God does not forsake the poor, miserable, and sick? That is the cross of Christ. It is in the flagellated, martyred, tortured body of the crucified that we recognize this side of God's glory and majesty, which God allows us to see. Luther is fascinated by the narration of Exodus 33: Moses asks God to let him see God's glory. God puts him into the cleft of a rock so that he would not perish when God passed by. Human beings cannot see the glory of God, since it would destroy them. The back of God (*posteriori,* it says in Thesis 20) is the side of God turned toward human beings. God is acting "through the opposite." So the cross, the misery of Jesus

---

4. *Luther's Works,* American edition, vol. 31, *Career of the Reformer,* I, ed. Harold Grimm, general editor Helmut T. Lehmann (Philadelphia: Muhlenburg Press, 1957), 10

of Nazareth, is the side of God that is turned to us. It does not destroy us, but it saves us, if we recognize it and hold on to it. God and God's nature are visible only through Jesus' suffering and cross. "Now it is not sufficient for anyone and it does him no good to recognize God in his glory and majesty, unless he recognizes him in the humility and shame of the cross" (Thesis 20). God wants to be recognized "through suffering."

According to Luther, Christ and God belong together, so that they become one person. Thus in Luther's famous Reformation hymn it says: "If you ask me who he is, his name is Jesus Christ and there is no other God." Christ is the God who is near to us; he is the side of God turned to us. That is why we should hold to the cross. The cross is our only hope — our only theology. Knowledge of God and of human nature are contained in it. By it God and human beings are held and tied together (cf. Thesis 21).

Medieval piety sought suffering, poverty, and the monastic life. By this the devout were trying to become more and more like Jesus. The imitation of Christ (*imitatio Christi*) was to lead to a mystical merging with Christ. Luther, however, does not mean this type of suffering. He does not refer to the poverty that is self-chosen, the pain that is a self-imposed exercise of repentance. No, just as the cross was imposed on Christ, in the same way Luther refers to the grief that is inflicted upon us, the pain caused to us. It brings us together with Christ. In such suffering I am to recognize God. The human being, however, has a different way of thinking. "He prefers works to suffering, glory to the cross, strength to weakness, wisdom to folly, and, in general, good to evil" (Thesis 21).

Luther's castigation of this "natural" attitude has nothing to do with masochism. The point is not a self-chosen piety of suffering (*Leidensfrömmigkeit*) but solely to follow God on God's way to human beings and to achieve recognition of God in this way. It is the humility (*humilitas*) of God to seek the lowly and sick in order to bear their grief. For this reason true theology and recognition of God can be found only in the crucified Christ (Thesis 20). Human suffering is not thereby glorified or considered praiseworthy. For Luther grief remains grief and misery remains misery. It achieves this other quality by the mere fact that I know: Here is God; it is here that God "takes effect," so to speak.

Whatever we today may call "the christology of solidarity" — a notion that came into existence under the influence of Latin American theology — was already laid down in Luther's Heidelberg thesis: God is present in suffering. Our cross is God's cross! And since God carries it with us, we are changed. The works of God are always active (Thesis 27). God's action is with us and within us. It changes us and enables us to do good works although we are evil and sinful. As radical as Luther is in his understanding of sin, just as radically does he take the view that through God evil is being extinguished and that God does the good within and through us. But then this is not my work but the work of Christ. Mine has to pass; his to begin. "He must increase, but I must decrease" (John 3:30). This sentence of John the Baptist applies to everyone. "My soul,"

Luther says in mystic language, "is turning empty," it is being "deflated," so that it may be filled with the works of Christ (Thesis 21). In this way the weak turns strong with the strength of Christ.

I shall try to illustrate the consequences to be drawn from this with an example from literature. In Dostoyevsky's novel *The Brothers Karamazov* the pious and pure Alyosha enters into a severe crisis after the death of the holy Staretz because he had expected — like all the others close to the holy man — that after Staretz's death a miracle would happen. He expected miracles to happen in his corpse and through it. But instead the dead body putrefied unusually fast; by the very next day the odor of putrefaction had already became overwhelming. Alyosha was overcome by fearful doubts. They literally knocked him down. Lying on the ground as still as death, he summarizes all his doubts, all his fears in one question (which previously had been uttered by his brother Ivan to express his disbelief): "I do not revolt against my God; it is only that I do not want to accept his world."

"I don't want to accept God's world as it is." We all have a strong desire to discover something of the beautiful, the good, a little bit of the glory of God in our world. The fact that even a saint's corpse ends up in putrefaction destroys this illusion. Luther's antithesis reads as follows: The cross liberates us to a realistic view of the world. The theologian of the cross sees things in an undisguised way, in their genuine nature. She or he "calls the thing what it actually is" (*dicit id quod res est,* Thesis 21). Such theologians try neither to enhance nor to disguise things. Turning to the world as ones who have been liberated through the cross, they see the world in its suffering. But they do not turn their backs on the suffering but instead turn to human beings in their grief. They love others as God does and thereby act like God. God sees human beings as they are; God sees and loves "sinners, evil persons, fools, and weaklings" (Thesis 28).

Human beings are supposed to act like God. What is meant by this? I will illustrate this with a short story. During the war a wounded soldier was taken to a military hospital where he was nursed with particular care by a nun. He expressed his gratitude, whereupon she answered with her personal devoutness: "I did it for God's sake." The wounded man, however, replied: "I thought you had done it for me."

The effect of the cross is to perceive and help human beings for their own sake. With this analysis of reality Luther makes close contact with Marx,[5] who rejects evaluating human beings by standards other than themselves, for example, by their exchange value or their individual working power. Human beings are not to be judged by their works, but instead we have to accept them as such. By this we acknowledge their dignity. This is what Luther refers to when he

---

5. E. Thaidigsmann has rightly made reference to this in his *Identitätsverlangen und Widerspruch: Kreuztheologie uber Luther, Hegel und Barth* (Munich, 1983), 43f.; Winston D. Persaud, *The Theology of the Cross and Marx's Anthropology: A View from the Caribbean* (New York and Frankfurt, 1991).

claims that the love of God changes human beings — exactly as our love of a fellow human being if we turn to that person and to the world with an open mind.

This view has great implications for the concept of freedom as well as for science and ethics. The world may be considered and studied as it is.[6] Labor will likewise be appreciated in a completely new way. A new type of professional ethics (*Berufsethik*) comes into existence. Could this also serve as the basis for a new social ethics? Does Luther realize the explosive political force implied in this "practical doctrine for battle," as Jürgen Moltmann calls the theology of the cross (*theologia crucis*)? E. Wolff answers this question in the affirmative; Moltmann, however, in the negative.[7] I am convinced that the socioethical dimension is very well indicated here. The threefold reference to the notion of "the poor and needy" within the final thesis (Latin text) underlines that. The theology of the cross aims at our turning toward the poor and needy. To do this means to be blessed. That is what God does, and the cross provides us with the proof. Thus the cross is both at the same time: the source of the recognition of God and of the source of the recognition of the human being: "This is the love of the cross, born of the cross!" (*Iste est amor crucis ex cruce natus*).

II

We have tried to grasp Luther's theology of the cross as a response to the issues of his day. In this context special attention has been given to the attempt to break out of the clutches of Aristotelian ontology — and to encourage people to live a life before God (*coram deo*) in liberty. It would be a life with eyes not closed to the grief of human beings. Instead we are to approach suffering persons and to look after them with loving care. Such love follows the way of God's love. To see the sufferer, to be precise, to see the one who is suffering, means to see God. Such recognition of God discloses reality in an objective way.

Is a theological decision in favor of the theology of the cross a road all theologians have to follow, if they want to be true Christian theologians? It has become obvious that Luther was of that conviction.

What is the reason for his assumption? It is not enough to say that Luther refers to Augustine, and it must be added that it is even debated whether Luther quotes him correctly. Not even the assertion that he quotes Paul is sufficient reason because citations of Paul remain empty words if they are only used as *dicta probantia*, proof texts degraded to a biblicism instead of cited according to their inner conviction and systematic theological implications.

---

6. On Luther's ethic of work, see to Gustav Wingren, *Luther on Vocation* (Philadelphia: Fortress Press, 1967).

7. E. Wolff, *Peregrinatio II* (Munich, 1965), 207ff. Jürgen Moltmann, *The Crucified God: The Cross of Christ as the Foundation and Criticism of Christian Theology* (New York: Harper & Row, 1974), 72ff.

Nevertheless the reference to Paul is quite important for us. After all, Luther learned from Paul. Paul was the first to develop a theology of the cross, and this occurred not in his dealing with Judaism but in his dialogue with Syrian religion. His "Gentile-Christian" theology of religion was here taking shape. In the wake of Paul — but independently from him — the Evangelist Mark did the same. And again this occurred in dialogue with Syrian religion. It is interesting to see how Mark refers to the Jewish-Christian Peter: "He does not understand a thing about the cross." It is of no great importance to him; he attaches relevance only to the Messianic Jesus (Mark 8:29).[8] He ignores the cross and consequently he is being frequently and bluntly criticized (Mark 8:31ff.; 9:6). Is it purely by chance that Mark situates the announcement of Christ's Passion, the Transfiguration, and the criticism concerning Peter outside Israel in the "land of heathens"? Again it surely is no coincidence that a pagan captain is the first to recognize Jesus as the son of God. This happens under the cross (Mark 15:39). Not in Judaism but in non-Jewish religions does one clearsightedly recognize that the cross is the distinguishing feature of the newly established religion, Christianity. Up to this day this has apparently remained true for those communities where Christians are a minority.[9] Does this mean that the essence of a religion may be grasped more quickly from the outside than from the inside? This seems to be the case, at least with regard to specific differences (*differentia specifica*) and the creation of symbols. The cross has turned out to be the symbol of Christianity as such.

This applies to Western Christian art in general. Now the question is whether there are paintings that indicate something like a pictorial representation of Luther's theology. If Luther's specific contribution to the reformation of theology is contextual and changes the spirit of the times (*Zeitgeist*) in a theological way, then this must be the case.

Here I shall proceed from a hypothesis I have already suggested on previous occasions, namely, that theology is anticipated in the interpretative and pictorial arts. This theory proves true with regard to the central altarpiece of the Isenheim altar which was created by Mathias Grünewald between 1512 and 1515, hence a few years before the Heidelberg disputation. I am convinced that a perfect representation of Luther's theology of the cross as expounded in Heidelberg is to be found in this work of art.

In this picture the crucifixion is reduced to its chief motif. There are no houses, no soldiers, not even the two evildoers at the right and left hand of

---

8. In this connection, see the dissertation at the University of Heidelberg of A. Feldtkeller, "Das Entstehende Heidenchristentum im religiösen Umfeld Syriens zur Prinzipatszeit: Ein Beitrag zum Verhältnis von Urchristentum und Religionsgeschichte," 1992. On Mark, see ibid., 235ff.

9. On Africa, see Theo Sundermeier, "Das Kreuz in afrikanischer Interpretation" in idem., *Das Kreuz als Befreiung: Kreuzinterpretationen in Afrika und Asien* (Munich, 1985), 45–72. On the same problem, see further U. Berner, *Zur Hermeneutik religiöser Symbole: Das Kreuzsymbol in der frühchristlichen und in der modernen indischen Theologie,* in Theo Sundermeier, ed., *Begegnung mit dem Anderen: Plädoyers für eine interkulturelle Hermeneutik* (Gütersloh: Gütersloher Verlagshaus, 1991), 94–108.

The center portion of the altarpiece at Isenheim
(painted by Mathias Grünewald between 1512 and 1515)

Jesus. The background is total darkness. Luther had used the notion of a hidden God (*Deus absconditus*). God is absent there; it is hardly possible to express this more clearly than through this huge cross in front of the black and hollow background. The cross — the rough, almost unhewn wood beams — bends under the weight of the crucified. Hardly ever has the corpse of Jesus been illustrated so precisely in detail (so much "without beauty," Luther quotes Isaiah 53), so dreadfully and dispassionately as in this painting. The painter reproduces the event as it was. His painting is no historical reconstruction of a unique event but rather the incredibly realistic portrayal of a sick and dying contemporary around 1500. Nothing is hushed, nothing enhanced. Mary, who as in most other medieval paintings, is here the symbol of the church, turns pale in view of this cross. She is staggering.

In fact Luther's theology of the cross shook the entire medieval church to its very foundations! It was this theology and nothing else that caused this. It is upheld and newly established by the disciple St. John, the evangelist who most precisely and passionately spoke of the love of God for human beings (*amor dei,* John 3:16). Furthermore John characterized the death of Jesus as the death of the sacrificial lamb (John 1:29). The theology of the cross (*theologia cru-*

cis) opens up the range of vision for the love of God (*amor dei*), as Luther shows in his Disputation. With his disproportionately large finger John the Baptist points at the crucified. He has to increase whereas he, the preacher, has to decrease (so reads the inscription on the painting). And so the cross is depicted disproportionately large.

The destitute, to be precise, the sinner Magdalene, understands the meaning of the cross. She kneels down. There is no posture more appropriate before the cross than that of the sinner Magdalene. In the painting she is the one who is most distraught; still it is she alone who has "color." She is the only pretty one. Luther states: God does not love the attractive, but the ugly, meaning the sinner. The love of God makes attractive. Therefore sinners are attractive because they are loved. Nothing other than this is expressed here.

The Heidelberg Disputation refers to preaching only indirectly (Thesis 20), but later on in the great Reformation writings of 1520 this changes drastically. There Luther emphasizes more clearly that the salvation we are granted through the cross also has to be shared. How may we gain this salvation? Through the sacraments and the preaching of the Word! The major event needs to be shared in such mean-looking elements as bread and wine and in the word of the foolish preaching that does not magnify the preacher but acknowledges none but the crucified (1 Cor. 1:21–23). On the basis of Luther's theology of the word, preaching gains more importance whereas the sacraments receive less weight. All this is expressed at the right side of the painting, which, in its smallest details, is an almost literal translation of this message into the picture. We could continue to interpret the details, but this is not necessary since it has become obvious how much picture and theology coincide here.

But let me refer to another situation. Grünewald was commissioned to paint the altarpiece for the hospital of the Anthonite monastery in Isenheim. The oversized centerpiece forms the center of a doubly foldable altar. The altar was built for the very sick, or even incurable, and was intended to release healing powers. We may wonder if such a realistic depiction of a martyred person and a dead body could have a positive effect on the sick. Could it be possible that the painting was rather meant to be a preparation for death and to impart comfort for the dying? The small text inscribed on the central panel, which portrays the temptation of St. Anthony, could give reason to believe this! "Where have you been, good Jesus, where have you been? Why didn't you come to me to heal my wounds?"

By now it is generally accepted that pictures have a positive effect on sick people. It has been shown that in the patients' encounter with pictures, the "non-attractive, the ugly" has a positive effect and that "archetypal symbols frequently have a healing and consolidating effect."[10] By means of the suffering

---

10. G. H. Ott, *Bildende Kunst in der Medizin: Wortlose Hermeneutik zwischen Arzt und Patient,* in Theo Sundermeier, ed., *Begegnung mit dem Anderen,* 145–50.

and troubled Anthony the sick person may call for Christ and ask for his healing presence. And we receive the answer to our question as soon as the altarpiece is folded out. Christ is present in this harsh and terrible picture of the crucified, whose body shows all the symptoms of a fatal disease. This disease, the death of Christ, is the side of God turned to human beings. It is here that God is revealed to human beings. Here the sick person may see the love of God. Love crucified (*amor crucis*)! It is healing and makes the ugly one pretty, the sinner blessed, it gives support and courage to the faltering and heals the sick.

Here Luther's theology of the cross has taken shape in a convincing way in this altar painting, even before it was expressed in words!

Through this picture the question of whether a contextual theology may be universalized gains a new, perhaps more precise context. The altar painting was created for a specific local context, which it does not ignore. It aspires to be neither ageless nor timeless, yet in its message it transcends all spatial and chronological dimensions. After all, it is one of the world's greatest pieces of art. In its artistic expression it may be understood everywhere even if it is detached from its original context. Its specific message has been universalized and it has gained worldwide significance.

Universalization, however, does not mean repetition. The point is not to copy this painting countless times, as happened with Leonardo da Vinci's "The Last Supper," which is to be found as print, embroidery, and copperplate engraving in luxury residences in the United States, in African huts, and in Catholic hospitals in Sicily and India. Imitation is not the aim and object of the matter, but the basic decisions made by the artist are relevant and set new standards.

A further illustration is appropriate here. We had arranged an exhibition in Heidelberg with the works of the Balinese artist Nyoman Darsane, whom I personally regard as one of Asia's greatest contemporary Christian artists. After growing up as a Hindu, he was converted to Christianity. With his art he has been contributing to the inculturation of the gospel in Bali. I remember asking him why it is that the cross hardly ever appears in his pictures. He contradicted me by drawing my attention to a painting in the exhibition. In its center it shows Christ with multicolored spears of eight persons (who form a circle around him) pointed at him. He dances, although he is gradually dying. The fact that the painting is a depiction of the cross becomes obvious because at the bottom of the painting the trunk of the cross is visible. If we take a closer look, we recognize the arrangement typical of Balinese-Hindu symbolism. Christ is located in the center of the lotus blossom — a position usually taken by the god Shiva. The eight figures in different colors are located exactly where Bali's pantheon is usually arranged (Vishnu at the top, black; Brahma at the bottom, red, and so on). Christ is active in regard to his death; he is dying for them and in their midst once and for all! Christ is located in the middle of the central symbol of Asian piety. There he is in his place. In general the lotus blossom is the symbol of purity; the beautiful flower blooms in the midst of the dirt of the world and yet remains untouched by it. Here it becomes the place of death. The purity is stained but thereby it receives its final purification.[11]

Does this painting represent a new instance of the theology of the cross in a Balinese context? I would answer this question positively. But so far I cannot give a final answer, not yet. All I can do at the moment is to make a suggestion, try to offer a solution for the problem. When saying goodbye, the artist told me that our discussions had made him think a lot. He said that for the next exhibition he might bring along some new pictures of the crucifixion. At the moment no one can tell what they will look like. The morning after our conversation Mr. Darsane gave me a sketch as a farewell present. He had drawn it into the catalogue we had issued for the exhibition. Maybe this indicates the direction we will have to follow: The dancing Christ on the cross. Only the future will show whether this will turn out to be an independent inculturation of the *theologia crucis* or something completely different.

We have come a long way. In dealing with Luther's theology of the cross we asked whether this contextual theology could be universalized. We have tried to answer this question by means of two depictions of the cross. This has shown that the gospel remains the same even in its changeability. The theology of the cross will always be fashioned as a contextual theology while, at the same time, being universally valid.

---

11. Contrast this with the paintings and the lotus symbol in the traditional art of Bali in Theo Sundermeier and Volker Küster, eds., *Das Schöne Evangelium: Christliche Kunst im balinesischen Kontext* (Nettetal, 1991), especially 64–68, 73ff.

Chapter 9

The Cross of Jesus Christ, the Unity of the Church, and Human Suffering

Winston D. Persaud

†

Because it is the crucified and risen Jesus Christ whom it follows, the church cannot but be involved in the alleviation of human suffering. The crucified Lord is to be found in the hungry, the naked, the sick, the imprisoned. The individual Christian and the church as a whole bear the marks of suffering, Christ's ongoing suffering in the world. The church's role as fellow sufferer, as protester against suffering, as advocate, as individual and institution that practice mercy and charity and work for justice and peace, is rooted in its identity as people of the cross. It cannot be otherwise. Unity of the church is derived from the one gospel and from our common following of the crucified Jesus in a suffering world. From this one gospel are born several strategies of faithfulness that do not necessarily cohere. Unity is not static. Fundamentally, it is both gift and task. The diverse strategies that emanate from the one gospel are in perpetual tension, if not outright conflict, against the very gospel that called them forth in the first place. The gospel cannot define the common good to be pursued across religious, cultural, economic, or political boundaries. Only Christians can be appealed to to live faithfully under the cross of the crucified.

Theology of the cross embraces a conception of reality which transcends the depths of socioeconomic and political conditions of life, but it also includes these conditions. It is concerned first and foremost with the praxis of the God who suffered the Son to die on the cross. It is a praxis whose

111

efficacy is through the contradiction of love in the crucifixion for the sake of the enemy. . . .

Theology of the cross does not call human beings to quietism nor to apathy based upon a reactionary ethic of the status quo. To speak of the praxis of transcendent grace is to exhort to radical praxis in order to transform the inhuman conditions which, in many parts of the world, mean the transformation of the socioeconomic and political realities of life. The acceptance of humankind's ultimate future in the hands of the suffering God is not to dismiss or to reduce the acute need for a more human future premised upon human praxis. On the contrary, radical forgiveness through the cross of Christ calls Christians to radical praxis. It is praxis which is always in danger of becoming legalistic and of reducing the gospel to a form of law through the justification of human beings by their works. Praxis for the transformation of the material conditions of life must be complemented by the praxis of celebration: celebration of the future of God which is already here in the presence of the crucified and risen Christ Jesus. At the Lord's table we are called to partake of the messianic banquet, of which the Eucharist is a prolepsis.[1]

Let me make clear at the outset that in this essay the following questions, which were provided by the planners of the consultation, have been at the core of my thinking: What is the role of the church in the face of human suffering? Does this role contribute to or counter the unity of the divided churches? In what way could the church's response to human suffering contribute to the unity of humankind? What is the relation between the unity of the church and the discipleship of the crucified Jesus in a suffering world? How is the discipleship of the individual Christian and the church a factor in the alleviation of suffering in the world? What is the place of the Eucharist in a world of suffering?

I must admit that, though timely, these are very difficult questions and each merits a separate and elaborate treatment. But that is not the task at hand. Having them has given me some sense of parameters within which I could proceed. I will not address these questions in a single fashion; that would be impractical and superficial. Such an approach would result in several "mini-essays" that would be a serious injustice to both the overall theme and each individual question. Instead, I will consider the overall theme with these questions as integral to it. Of course, it should be obvious to the reader that some of the questions are more explicitly addressed than others.

If the unity of the church is derived from the one gospel of Jesus Christ, then consideration of what conduces to unity is consideration of what the gospel is. Yet, it should be admitted that increasingly it appears that while we Christians are agreed that we are judged by the gospel, we are not agreed on what

---

1. Winston D. Persaud, *The Theology of the Cross and Marx's Anthropology: A View from the Caribbean* (New York and Frankfurt, 1991), 128, 131ff.

the gospel is! In other words, we are faced with the discomfiting contemporary crisis of defining and confessing the gospel. Both defining and confessing go together.

Historical Conditionedness and the One Gospel

At first glance, our theme and the attendant questions suggest *a discrete, discernible universal context*. To many, such a universal context is as ephemeral as the morning mist in Guyana. It is as real as one's grasp of it, but that is always fleeting. But the elusiveness of perceiving and conceptualizing a universal context is not the only problem. Assuming a universal context has generally meant that I (the interpreter) could simply proceed without any serious consideration of the "historical conditionedness" of what I thought in response to those questions. But recognition of such "historical conditionedness" is precisely at the heart of the dilemma of finding unity in the midst of such diversity of "conditionedness." It is not merely that the dilemma stems from the fact that the interpreter is a discrete individual, who posits his or her personal viewpoint. It is that and more. The individual is a sociocultural being, with all that implies.[2]

In the contemporary postcolonial world, in which one of the "causes" passionately championed is that of retaining and celebrating one's cultural rootedness as one fundamental way of overcoming one's suffering, to posit a universal context is simultaneously experienced as a liberating celebration of unity and an oppressive remembrance of a particular "historical conditionedness" as the unifying universal. For many, insisting on retaining and celebrating one's cultural rootedness is "out of sync" with the times (indeed, anachronistic), and it is tantamount to imposing certain cultural standards as superior and normative and dismissing others as inferior and non-normative. But no culture is beyond criticism. To be candid, this criticism is applicable to so-called oppressed non-Western and Western cultures and "subcultures" as well as so-called oppressive Western cultures.

It cannot be otherwise, if we are serious about the meaning of the cross of Christ and the role of the individual Christian and the church in relation to the alleviation of human suffering. Theology of the cross *(theologia crucis)* becomes theology of glory *(theologia gloriae)* when theology of the cross stops at pointing out the idolatrous and demonic in the dominant cultures. Theology of the cross becomes theology of glory when it does not distinguish between, on the one hand, the celebration of the oppressed and their cultures as equally legitimate media of God's paradoxically hidden grace for all and, on the other hand,

---

2. In using the term "historical conditionedness" I wish to convey an expanded meaning of *Sitz im Leben* to include the ongoing and decisive shaping influence on the interpreter of such factors as sociocultural, political, economic, gender, race, color, religious, etc. forces. Throughout this paper, unless otherwise indicated, the inclusive meaning of "sociocultural," "historical conditionedness," and other variants will be used with this inclusive meaning in mind.

how the oppressed and their cultures have been and are themselves oppressive. "Historical conditionedness" applies both to the oppressed and suffering and to those who oppress and inflict suffering. Consequently, we would be less than thoroughgoing and evangelical and would serve the cause of the suffering less if we were to disregard the full scope of judgment of theology of glory.

No culture is so superior and triumphant or has suffered so much that it thereby has the authority to disregard the good in another culture or even in its own. No one, no people, no nation is more special in God's eyes on account of such factors as innate, natural characteristics; superiority or superabundance of one's, or a people's, or a nation's gifts, material resources, development, or culture. St. Paul's words are still true: "But God proves his love for us in that *while we still were sinners* Christ died for us" (Rom. 5:8; emphasis added). The individual Christian and the church as a whole need to remember that Paul's words are applicable to them as well as to the whole human community. Both the individual Christian and the Christian communities within the one, holy, catholic, and apostolic church acknowledge and appreciate the image of God *(imago Dei)* in which we were created and the likeness of Christ *(conformatio Christi)* into which are re-created and continue to be made within particular cultural milieus. That is an indispensable given. It cannot be otherwise.

We hear and proclaim the gospel as people living within communities that have cultural, socioeconomic, political, or other peculiarities. But there are only two basic truths: *there is only one gospel of Jesus Christ* and *there are many cultures and many sociopolitical and economic strategies derived from the one gospel.* Indeed, it would be more accurate to speak of strategies derived from the law of love. "The gospel does not build structures but relations and transforms them from the bottom up. The gospel is not a structure."[3]

While, of necessity, there are several expressions of the gospel in a variety of cultures and contexts, there is only one gospel. Even a cursory glance at the history of the church tells the story of the ongoing struggle to know, define, and confess, in word and deed, individually and corporately, the one gospel of Jesus the Christ. The contemporary crisis in defining and confessing the gospel is a symptom of the inevitable, ongoing struggle in which the community of faith has to engage, once it persists in announcing salvation and liberation, reconciliation and renewal, in and through the life, death, and resurrection of Jesus the Christ.

Here, let us be clear: the problem of inculturation is not only a North-South phenomenon; it is also a South-South phenomenon. Dominance of South over South is a reality that we cannot ignore. Within countries in the southern hemisphere, there are groups whose cultures are being forcibly suppressed. Churches are not exempt from this dilemma. This recognition is liberating and not self-defeating.

---

3. Josef Hromadka, "The Witness of the Church in a Changing Czechoslovakia," public lecture, October 9, 1991, Princeton Theological Seminary, Princeton, New Jersey.

The contemporary dilemma in defining and confessing the gospel in the face of human suffering, the divisions between the churches, and divisions within the human community might be best summarized thus: what we have today is a better and clearer grasp of what the gospel is *not* than what it is! Gospel has come to mean a transcendent historical referent that increasingly is a negation of what is considered negating, evil, or dehumanizing. In such cases, there is a pressing necessity (it would appear) to spell out clearly what the gospel is. Where it is spelled out, that, too, falls under the very negation that it intends for another set of prevailing circumstances. Consequently, there is the increasing danger that our contemporary usage of "gospel" will make it devoid of any critical, essential substance and meaning. This essential substance and meaning is necessarily centered in the Triune God, known and revealed in Jesus the Christ in the power of the Holy Spirit. It is not centered in some monarchic or egalitarian theistic referent, a mere human projection, which arises out of interpreted subjective need with, consequently, no fundamental, evangelical connection to Jesus the Christ, God the Son, who became human, suffered, died, and rose again.

Where interhuman justice can add to God's justice and righteousness in a redemptive sense, the gospel is threatened. By the same token, where the pursuit and practice of interhuman justice is merely a matter of personal whim or fancy, or it is an addendum to the gospel, then God is made out to be a liar when Yahweh claims to be a God of justice, righteousness, and compassion. That the Triune God, known and revealed in the cross of the crucified and risen Jesus Christ in the power of the Holy Spirit, is made out to be a liar is a conclusion based on the nature of the community whose God is known in the cross of Jesus Christ. Every community of faith mirrors (albeit partially and not without distortion) who its God is. That the Triune God is compassionate, righteous, and just is to be known by the character, life, and praxis of the community of faith.

Paradoxically, intrinsic to this "good news" is the message that God sides with the poor and the oppressed, the suffering and the "sinned against." This is good news for both the poor and the powerful. Only the God who gives life to those denied life or who experience life only in its material and spiritual distortions can give life to the powerful, the so-called non-needy and the non-poor, as well as give "life to the dead and [call] into existence the things that do not exist" (Rom. 4:17). It is this God who "raised Jesus our Lord from the dead, who was handed over to death for our trespasses and was raised for our justification" (Rom. 4:24b–25). If this is not true, then the "truth" is that the powerful find their life through the creation of their own gods who safeguard their illegitimate assumption and wielding of power. By the same token, the weak, the oppressed and exploited, the suffering, indeed the whole creation, are without hope.

When the "Spirit-prompted" praxis of an individual Christian or a community of faith in Christ contradicts my/our own "Spirit-prompted" praxis or that of another community's, the ensuing dilemma is theological. On the one hand, one or both praxes may be ethical quietism in the face of blatant human oppression and sin; or, on the other hand, it may be that one or both are the active, "radical" pursuit of the common good. Whatever the case might be — the clash between quietism and activism or between two basic visions and strategies for interhuman peace and justice — the verdict remains that the dilemma is essentially theological, since what is at stake is the identity of the God who is agent of the former as well as the latter. Which, then, is authentic Christian praxis? Which socioeconomic posture is evangelical and necessary for determining what the gospel is or is not? Does the proclamation of the Word, both law and gospel, inevitably lead to the raising up of some and the putting down of others on the basis of socioeconomic factors? These are sobering, critical questions that defy easy solution. But they continue to beg of radical response from the "evangelical" community.

It is sobering to remember that praxis as strategy, as the life of faith in pursuit of holiness, both emerges from and mirrors identity; it is not identity. Yet, paradoxically, since praxis as strategy mirrors identity, it cannot be separated from identity, since it participates in its substance. But neither can Christian identity be devoid of praxis. To be so would result in a docetic discipleship, meaning one in which it merely appears that we are disciples of Jesus the Christ, but in reality we are not.

We are back to the dilemma of suggesting strategies as expressions of the law and the gospel, without saying this is law and not gospel. Added to this is the issue of determining what to support and what not to support on a sound theological basis. Undoubtedly, the church has resources that are appropriated in ways that are both just and unjust. By what right does it speak to the world? Is it its own story in providing an alternative way of successfully being a community of love, justice, peace, and mutuality? Or, is it, in the final analysis, the Divine call to do so? In other words, we cannot but live and speak the truth of the gospel that announces and calls forth a new creation — the reign of peace, forgiveness, reconciliation, and justice. Many, both in the church and outside, long for such a new creation. At the same time, many across the spectrum of "historical conditionedness," to which we referred above, wonder whether the new creation is not wishful thinking, like waiting for Godot! Thus, the question is sounded once again: *What is good news?*

Taking due cognizance of its "historical conditionedness" means that in the face of human suffering the church cannot simply announce its reason for being and its right to its particular mission as distinct and separate from its consequent role in the face of human suffering. Clearly, it is already an empirical reality, called by the Holy Spirit to be the community of Jesus Christ. But, for some, it is simultaneously constituted by the very role of proclamation and service (*diakonia*) it plays. The *a priori* of its distinctive identity, its essence, does not exist outside of the concreteness of its empirical manifestation in the "historical givenness." This is another way of saying that there is no formulation of the gospel apart from any cultural wrappings. At the same time, cultural wrappings as form cannot be equated with the gospel. When the sociocultural wrappings are suffering and the perceived sources of such suffering, the underlying kernel of the gospel can appear to be patently divisive. How can it be that the gospel of healing and liberation gives rise to suffering that destroys rather than heals, dehumanizes rather than liberates? On the basis of the gospel, some forms of suffering are patently anathema, while other forms of suffering stem from faithfulness to the gospel. So, is there a gospel centered in the cross of Jesus Christ that transcends the "historical conditionedness"?

Particularity of the Gospel: Unity and Diversity in the Spirit

The church, as a community of faith and life "in Christ," by its unity in confession and service helps to dismantle the systems — ecclesial, religious, and secular — that cause, legitimate, and further human and non-human suffering. This is not to say that mere cosmetic unity will automatically bring an end to suffering. The premise on which unity is founded is decisive for liberation rooted in and sustained by the power of the powerless cross of Christ.

The church is in the world and participates in the world's sufferings. At the same time, the church is also a source of suffering. It is righteous and sinner at the same time (*simul justus et peccator*). Its own history is replete with tragic examples of such suffering. Indeed, the five-hundredth anniversary of Columbus's arrival in the "New World" provides us with a singular opportunity to face this tragic irony of the church as inflicter of suffering and the church as sufferer and as agent of healing. It cannot be otherwise, since the church is in the world as well as not of the world. As Roger Haight, S.J., in his appraisal of Latin American liberationist ecclesiology, correctly observes,

> The church exists in a double relationship, to God and to human society or the world. The world here stands for the whole sphere of history and society that are not the church. The church must be defined by this double relationship, and its nature can only be adequately understood as some kind of medium between God and the world, as an instrument of the purposes of God for the world.[4]

The complexity of the church's role in the face of human suffering is that in making choices to side with and help alleviate the suffering of a particular group (masses!) of sufferers, the church may, and has in fact often, worsened the conditions of other sufferers. Many have noted with sadness and anger that, while the churches through the World Council of Churches rightly and sympathetically dealt with the predicament of Christians and people of other faiths in

---

4. Roger Haight, S.J., *An Alternative Vision* (New York: Paulist Press, 1985), 164. Unless otherwise specified, throughout this paper "liberation theology" refers to Latin American (liberation) theology.

many parts of the world, they were deafeningly silent in the face of the appalling suffering of the people in Romania and elsewhere.[5]

The particular stance the church takes is always ideological. It is hoped that it is a theologically centered ideology, meaning an ideology centered in and critiqued and judged by the cross of the crucified Jesus Christ, who continues to suffer in those who are not embraced in the stance that is made and whose suffering is thereby made worse. How the churches negotiate the variety of ideological postures is a primary determinant in contributing to or countering the unity of the divided churches. One overarching, universal praxis (if it can be found) cannot guarantee unity or sustain unity. Such a praxis can only become tragically demonic as human beings are trapped in insuperable bondage. Only a theological vision out of which spring several praxes, indeed conflicting ones, can truly contribute significantly to the unity of the divided churches. Of course, even such a universal theological vision is not derived from abstract speculation but from authentic engagement and reflection in the concrete conditions of life. They are praxes that reflect the cultures in which they are shaped.

The resultant vision is not ecclesiocentric but theocentric; more particularly, it is Spirit-centered. The center is the Creator Spirit who is sovereign even over the church and works both within and outside the church. In this vein, Haight argues:

> A second principle of liberationist ecclesiology is that the church is not the center of the world; the church is in Gutiérrez's phrase "uncentered" in human history. A concrete historical point of view engenders the empirical perception that the church has not and does not command this position. And from a theological perspective the recognition of the universally operative will of God for human salvation led to the conclusion that, if this be the case, the saving grace of God's Spirit must be mediated by other means than historic Christianity. This implies that the traditional symbol of the reign of God must extend beyond the sphere of the church. And thus one is led to an ecclesiology that ironically is not ecclesiocentric. Its center is God and God's Spirit. The church has a special relationship to and knowledge of the working of God's Spirit though the revelation of Jesus Christ. But the church also has a responsibility to witness to this Spirit of God and cooperate with it insofar as it is active in the world and history at large.[6]

---

5. See Eberhard Jungel: "To this day it irritates me that in this regard something like a liberation theology for the oppressed people in the world of 'realized socialism' was apparently never considered. Even in the headquarters of the World Council of Churches on the Genevan route de Ferney, where injustice in other parts of the world was courageously identified by name and resistance movements were energetically supported, one feigned blindness to the conditions in Romania, for example, right up until the end. This is an ecumenical scandal. And one can only hope that this dark shadow will not darken the undeniable achievements of ecumenism" ("Toward the Heart of the Matter," in James M. Wall and David Heim, eds., *How My Mind Has Changed* [Grand Rapids: Eerdmans, 1991], 148).

6. Haight, *An Alternative Vision,* 164.

But, it may be asked, has the church not always been concerned with the social dimensions of the faith? Is that a recent phenomenon? While criticizing the phenomenon of "Christendom," is not the call for the church to radically reshape society through and for the alleviation of human suffering another call for a modern, "enlightened" reformation of "Christendom"? If this is so, what sanctions are indispensable to safeguard and promote human freedom and plurality — in short, to avoid the "evils," old and new, of Christendom? These are crucial questions that are particularly relevant to the unavoidable dilemma of how we will determine what, without as well as outside the church, is of the Creator Spirit.

Haight recognizes that the liberationists' views of the church include "opposition to sin, especially social sin and dehumanization." In addition, "There are also the much more traditional and standard themes of the church as the mediator of grace through the sacraments." Notwithstanding this, Haight insists that "the three principles concerning the church's relation to the world, its uncenteredness and its role in human emancipation define as it were distinctive features of liberationist ecclesiology. Indeed they imply or include and color most of the others."[7]

Hitherto, the churches have been divided over faith and practice. Liberation theology is in a significant way a reconstitution of the basis of those divisions while forging new unities based on orthopraxis. But to focus exclusively on the doctrinal divisions is to lapse into "doctrinal reductionism," which ignores the concrete, social, and institutional reality of the church. This would be to place the church totally outside the critical scrutiny "of the variety of viewpoints that are provided by the human sciences such as philosophy, social psychology and so on." Haight maintains that

> the subject of ecclesiology, that which is spoken about, is the empirical church, the church as a phenomenon of history, the church that we see. Even though the church cannot be adequately understood theologically as merely an empirical organization, the fact that the church exists in the world and in relation to history forces one to keep the empirical church as one's point of reference and to avoid doctrinal reductionism.[8]

The critique of "doctrinal reductionism" is soberingly appropriate. The church is not its doctrines, and neither is the church confined to its empirical manifestations. If the empirical manifestations of the church alone were the church, then unity is an insuperable and futile task and unity as gift is hollow and empty. It is axiomatic that the church is created by the gospel, and it precedes the gospel that it proclaims. Both that which is created by the gospel and that which precedes the gospel are the one church that exists in the world. But

---

7. Ibid., 165.
8. Ibid., 167.

the church as empirical reality continually has to distinguish between gospel and "ceremonies," recognizing that both the pure gospel and human-made ceremonies[9] have the stamp of "historical conditionedness" upon them. In addition, while "the holy Christian people are externally recognized by the holy possession of the sacred cross...and the only reason they must suffer is that they steadfastly adhere to Christ and God's word, enduring this for the sake of Christ,"[10] in the cross of Christ the whole of creation is held together (Col. 1:15ff., esp. v. 20). Where the church suffers for the sake of the gospel, the church's (and the individual Christian's) suffering is (has been) taken up in the cross of Jesus Christ for the sake of the whole creation. The unity of humankind is neither absent from the cross of Christ nor the cross of the Christian (church). Indeed, it is precisely because this unity occurs through the reconciliation God creates "by making peace through the blood of [Christ's] cross" (Col. 1:20), that human suffering, for which culpability is laid at the feet of Christians (as well as people of other faiths), is judgment upon the church (as well as others). The church must constantly and vigilantly work at removing the barriers that exclude people from the grace and goods God gives.

Again and again, the church has to consider what kind of message and posture constitutes good news, especially to and among the poor, suffering, and oppressed. It is a serious problematic of whether the unity of the church and the unity of humankind are enhanced through the proclamation of a partisan God of the poor, suffering, and oppressed. The biblical witness to God's partiality is ambiguous: it points to both division and ultimate separation (Matt. 25:31ff) and to the insuperable unity of all that occurs through the blood of the cross of Jesus Christ (Col. 1:15ff). Therefore, to posit the thesis that division and separation are not ultimate and irreversible is to overlook significant biblical texts.

Suffering — including tragic forms — that is to be transcended can come from the violent imposition of forms of unity that leave little or no room for dissent, difference, and individual creativity. The cross of Jesus Christ is itself the epitome of tragic and at the same time liberating suffering. To follow the crucified and to protest against suffering results in suffering. Hence, we distinguish between "protest" suffering and "passive" suffering as victim. It should be made clear, however, that "protest" suffering does include victimization. The crucial difference here is that the victim protests in the name of the crucified and risen Jesus Christ. To follow the crucified and risen Lord is to follow in faith; it is living out in love the justifying trust we have in him. But the lived dynamic of that trust is not a peripheral matter, mere adiaphora. How we live is testimony to what our freedom in Christ implies and what participating in Christ calls forth. We may make wrong judgments. Our discernment may be

---

9. See The Augsburg Confession, Art. VII, in *The Book of Concord*, trans. and ed. Theodore G. Tappert (Philadelphia: Fortress Press, 1966), 164f.

10. "On the Councils and the Church," 1539, trans. Charles M. Jacobs, revised by Eric W. Gritsch, in *Luther's Works*, American Edition, ed. Eric W. Gritsch, with an introduction by E. Gordon Rupp (Philadelphia: Fortress Press, 1966), 164f.

wrong (and more often than not it is wrong); but whether it is radical activism or quiet passivism, the path of our discipleship is inextricably bound up with our discernment of the way of Jesus. Does the church proclaim and is the church servant of a partisan God?

"God is the One who suffers for the healing of humanity and the whole creation."[11] The church is the community that is born out of and has its life in unconditional love.

> While love and solidarity might be born out of common suffering, there is no way of guaranteeing the continuation of such love and solidarity after the revolution has been successfully completed (or defeated). Love of human beings for one another does not come from within human beings themselves. Its source is the suffering God, not the human creature.[12]

The question of the unity of the church and of humankind is the crucial question of how enemies are transformed into friends!

Following the crucified and risen Jesus Christ is authentic to the extent that the church and the individual Christian are found *among* the suffering, for that is where the crucified and risen Christ is to be found. By taking on humanity, the incarnate One takes on the tragedy and reality of human suffering. He could not be human and live outside the reality of human suffering. That would be a contradiction. His solidarity in suffering is salutary and liberating. However the church and the individual Christian participate in Christ's solidarity with the suffering, solidarity *with* the suffering will be incomplete, indeed pretentious, if it fails to be a solidarity *among* the suffering in their varied "historical conditionedness." Only in this way can we speak of a genuine family resemblance among the suffering — a family resemblance that includes but is not limited to race, gender, skin color, class, ideology, culture, etc. "And the Word became flesh and *lived among us,* and we have seen his glory, the glory as of a father's only son, full of grace and truth" (John 1:14; emphasis added). This understanding of solidarity is a sobering reminder that even the perspicacious intellectual stands under the judgment of this thesis.

For liberationists, it is crucial that that role be seen as constitutive of the very gospel itself. Anything short of this is at best adiaphora. But it needs to be noted, at the same time, that any implied or expressed theory of social change cannot be taken as intrinsic to the gospel. Notwithstanding this, there is no kernel of the gospel apart from its intrinsic groundings in the sociohistorical realities of the world in which we live.

Communities of faith in Christ define the gospel contextually in the midst of sociohistorical realities that shape them and are in turn shaped by them. Unity of action, in contradiction to unity in the gospel, is ideological. But unity in the

---

11. Persaud, *The Theology of the Cross and Marx's Anthropology,* 127.
12. Ibid., 128.

gospel does not imply a single, uniform, homogeneous response to the gospel. That, too, would be ideological, and in that case negatively so. It is conceivable that agreement on the gospel necessarily implies plurality of praxes. If there is no place for such plurality of praxes, then the unity in the gospel is not evangelical but ephemeral and fanciful. Moreover, it is not liberating.

Here, it is instructive to our purposes to consider the current phenomenal growth of evangelical and Pentecostal Christianity in Latin America. It is a phenomenon that especially, though not exclusively, touches the masses of the suffering, poor, powerless, exploited, marginalized, and dislocated. It is a phenomenon of liberation, of newfound spiritual and sociopsychic healing in the midst of fragmentation and chaos; and, it is a phenomenon of division, of spiritual and social separation. In short, both centripetal and centrifugal forces are at work simultaneously in the churches and the societies as a whole.

David Martin, in his seminal sociological work on evangelical and Pentecostal Christianity in Latin America, poignantly analyses the obvious tension between unity born out of a voluntarily appropriated faith (as in evangelical and Pentecostal Christianity) and organic social unity founded on the Catholic church's overarching domination of the sociopolitical and cultural milieu.[13] Martin finds that the former, as in Brazil, "cut people off from the wider society in order to raise them within a new religious framework. They were 'peculiar' in order to be something different."[14] Martin provides a provocative, insightful, and discomfiting picture of another explosive alternative to traditional Roman Catholicism in Latin America. Correctly observing that the clash between Hispanic and Anglo-American cultures is a clash between two "civilizations," he perspicuously shows how evangelical and Pentecostal Christianity is creating new "unities" precisely through voluntary rejection of old loyalties based on hierarchy and involuntary unity. Martin writes:

---

13. David Martin, *Tongues of Fire: The Explosion of Protestantism in Latin America*, with a Foreword by Peter Berger (Oxford: Basil Blackwell, 1990). We cannot do justice to Martin's brilliant and informative discussion of the "voiceless," including women (cf. pp. 181ff.), being given a new tongue within Pentecostal circles; the significant appeal to and among the poor that Pentecostals have on account of their lack of sophistication; and Pentecostal appeal among Brazil's Afro-citizens, most of whom are very poor. Here the blending of "Pentecostal" and "African," Indian and Hispanic does not go unnoticed. For example, Martin writes: "Whatever may be the truth about the pool of US power, it is evident that Pentecostalism (as well as other forms of evangelicalism) enables many of its followers to achieve a power in their lives which can simultaneously infuse them with the possibility of 'betterment' and of new goods of every kind, spiritual and material, and also puts them in touch with spiritual charges and discharges lodged deep in the indigenous culture, black, Indian, or Hispanic. The long-term resources now drawn upon in people's lives run back both to the traditions of Protestant revival and to the ancient spirit worlds of Indian peasants and African slaves" (p. 204). Another highly significant work is David Stoll, *Is Latin America Turning Protestant? The Politics of Evangelical Growth* (Berkeley: University of California Press, 1990). Richard Shaull's article, "Three Responses to a New Historical Situation" *Interpretation* 46, no. 3 (July 1992): 261–70, contains a welcome, insightful, and positive appraisal of Pentecostalism in Latin America.

14. Martin, *Tongues of Fire*, 65.

Thus, seen from a certain angle, the emergence of Pentecostalism and of evangelical Christianity generally represents a first incursion of Christianity understood as a biblically based and personally appropriated faith, propagated by a distinct body of committed believers. Catholic observers candidly admit this when they speak of the spiritual vacuum which opens up once the external forms and localized practices collapse under the intense pressure of rapid social change.[15]

Summarizing Ivan Vallier's apposite description of the meaning at the local level of such religious and social chaos, Martin writes: "When people came to church not only was the celestial hierarchy made manifest but the social hierarchy was also on parade. Those who worshipped regularly in the same church building did not constitute a solidarity based congregation but a random assortment of differential social statuses juxtaposed in proximity for the duration of the mass." Martin adds that Vallier "goes on to point out that there was no need to create an active and enthusiastic lay body, since everyone was gently cradled in one and the same religious universe." This situation, Martin correctly points out, parallels that "in England up to the eighteenth century, and for Pentecostals and Catholics today one only has to substitute Methodist and the church of England two hundred and fifty years ago." Martin concludes that "what the Pentecostalism of today offers then is a body of committed lay persons, actively brought into being rather than passively existing, and enjoying a solidarity based on social affinity."[16]

Ironically, it is precisely in response to human suffering that new unities are being forged, while concomitantly the unity of the church, as expressed in its hitherto seriously uncontested primacy in shaping the lives of the people of Latin America, suffers divisions and fragmentations. The question is: how do these divisions and fragmentations revitalize the church? Are they inimical to the unity of the church? In this vein, Catholic Action and liberation theology, within the Roman Catholic church, and evangelical and Pentecostal Christianity outside the Catholic ambit, are significant movements to be considered. Martin notes the curious contradiction that "Catholic Action divided the self-conscious Catholic from the automatic ritual conformity of established strata. So while it was hegemonic in aspiration it was sectional in organizational form." Martin therefore concludes that Catholic Action "was proto-Protestant insofar as it was lay and depended on specific commitment. But beyond that it could develop in a radical direction and give birth to troublesome fraternities of revolutionary Catholic youth."[17]

Thus Martin says that "liberation theology represents a continuation both of

---

15. Ibid., 289.
16. Ibid. (Martin references Ivan Vallier, "Religious Elites," in Seymour Martin Lipset and Aldo Solari, eds., *Elites in Latin America* [Oxford, New York: Oxford University Press, 1967], 196–97).
17. Ibid.

sectarian Protestant motifs and of this political and ecclesiastical radicalism."
He continues:

> The point is that Catholicism itself was bringing into existence elements of
> Protestantism through Catholic Action and liberation theology. What was
> forming outside the walls of the Catholic Church was also germinating
> within: a parallel development. Yet what stayed within was marked by its
> Catholic inheritance, in particular the idea of the church as promulgating
> norms for society as a whole and acting as moral mentor. It was adjusted
> to political reality in a characteristically Catholic manner and was, there-
> fore, ready to provide political translations of the Bible, especially of the
> Old Testament, as well as to reformulate the doctrine of the just war to
> encompass revolutionary violence.[18]

While Martin finds that "liberation theology is, therefore, a major rival to
Pentecostalism," he is more convinced that it "is not so successful a competitor
as might be expected." Ironically, in the role as a major rival to Pentecostalism,
"it probably has a modest welcome even from the more cautious members of
the hierarchy, however much they are alarmed by its attitude to traditional Catholic organization and the primacy it affords politics." Martin spares no effort in
identifying what he feels are some of the glaring shortcomings of Latin American liberation theology. Thus, for him, the greater irony concerning liberation
theology is that

> there are even those who see its existence as indirectly helping forward
> the expansion of evangelicalism. The reason is that however much it rep-
> resents "an option for the poor" taken up by hundreds of thousands of
> the poor themselves, that option is most eloquently formulated by radi-
> cal intellectuals like the Boffs and the Cardenals. However idealistic and
> decently concerned and shocked the leaders of "liberationism" may be,
> they are not usually "of the people." Liberation theology has a decided
> middle class and radical intellectual accent alien to the localized needs of
> "the poor." It claims to be Latin America [sic] but it is, in fact, at least
> as "foreign" as Pentecostalism, if not more so, with spokesmen — yes,
> spokes *men* — who are part of the international circuit of theological lec-
> turers. This means that while the language of Pentecostalism is "odd" and
> many of its practices initially unattractive, the language of liberationism
> can easily remain remote. Beyond all that, it promises to pull poor people
> struggling mainly for survival into much larger and bloodier struggles of
> which they have often had more than enough.[19]

---

18. Ibid., 290.
19. Ibid.

To be candid, Martin's open attack here on "the Boffs and the Cardenals" is unwarranted and unnecessary. It does not enhance his argument, nor does it take cognizance of the fact that Latin American theologians themselves have observed with profound concern the gap between "middle-class leftists" and "the grassroots people" that characterized "the first theology of liberation." Notwithstanding Martin's harsh critique, liberation theology's determined promotion of "the church of the poor" or "the preferential option for the poor" has been positively and intentionally addressing this gap.[20]

Liberation theology is self-consciously a theology of redemptive, liberating suffering for the oppressed, the poor, and the marginalized. It is arguable that it is less a theology of reconciliation — unless it is reconciliation preceded by liberation, which would thereby imply that such reconciliation as would be necessary is authentic. Evangelical and Pentecostal Christianity, in its primary emphasis on personal renewal — becoming a new person in Christ (as evidenced by speaking in tongues for the Pentecostals) is the new "free space" — is, in Martin's view, no less radical in its implications for socioeconomic and political transformation. Such transformation occurs, despite the obvious apolitical character of evangelical and Pentecostal Christianity. In it liberation is first and foremost personal, individual reconciliation with God. Those who suffer at the hands of powers and systems that are evil and human capacity for their transformation is suspect. Hence, a reinforcement of the priority of inward change, indeed, radical change![21] However, what remains unchanged are the patterns of leadership. Among Pentecostals, the emerging pastoral leadership continues in the mode of the hierarchical, authoritarian, "patron-client" relationship so pervasive in church and society.[22] This is in contrast to newly received gifts of the Spirit of equality and individual dignity.[23]

As a definitive theology of the church, the theology of liberation does not purport to have an all-encompassing prescription for all ills, individual and societal. It is acutely aware of its "historical conditionedness," and, increasingly, it is becoming more aware of some of its endemic and severe short-comings. It was never as pluralistic as the world of religions actually is. Certainly in its parent, progenitive form in Latin America, it did not reflect on the reality

---

20. See Juan Luis Segundo, S.J., "The Shift within Latin American Theology," *Journal of Theology for Southern Africa* 52 (1985): 23; and Leonardo Boff, "Teologia a escuta do pove," *Revista Ecclesiastica Brasileira* 41 (March 1981): 55.

21. See Martin, 264, where Martin summarizes Bobby C. Alexander's conclusion on the latter's study of a Pentecostal community in New York. "Alexander concludes that there is enough evidence from his own research and that of others to refute the notion that the release of tension in the worship of the congregation necessarily diverts psychic power from the pursuit of political redress." Presumably, this marriage of ecstatic worship and political action is more widespread than is often recognized. The dilemma of what strategies for sociopolitical and economic change are more liberating remains.

22. Ibid., 229. Elsewhere (p. 264), Martin writes: "Their style is authoritarian and this makes them useful allies for the national security state and its military rulers, as well as pawns of the 'Manifest Destiny' of the United States."

23. Ibid.

of the great world religions. What it did overwhelmingly was to reflect on the deleterious and oppressive legacy of Iberian Catholicism, in both its religious and secular expressions, that obtain in Latin America today. It is clearly not a Caribbean phenomenon that includes reflection on the ethnic and religious diversity there.

With all its liberating potential, liberation theology as the great leveler — by focusing primarily, though not exclusively, on human reality as systemic socioeconomic and political oppression — militates against the very justice it pursues. There is no question that Latin American theology falls within the ambit of "Western." This means that the church outside the Western hemisphere has to deal with the injustices that arise even when the primary focus and strategies of Latin American theology are borrowed and adapted in new contexts. For example, liberation theology exclusively builds its socioeconomic and political analysis on the dependency theory. Thus, the clash between Western capitalism, on the one hand, and Latin American theology, on the other hand, is viewed as a clash over the permissibility of so-called democratic, exploitative capitalism to pursue courses of action that do not have the welfare of the impoverished, exploited, and oppressed masses of Latin American people at the center of its primary concerns. I cannot go into an elaborate treatment of the dependency theory. I have neither the expertise nor the space for such a treatment. It should be pointed out, however, that the dependency theory masks the culpability of national and other local decision-makers for a great deal of the suffering of their people.

The unity of humanity is not a by-product of the gospel, nor should it be confined to the doctrine of creation. It is central to the doctrine of redemption. At the same time the church's response to human suffering is not so unique that it is totally different from the diverse responses emanating from the world. Through Christ's life, death, and resurrection, forces for healing, liberation, and reconciliation have been unleashed. To stand with those outside the church is to be faithful to the law and the gospel.

Derived from and centered in the gospel, the unity of the church calls forth a plurality of responses for the alleviation of suffering by those who follow the crucified Jesus. Unity of the church is not suprahistorical. Even as eschatological reality,[24] unity of the church implies a life of imitation of the crucified Jesus. But the very plurality of responses to discipleship, necessary though it is to the unity of the church, is a primary threat to that very unity. Is unity sustainable or realizable, given the centrifugal forces of plurality? With this in mind, we turn our attention to the Eucharist and the common good.

---

24. As an example of what I mean by eschatological unity when considering the "historical conditionedness" of the Caribbean man and woman, see Persaud, *The Theology of the Cross and Marx's Anthropology*, 241.

The Eucharist:
Celebration of the Common Good[25]

The liberating power of the crucified and risen Jesus Christ is present in the anticipatory celebration of the transformation of sin and alienation. The genuine urge for wholeness emanates from God. It is not the product of historical circumstances. It is not the result of human achievement nor is it sustained or heightened by optimistic hope in humankind's capacity to transform ultimately the human condition. Through the Holy Spirit, human beings "become" the power and love of God in Christ in the world. Openness to God is completely and totally the gift of the Triune God, who brings the Absolute Future. This does not deny the celebration of the real liberating Divine-human activity in history. To do so would be to distort the theology of the cross into a form of docetism. The cry for wholeness in history is the cry for the salvific presence of God, which is already available to the "eyes of the faith."[26]

The Eucharist is thanksgiving for redemption, which no one could accomplish for himself/herself or for others. Only God through the Son in the Spirit could and can accomplish redemption. The Eucharist is also sustenance for mission, a mission defined by the Giver of such sustenance. It is God's mission in which we participate. At the Lord's table, variously understood, the suffering are present. Those more characterized as inflictors and benefactors of the suffering of others and those more characterized as victims of suffering all meet together at the Lord's table. There are not two tables. Participants are irrevocably bonded; to leave the table together as sisters and brothers radically contradicts the systems of suffering that make us antagonists. How our identity is determined, by the latter (as antagonists) or by the former (sisters and brothers), significantly determines whether the Eucharist is a sham or the radical meal of thanksgiving, equality, and community. The Eucharist is a foretaste of the unity we have in Jesus Christ.

The Christian community is peculiarly a community of memory. In its liturgy and worship, in the Thanksgiving, it recalls the drama of God's divine love affair with the world, a love affair that includes the death of the Son, as well, and his resurrection. In recalling this drama, the Christian community is again and again reminded that God is the source of its life and being. Such remembering empowers the community both to see and live in the world differently, not dominated by self-interest but freed for the pursuit of the common good, which transcends national, gender, race, or class divisions and boundaries.

---

25. This discussion includes some material that appeared in the Fall 1992 issue of *Word and World*, which has been appropriately modified.
26. Ibid., 132ff.

The appeal to the Christian community to pursue the common good for the sake of the suffering is premised upon the twofold responsibility as citizens of respective nations, and, more important, as members of the household of God through the life, death, and resurrection of Jesus Christ. Through our baptism into the body of Christ we have joined people of various sorts and conditions. In the Apostle's Creed we confess, "I believe in the holy, catholic church, the communion of saints...." Thereby, we acknowledge that our identity in Christ is bound up with a host of others who are materially poor and oppressed. Ironically, their poverty and misery may be connected to socioeconomic and political systems that benefit some nations and some groups within those nations more than others. Because of its peculiar identity — a people who follow the suffering, crucified, and risen Lord, Jesus Christ — the Christian community cannot silently stand by and allow such inequity to remain unchallenged. Even national economic and political self-interest must not stand in place of solidarity with the poor and the suffering. The discourse on the last judgment (Matt. 25:31ff.) is a salutary reminder that solidarity with the poor in pursuit of their good is surprisingly solidarity with Jesus the Christ! Not to stand with the poor and the suffering is surprisingly not to stand with Jesus.

In the face of the appalling suffering in the world, and our witting and unwitting participation in economic and political systems that tear away at the inextricable unity that Christians share in Christ, the Eucharist *re-presents* the suffering of Jesus the Christ for the sake of the world and simultaneously *presents* the world of suffering in need of healing. In the Eucharist, the community gathered around the table lifts up its hearts in thanksgiving for God's redemption. Simultaneously, Jesus Christ *presents* the community with the needs of the suffering. Christ's presentation is both gift and task. It is gift in that those who suffer are also included in the reign of God. It is gift because the suffering still hunger for bread, physical sustenance, for the fullness of life God offers in Jesus Christ.

The scriptures are unequivocal in their call to the people, whose God is the crucified and risen Lord, to celebrate their superlative, new, and divinely given status and identity. The Christian is called to celebrate his/her new, exalted state in Christ. Celebration is intrinsic to being Christian, but to detach the "exalted" status and to focus inordinately upon it is idolatrous and leads to disastrous consequences. True exaltation is in God who is the source of the exaltation. The new creation in Christ (2 Cor. 5:17), which the Christian celebrates, is intrinsic to the very reality of the gospel. Consequently, to say, "Once you were not a people, but now you are God's people..." (1 Pet. 2:10; also, v. 9), or "not many of you were wise by human standards, not many were powerful" (1 Cor. 1:26) is to place supreme value on the God who gives the new in place of the old. To make this new life a badge of superiority, which is expressed in an ethic of dominion as domination, exploitation, and stereotyping, is contrary to the gospel. But for the grace of God, we are nothing.

Admittedly, one of the dominant myths that shapes our lives is the myth that taking care of my needs will necessarily include caring for the needs of others. Luther's emphasis on the Christ for me (*pro me*) is misappropriated when it is taken to mean "me first," then others afterward. This applies no less to those of us who engage in the issues of justice and peace than those who rest secure in the benefits of the status quo. Engagement in the issues of justice turns the spotlight even more brightly on all the beneficiaries of the very systems that are "blessed" by some and condemned as "unjust" and "inhuman" by others. I know of no way of avoiding this irony.

Yet, the Eucharist is a seeing through the eyes of the crucified and risen Jesus Christ. For example, as we witness the phenomenal growth of evangelical and Pentecostal Christianity worldwide, questions, old and new, concerning doctrinal, political, and ideological faithfulness to the gospel and to authentic liberation inevitably arise. (Of course, these are not the only crucial questions.) We are seeing old walls of division crumbling and we are witnessing the emergence of new walls of separation. The Eucharist as a seeing through the eyes of the crucified and risen Jesus Christ is a seeing that beholds the Christ in the bread and wine present outside the walls of division! Thus, the individual Christian and the church as a whole that would be faithful to and receive from its Lord cannot but be present in both places.

Chapter 10

Christian Mission toward Abolition of the Cross

Choan Seng Song

The topic assigned to me was "Christian Mission under the Cross." I took the liberty of changing it to "Christian Mission toward Abolition of the Cross." I realized I had to reframe my topic in this way when I had almost reached the end of my essay. This rather unusual title may surprise some of those who have acquired the theological stamina not to be surprised easily. As a matter of fact, it did surprise me and even unsettled me. It seemed to run counter to the very concern of the theology of the cross and its implications for our world today. But I invite the reader to join with me in this adventure of theology into Christian mission whose task, as I came to see in the exercise of this essay, is to work toward the abolition of the cross.

Our concern here is Christian mission, not just mission, not just any mission, but *Christian* mission, the mission of the Christian church. And it has a clear focus: the cross of Jesus. Christian mission and the cross of Jesus: what could be a more sound theological equation? Is this not the way it should be when we apply ourselves to the subject of Christian mission? Is it not the way it has been in the history of Christianity in Europe and America? And is it not the way Christian mission has been initiated and practiced in Africa, Asia, Latin America, and the Pacific?

Here history seems on the side of the Christian mission carried out as the missiological mandate of the Christian church. In the year 312, so we are told, Constantine the Caesar defeated Maxentius his rival in the Latin West and entered Rome in triumph, "the event which was to change the course of the history

130

of the church and empire alike."[1] Change it did, both the glory and the bane of the church, more bane than glory as a matter of fact, in its ecclesiastical development and its missionary expansion. But how did Constantine conquer the empire? By the sign *Chi* and *Rho,* so the story goes, the initials of the name of Christ, which he is said to have seen in a dream on the eve of the battle at the Mulvian Bridge and which he had painted on the shields of his soldiers. Do we not find in this political and military episode of legendary nature the "secular" root of the theological and missiological mind-set of the Christian church in the history of its expansion? Has not the image of Jesus as conqueror dominated the Christian missions of the churches in the West? And is it not this image of Jesus that the churches outside the West have projected in relation to the people of other religions?

Several hundred years after Constantine the Great, the Christian church in Europe, well established as "powers that be" not only in spiritual matters but also in secular matters, was to be entrenched in one of the most tragic, brutal and futile religious wars in human history. I am of course referring to the crusades of the Middle Ages that lasted almost two centuries. The religious fervor, the pious vision, the religious zeal, may not have been totally lacking in these military operations to retake the holy land for Christianity, but these were of dubious nature at best. What moved the crusaders were "love of adventure, hopes of plunder, desire for territorial expansion, and religious hatred [toward Muslims]."[2] Note particularly "religious hatred" in this list of things that moved the church and the crusaders. It was directed to what they called "infidels," the Muslims. They went to the crusades against the latter by "a cross sewn to their clothing."[3] Contempt for infidels and hatred for Muslims by the sign of the cross! And how has that sign of the cross continued to play a negative role in the dealings of Christians with the people of other faiths for all this time!

Mission Impossible

The cross is the key symbol of Christianity, just as the lotus is the chief symbol of Buddhism. A church is recognized as a Christian church in a Buddhist country such as Thailand by the cross set on its roof. A priest is identified as a Christian priest in distinction from a Taoist monk, for example, in Taiwan, by the cross he wears on his chest. Christianity without the cross would not be Christianity, just as Buddhism would not be Buddhism without the lotus. To confess the Christian faith is to confess faith *in* the cross. To speak of the Christian church is to speak of the church *of* the cross. To be engaged in Christian theology is to be engaged in the theology of the cross. But how Christians

---

1. Wilston Walker, and Richard A. Norris, David W. Lotz, Robert T. Handy, *A History of the Christian Church,* 4th ed. (New York: Charles Scribner's Sons, 1985), 125.
2. Ibid., 284.
3. Ibid.

have all too often misrepresented the cross as a sign of conquest! In the modern history of the Christian church, how many Western missionaries have gone out to conquer even the remotest parts of the world by the sign of the cross! How has the political image of the cross rather than its biblical image influenced our faith, dominated our church, and shaped our theology!

But the cross has not conquered the world. This is a factual statement. It has not even subjugated the part of the world called Asia, for instance. Perhaps the cross itself, the cross in its true meaning, that is, the cross of Jesus, has not meant to conquer any body of land with the covert and overt protection of political and colonial power, be it that of Constantine the Great in the fourth century or that of Europe and America in the nineteenth century and the first half of the twentieth century. Does this mean that the entire missionary enterprise of the Christian church has been misdirected? This is a disquieting thought after so much material and human resources have been poured into it. This is a question one is not supposed to raise after so much heroic sacrifice has been made by Christians at home and missionaries in the "field." Ought not the question be dismissed as an expression of unbelief on the one hand and ingratitude on the other?

Unbelief or not, ingratitude or not, the question just does not go away. It came back over and over to haunt me as I was working on this essay, not in America but in Japan. Has not the history of the missionary expansion of the Christian church in the West, to put the question once again in a slightly different manner, in the name of "the great commission" based on Matthew 28:18–19, been a history of the Christian conquest of the world miscarried and unfulfilled? The vision to Christianize the world — has this been God's own vision or the vision of the Christian church that came to be allied with the power of the Roman Empire in the fourth century, ironically the power that sentenced Jesus to die on the cross three hundred years earlier? The mission to convert to Christianity the people nurtured and shaped by cultures and religions other than Christian religion and culture — has this been the mission of God who, according to the Genesis story of the Hebrew scriptures, created heaven and earth? Have we not too easily identified our theology of Christian mission with God's own theology of mission?

I just said that I worked on this essay not in the United States of America but in Japan. And this is important. My sabbatical leave from the Pacific School of Religion in Berkeley, California, brought me to Kyoto, Japan, where I have been teaching at the School of Theology, Doshisha University, as visiting professor of theology. This ancient capital of Japan is a fascinating city in every way. It is truly a city of "ancient color and fragrance" (*ku se ku hsiang*), to use a Chinese expression. But hidden deep behind its colors and fragrance one encounters in Kyoto the history of Japan at its noblest and at its bloodiest. It is a city that housed the splendor of feudal Japan on the one hand, while on the other it seems still restless with the souls of thousands of men, women, and children fallen victim to the ruthless struggles for power among the feudal lords. Walking the streets of downtown Kyoto, one is at once amazed and sobered — amazed because of the tenacity of human beings to survive in spite of cruel adversities, and sobered because of the horrendous brutality human beings are capable of inflicting on one another.

But it is the fate of Christianity in Japan that makes me think deep thoughts about Christian mission. Japan was forced to open its door to the West in 1858. Already in the following year the first Protestant missionaries arrived from America to inaugurate the era of Christian mission in that country. After more than a hundred years of missionary labor of preaching the Christian gospel, establishing churches, introducing modern education, and building hospitals, Christians in Japan today still make up only 1 percent of the total population. There are scarcely signs that the situation will improve in the future in favor of the cause of Christianity. The cross as a sign of conquest that inspired militant activities of Christians and churches has not conquered and will not conquer Japan. This is the strong impression a city such as Kyoto makes on outside visitors.

Kyoto is a city of temples and shrines. In this city with a population of 1.5 million there are more than a thousand temples and shrines, big and small. The number of Christian churches, all denominations and confessions included, is said to be about sixty. But it is not just a matter of numbers. In Kyoto one breathes the Buddhist air, observes Buddhist ceremonies, takes part in festivals of a religious nature different from Christianity. Even the atmosphere of Christmas is very subdued, much more subdued than in any other Asian city I have come to know. In Kyoto, in other words, one lives in a world shaped and defined largely by Buddhism and its ethos. One may contend that the Buddhism one meets in Kyoto is a form of what historians of religion would call "diffused religion." Most citizens of Kyoto would be at a loss if asked about the history of Buddhism in Japan, doctrinal differences that distinguish one Buddhist sect from another. They would not be able to explain the religious significance of the tea ceremony that takes much discipline and patience to learn. But the unmistakable fact is that it is the Buddhist and not the Christian cultural ethos that penetrates deeply into the life of people and the texture of society both in its religious and secular dimensions.

For me this is a thought-provoking experience, because I, like any one else from outside Japan, has to witness how modern science and technology from the West have transformed Japan and made it an economic power second only to the United States in the world today. What one finds in Japan is a living example of defiance of the Protestant thesis that Christianity is the primal mover in the construction of a modern culture of prosperity. That might have been the manifest destiny of Christianity in Europe and America but not in Japan. If this is true with Japan, it is also true with Singapore, Hong Kong, Taiwan, and South Korea, known as the "four small dragons," which have come to play a considerable role in the economic order, or perhaps disorder, of the world in recent years.

Even Thailand, which has remained a Buddhist country, is no exception to what I just said about Japan. Thailand is not far behind in the culture of modernization imported from the West. But it has kept Christianity at bay despite years of missionary endeavors of the churches of America. Speaking of Christian mission in Thailand in Berkeley two years ago, a Thai Christian church historian had these words attached to his lecture title, "Mission Impossible," with a question mark. From what he had to tell us as a Thai church historian and not as a Christian missionary, we knew he meant that question mark to be rhetorical. To carry out Christian mission in Thailand, he was saying, at least in the way it had been done in the past, is an impossible mission.

Raising Theological Questions

Christian mission in those parts of the world shaped by other religions is mission impossible, and will remain mission impossible if it is motivated, even if not by territorial conquest, by spiritual conquest of other people. The words of a Japanese historian of science, who is also a Christian are relevant here: "Why," he asks, "does Christianity have always to be associated with things European?" He then goes on to say: "As long as we neglect to grapple with what Christian faith really stands for, we may be able to continue living in the house built by European Christianity but will not be able to live the life of Christ with Christ."[4] These words hit the nail on the head, as it were. I believe this is the crux of the matter that faces us Christians today in Asia. But do not these words also make Christians and theologians in the post-Christian West ponder deeply on the authentic meaning of the Christian faith and on the role of Christianity in the world of cultural and religious pluralism today?

What I am raising here is a theological question. To grapple with what Christian faith really stands for — is this not a theological question first and foremost? As we Christians in Asia realize that the Christianity brought to our shores is much less than what it should be and much more of what it should not be — does this not amount to a theological awakening? When we resolve to know for ourselves what the faith in Jesus means for us — is this not the beginning of our theological journey? Christian mission does not have to be impossible. The question is, of course, what kind of Christian mission? It has finally dawned on me that for Christian mission to be really possible it has to be predicated on our theological inquiry into what Christian faith is really about, what Jesus of Nazareth really did, and why he had to end up on the cross. Yes, the cross on which Jesus died, not the cross on the roof of a church but the cross used by Roman colonial rulers for the execution of criminals, not the cross hanging on the wall inside the church but the cross standing on Golgotha, the place called

---

4. Yoichiro Murakami, "Modernization of Japan and Christianity," in Kiroku Echimae and Yichuko Saito, eds., *The Japanese and Christianity* (Tokyo: Women's Paul Association, 1979), 289–313; translation from the Japanese by C. S. Song.

the Skull, on which Jesus died. Does not this lead us to a new quest for God? Does not this demand that we direct new questions to the church and the role it should play in the world today, the world liberated from the political and cultural domination of the West?

It must be clear to you by now that I am dealing with the relationship between theology and mission in that order and not the other way round. It is a mystery to me why even today most Christians, even missiologists, are confused about this relationship of theology and mission. In words that summarized an event as recent as the conference on world mission and evangelism held by the World Council of Churches in San Antonio, Texas, in May 1989, one finds these words:

> The missionary calling of the church must become the underlying perspective and organizing principle of all that goes on in ministerial formation. Such a rethinking and restructuring of theological curricula and method in the light of the perspective of the missionary nature of the church will then lead us to a new understanding of the ministry itself.[5]

These words might have stirred up certain churches and Christians for missionary actions in the good old days, but they sound hollow and unauthentic today when the very concept and practice of mission are under close theological scrutiny.

The missionary calling of the church. The missionary nature of the church. Phrases such as these used to be on the lips of mission executives in the heyday of the missionary enterprise of the churches in the West. Although local congregations were never quite mobilized to be "missionary" congregations, at least their missionary calling was fulfilled in the persons of missionaries they helped to send overseas with their contributions to the mission funds. It is in fact more true to say that missionaries sent overseas carried out vicariously the missionary calling of the church at home. No wonder the so-called missionary nature of the church at home has never been clear. This has never been so evident as today when the churches and Christians in Europe and America have found, to their bewilderment, those people of other religions and cultures to be their neighbors worshiping in their own temples and mosques — those very people their missionaries were supposed to have converted to the Christian faith a long time ago.

History has a curious way of making fools of us, and this is one of the examples. What is the missionary calling of the Christians in Europe and America toward those Buddhists, Muslims, or ancestor worshippers who have come to live in the midst of them and who continue to believe and worship the way they used to in the lands they left behind? How are we to speak of the missionary

---

5. See Frederick R. Wilson, ed., *The San Antonio Report: Your Will Be Done, Mission in Christ's Way* (Geneva: World Council of Churches, 1990), 145.

nature of the Christian church when our church does not seem to offer a viable alternative to meet the spiritual needs of those new neighbors of ours who have brought with them the gods and lords that protected their people for centuries in the past and will protect them in their land of adoption for centuries to come?

These newcomers from the distant shores have compounded the matter for the churches in Europe and America. The churches have had to witness helplessly as the world they thought they had Christianized has been secularized by leaps and bounds. They were not able to stem the mighty tides of secularization, the stepchild of Christian civilization, and they have been on the defensive in the face of it. Have they developed the missionary nature of the church in the secularized West? Have they been able to rediscover their missionary calling toward their own secularized society? The answer, unfortunately, is not clear. And now the world of cultures and religions has found its way into their secularized "Christian" world. By and large the people from the other side of the world appear to be more religious, more conscious of the spiritual heritage of their old world than of the Christian heritage of their new world.

What is the problem here? Why this dilemma of the Christian church? The problem, it seems to me, is that we are still talking about the very missionary calling we inherited from the past. Our dilemma comes from the very missionary nature we thought our church should have when Christianity was riding the waves of the Western domination of the world. This missionary portion of the history of Christianity has to be carefully scrutinized, and there are church historians in the Third World scrutinizing it carefully. This whole chapter of the missionary expansion of the Christian church outside the West has to be critically reexamined, and there are theologians in the Third World reexamining it critically. Their scrutinizing begins to tell us stories of Jesus, God, and nations different from the stories with which we are familiar. But most of us schooled in the traditions of Christian mission find it difficult to listen to them.

Their reexamination too is disclosing to us accounts of how Jesus would have dealt with peoples who are not Christian because of the ways in which God has been dealing with them — accounts that are not quite the same as those told us in the theological writings from the West. How can we, then, speak of our missionary calling and the missionary nature of the church without first listening to these strange stories? How can we issue a call for Christian mission unless we first learn from those unfamiliar accounts of the ways of God? Christian mission is possible only after we have listened to these stories and learned from these accounts. But then ours will be a Christian mission very different from that which the churches in the West practiced for the past two hundred years. It will of course be radically different from that carried out by those Christians and evangelists today who believe themselves to be entrusted with the burden and responsibility to save the so-called lost souls. What a heavy burden to bear — burden perhaps God has not asked them to bear! What awesome responsibility — a responsibility perhaps God has not entrusted to them!

From Theology to Mission

The Christian church today, East or West, South or North, stands at the threshold of a different theological era. It is an era ushered in by the East and an era in which the South plays a leading role. The implications for the theology and the mission of the Christian church are obvious but enormous, self-evident but breathtaking. At long last people in the East and in the South are telling us what theology is and how to go about it. They are not just "subjects" to be studied by theological anthropologists from the West, but themselves "subjects of theology." They are not the souls to be salvaged for God by well-meaning Christian preachers and evangelists; rather they reveal to us what God is doing in the life and history of the nations.

The stories they tell us, the experiences they share with us — are they not the very subject matters of Christian theology? Professional theologians have always wanted to know what God is doing in history and told us in so many words what they think they do know. Tireless evangelists have always been curious about the saving ways of God and pronounced with conviction at endless evangelical rallies what they believe that way must be. But people from the East and from the South are telling us something quite different. They are showing us that God may not have the same concerns we have had all along, that God may be not quite interested in the ways we have been doing things for God. Are they not in fact telling us what that prophet who has left us no name told his people in exile a long time ago? "My thoughts are not your thoughts," that prophet we call Second Isaiah found himself saying on God's behalf, "nor are your ways my ways" (Isa. 55:8).

If those women, men, and children — their life and their history — are subject matters, or contents, of theology, they are doing theology in ways very different from our ways. Theirs are so different, as a matter of fact, that we tend to dismiss what they do as not theological. Their theological logic is simply illogical to us and we do not consider what they tell us deserving the name of theology. We may be tempted not to take them seriously just as that prophet called Isaiah was not taken seriously by the false prophets, priests, and leaders of his day. In fact they went so far as to ridicule him saying:

> Whom will he teach knowledge,
>   and to whom will he explain the message?
> Those who are weaned from milk,
>   those taken from the breast?
> For it is precept upon precept, precept upon precept,
>   line upon line, line upon line,
> here a little, there a little. (Isa. 28:9–10)

Of course we are not as rude as the religious leaders of Isaiah's day. We may lend sympathetic ears to the stories of people from the East and the South. We may even think that these stories call us to missionary actions. But we are not so sure whether they can constitute what we know to be theology.

But if these stories from the South and the East are not theological enough, what is theological enough? If the accounts of the people from those regions of the world are not considered to be the very stuff of theology, what then will be? These questions have, in fact, to do with the fundamental nature of theology. What is Christian theology? How is it related to life, not life in abstract but the life of you and me, Christian or not? How does it understand history, not history in general, but history of this nation and that nation, again Christian or not?

And there is something more, something that we in our sound theological mind have not dreamed of. Those stories that come out of the life and experience of people in the East and the South *naturally* get linked with the stories of our Bible. I emphasize the word "naturally." The reason is that those people who tell their stories do not contrive, do not strain, do not manipulate, like most of us theologians trained in traditional theology do, to relate their stories to the stories of the Christian Bible. Is this not strange, considering the fact that the majority of them are not Christian, at least 95 percent of Asia's population, for example? Why is this so? One cannot but be curious.

How is it possible that the stories of these men, women, and children who are not Christian naturally get related to the stories of our Christian Bible? But is this not a wrong question? Should we not rather ask: Why is it not possible? If it is not possible for our traditional theology, it must be possible for the kind of theology God must be wanting us to do today, theology that deals with the Word that became flesh and dwelt among the people of the South and the East as well as among those in the North and the West, and perhaps more among those in the South and the East than those in the North and the West. This is a theological discovery of momentous significance and far-reaching implications. It makes us question, for instance, whether it still makes sense to define Christian mission in terms of reaching "the unreached people." It inspires us to wonder whether or not only Christians have a mission toward other people, but other people too have a mission toward Christians. It also compels us to think out loud whether ours must be a mission with missions of other people within one mission of God.

It seems to me this is a clear testimony of how theology must precede mission, how mission must be premised on theology. At first I thought I was getting at something new, but I soon realized that, in fact, it has never been otherwise in the history of Christianity from the earliest Christian community of the Apostles to the church of the present day. Peter is our first example. The central message of the sermon he preached at Pentecost was that "God has made him both Lord and Messiah, this Jesus whom you crucified" (Acts 2:36). Jesus is Lord! Jesus is Messiah! Jesus is the Christ! This was Peter's theology, or his christology. Then came his missionary appeal. "Repent, ... every one of you, in the name of Jesus Christ so that your sins may be forgiven ..." (2:38). I see here a movement from theology to missiology. Put differently, missiology is a product of theology. The kind of theology determines the kind of missiology.

I discern a similar pattern of movement in Paul. In Paul we have a great deal more, in fact a whole lot more, of how his theological understanding of Christ shaped his missionary career. We have of course a Lukan portrayal of Paul in the Acts of the Apostles. But it is the letters he wrote to the churches that allow us to know quite a lot of what was going on in his theological mind. At the beginning of his great letter to the Romans, he commended to the Christians in Rome the gospel "about Jesus Christ our Lord," who was "designated Son of God in power . . . by his resurrection from the dead" (Rom. 1:4, RSV). This theology of his, or this christology of his, was the heart of his missionary calling. "Through him [Jesus Christ our Lord]," Paul went on to declare and say, "we have received grace and apostleship to bring about the obedience of faith for the sake of his name among all nations" (1:5, RSV).

I wondered what inspired both Peter and Paul, and for that matter the earliest Christian community, to dwell more and more on Jesus as Lord, Messiah or Son of God in the place of Jesus of Nazareth. It must have been their experience of the risen Jesus. That Jesus is alive, that he is present with them, became the core of their faith and motivated them to be engaged in mission. True, Paul made much of the crucified Jesus in his letters. He wrote to the Christians at Corinth saying: "For I decided to know nothing among you except Jesus Christ, and him crucified" (1 Cor. 2:2). And again in that famous passage in the same letter: " . . . we proclaim Christ crucified" (1:23). Still I cannot escape the impression that for Paul as for Peter and those early followers of Jesus, "Jesus nailed to the cross" was to come under the shadow of the risen Christ and finally to be overshadowed by the latter.

This theological movement — movement from the crucified Jesus to the risen Christ, from the Jesus of the Crucifixion to the Christ of the Resurrection — came to affect the theology of the church and its mission in a fundamental way. What brought about the movement, it is commonly held, is the experience of the risen Jesus. The appearance stories of the risen Jesus in the gospels point in that direction. Even Paul himself had a dramatic encounter with the risen Jesus (Acts 9). It must have been with much passion when he wrote to the Corinthian Christians: "Now if Christ is proclaimed as raised from the dead, how can some of you say there is no resurrection of the dead? If there is no resurrection of the dead, then Christ has not been raised; and if Christ has not been raised, then our proclamation has been in vain and your faith has been in vain" (1 Cor. 15:12–14). This is his logic of faith. Everything hinges on the resurrection of Jesus.

But is this all there is to it? I ask myself this especially when I reflect on Paul as a missionary to the Gentiles and on the history of Christian mission. There must be something else that motivated Paul to devote himself to his missionary work. It is "salvation" as he understood it as a Jew within the tradition of the faith in the Hebrew scriptures. "Most of what Paul says in the very divergent circumstances of his surviving letters," it has been pointed out, "is controlled by certain central and identifiable convictions: that God had sent Jesus Christ to provide for the salvation of all; that salvation is thus available for all, whether Jew or Greek, on the same basis."[6] In Romans 9–11 Paul grapples with the relation between salvation of Gentiles and salvation of Jews with great brilliance and also with some deep confusion at one and the same time. Eventually he has to deny "two pillars common to all forms of Judaism: the election of Israel and faithfulness to the Mosaic law."[7] Salvation for him consists in faith in Jesus Christ the Jewish Messiah.

And what did Paul and early Christians understand by salvation? There does not appear to be anything special about this question. The answer for the early Christian community as for the church today is self-evident: salvation consists in life eternal and imperishable, in becoming members of "true Israel," in entering the blessings of God at the end of time. The new element in the apostolic kerygma is Jesus Christ. It is in and through faith in Jesus the Lord that one is given access to salvation. Is it, then, accidental that both Peter and Paul seldom referred to "the reign of God," the heart of Jesus' proclamation? The few times Paul referred to it in his letters had little to do with what Jesus meant by it, for example, in the Sermon on the Mount, or in parable after parable Jesus told to drive home to people what the reign of God was about.

Nor is it by accident that themes such as sin, judgment, repentance, and forgiveness came to play a dominant role in the thoughts of Paul and in the theological traditions of the Christian church. And of course these themes make up almost solely the contents of the message of missionaries and evangelists. They have shaped the mind-set of most Christians and their churches in parts of the world such as Asia even to this day. Most of them cannot think of salvation except in terms of deliverance from sin and entry into God's everlasting life. Christian mission then consists in nothing less than preaching the good news of eternal life for Christians and the bad news of eternal death for those who are not Christian. Ironically, Christian preachers, dwelling on salvation in this way, have much in common with what teachers of other religions also inculcate in their devotees. But they despise and condemn these religions as superstition and idolatry.

The Cross of Jesus

This understanding of salvation is coupled with the way Jesus came to be understood theologically. As we are well aware, for the Christian church, beginning with Paul and early Christians, "Christ is represented as paying our ransom,

---

6. E. P. Sanders, *Paul, the Law, and the Jewish People* (Philadelphia: Fortress Press, 1983), 4–5.

7. Ibid., 208.

or as offering the sufficient sacrifice for our sin, or as winning a victory over the demonic enemies who through Adam's disobedience got us in thrall."[8] But we must ask: Is this what the death of Jesus is really about? Is this the way the cross must be understood? We must further ask: Does Christian mission developed out of such a theology of salvation and shaped by such an understanding of Christ have to do with the cross of Jesus? Does it represent what Jesus sought to do in his life and ministry? Questions such as these point to a critical issue that is very much at the center of our topic.

If our answer to these questions is in the negative, that is, if the death of Jesus does not mean God paying ransom for our sin, if the cross is not God offering sufficient sacrifice for what we have done against God, and if Jesus' death on the cross does not bring about victory over demonic enemies, *then,* do we not have to reformulate our theology of Jesus' death? Do we not have to reconstruct our theology of the cross? What about Christian mission? Can we still have at the center of our theology and practice of Christian mission salvation in the sense of gaining eternal life, of entering the state of eternal bliss in the afterlife, though these are the main preoccupations of most religions, including Christianity?

What is, then, the cross on which Jesus was sentenced to die? What does it mean for those of us who confess our faith in him? And what does it symbolize for those who are not Christians? It cannot mean one thing for Jesus himself, who had to go through the pain and agony of it, and another for those of us who are members of the church gathered in his name, and yet another for the people of other faiths and no faith. For all the parties concerned, Jew or Gentile, white or black, yellow or brown, women or men, the cross of Jesus should not be a religious idea. It has never been and it will never be. Nor is it a theological construct unrelated to the realities of life and history. It has never been and it will never be.

The cross is a most cruel and inhuman form of execution, endured by Jesus of Nazareth two thousand years ago outside the city walls of Jerusalem in Palestine. It is what Roman colonial rulers meted out to criminals and slaves and to the nationalists who dared to challenge their power and authority. It is a hideous tool of oppression used on the victims of social and political oppression. In the particular case of Jesus the cross was even more atrocious because it was engineered by the leaders of Jesus' own religion to get rid of him. There on that cross, the political power and the religious power entered a most unholy alliance to rid themselves of Jesus for their own respective reasons. And what could be more horrible and frightful than when religious and political powers join forces to fight those opposed to them! In that event, political authorities gain a religious sanction to enforce their rule of terror. They are given the assurance that

---

8. John Knox, *Chapters in a Life of Paul,* rev. ed. (Macon, Ga.: Mercer University Press, 1987), 111.

God is on their side. The religious authorities on the other hand can rely on the political powers they do not have to achieve their evil purposes. The condemnation they pronounce on those who differ from them now acquires legitimacy in the eyes of the law.

If this is what the cross of Jesus was, and it was just that, we cannot theologize it away, that is, we cannot, as generations of Christian theologians have done, make God responsible for it. We cannot justify it as a ransom God has to pay to the devil in exchange for our freedom from its control. Nor can we concoct a theology of the cross, as many of us have done and are still doing and teach that God allows Jesus to die on the cross in order to grant us forgiveness of our sins. If we cannot do this, if we cannot create a theology such as this from the cross on which Jesus died, then we cannot go on doing Christian mission as if the only thing that matters is to believe in Jesus and escape from eternal punishment in hell. There is in fact much more of John Bunyan's *Pilgrim's Progress* in the theology of mission preached and practiced by many Christian evangelists today in Asia than Jesus' life and ministry of God's reign in the gospels of the New Testament.

If God has not engineered the cross of Jesus, what would the cross mean to God? The cross, one can say, becomes God's indictment of the inhumanity of the powers of this world, be they religious or political. And if we are allowed a glimpse of the heart of God, we would be seeing it bleeding as Jesus bled to death on the cross. Instead of forsaking him, as most Bible exegetes and theologians would have us believe, God must have never been so close to him as when he was dying a most humiliating, agonizing, and painful death on the cross. The cross is the manifestation of evil power lurking in the depths of humanity. It brings out into the open the dark side of human existence. It exposes the pretension of human beings to be true, good, and beautiful. In fact it is the mockery of the truth, goodness, and beauty to which human beings piously aspire. And insofar as the cross is just that, it is a mockery of God, an insult to the God who created human beings in God's own image, and the defacement of the creation God created to be good, to use the language of the creation story in Genesis 1. The cross is the self-destruction of human beings. It is human beings denying their own human nature. It is human beings become less human, inhuman, even anti-human.

Stories of the Cross

If this is the story of the cross of Jesus, we at once realize that this story is repeated over and over in human history both before him and after him. The story of Jesus' death on the cross is to be identified in story after story of men, women, and children who suffered and died under oppression and injustice. It is multiplied in many stories, countless stories, as a matter of fact, of people suffering and dying today because of the selfishness and greed of the rich, because of those in power who achieve their ambition and maintain their privilege at the expense of the powerless. The story of the cross of Jesus is not confined to the Christian church, recounted only by Christians during Passion week year after year, preached by ministers on Passion day.

The fact is, if we Christians want to listen to the true story of the cross of Jesus, meditate on it, craft a sermon on it, even construct a theology of it, do we not have to listen to a story such as told by a Malaysian lawyer and poet in his poem called "The Continent of Hunger"?

> The Continent of Hunger
> has no boundaries
> Its Capitals stretch
> from Rio to Chicago
> Kingston to Addis Ababa
> Naples to Buenos Aires
>
> Its children are
> of every race
> creed and color
> but have no difficulty
> in recognizing each other
> by their uniform of rags
> and their universal birthmarks:
> bamboo limbs,
> saucer-eyes, pumpkin bellies . . .
>
> The enemies of the Continent
> of Hunger are many . . .
> Besides having to fight
> these Big Businesses
> and Multinationals
> the citizens of Hunger
> have to contend also
> with twisted politicians
> purblind clergy
> corrupt generals
> and the fat greasy men
> who traffic in human misery . . .
> Gentlemen, you have the facts
> I now demand full
> and immediate recognition
> of this Continent of Hunger![9]

---

9. Cecil Rajendra, *Songs for the Unsung* (Geneva: World Council of Churches, 1983), 38–40.

This is a story of the communities of hunger in the world of exploitative economy. We read it in newspapers and see it on television. But what does it have to do with the theology of the cross and the Christian mission?

There is a line in the poem that refers to "purblind clergy." Does it not make us rather uncomfortable? We know big businesses and multinationals take advantage of political anomaly and exploit cheap labor of the country to make enormous profits for themselves and leave behind them economic chaos. We know "twisted politicians and corrupt generals" are hand in glove with each other and with the multinationals to make themselves rich and powerful. We also know heartless merchants who force young girls and boys from poverty-stricken villages into prostitution and create endless human miseries. But clergy? Christians? the church? What have we to do with it all? It may be a concern for a department called "church and society," for the National Council of Churches and other ecumenical bodies. Is that not enough? Do we not have important things to do, such as preaching the good news of salvation and leading people to Christ?

But the poem just cited is a contemporary "christological" hymn — a hymn that points to that great christological insight of John the Evangelist who said: "The Word became flesh and lived among us" (John 1:14). Stories in the gospels tell us that the religious leaders of Jesus' day were "purblind" to human miseries. Part of his mission was to awaken them from their self-righteousness and to open their eyes to the poverty, hunger, and discrimination that people were suffering. He associated himself with the poor and the outcast, proclaiming that the kingdom of God belongs to the poor, to the hungry, to the persecuted, and not to the rich or to the powerful (Luke 6:20–25; Matt. 5:3–12). Was this not also the mission of the prophets of ancient Israel? And should it not also be the mission of the church today? How can we carry on Christian mission when we are "purblind" to the fact that we as the church have also contributed to "the Continent of Hunger" by pursuing economic prosperity as the sign of God's blessing on us and on our church? Does this not mean that Christian mission must begin with us Christians and our churches and not with those outside the church, just as Jesus' mission was directed first and foremost to his own religious community?

The truth of the matter is that if the story of the cross in the poem of "The Continent of Hunger" does not sound right for our theological ear, then the story of Jesus' cross in the New Testament will not sound right either for our ear attuned only to traditional theology. But let us listen on. Perhaps if we listen more and more, we may be gripped more and more by the theology of the cross that people do and the "Christian" mission they practice. Let us listen to the story of "Sonny Flynn" from Australia:

> My name is Eugene Patrick "Sonny" Flynn. I was born in Darwin on 6 August 1938 and am of Aboriginal descent . . . I owned and operated my own taxi, cleaning contracts, and postal contracts, then I briefly joined the

public service. After the 70s I realized that a lot of my people, friends, were destroying themselves and their culture through the white people's baggage, for example, alcohol and modern living. I came to Adelaide 12 years ago and commenced my tertiary studies. . . . In this period I became active again in the church and community. I decided to be active to somehow Aboriginalize the church which for most of my life had fed, educated, and directed me, but which left out the most important part of my life, what makes me who I am — our spirituality and culture, our ways of being Aboriginal. The spirituality of my people is a very difficult subject to write about because it is deep in each of us. . . . It makes me proud and humble to see, feel and hear this spirituality because it is everywhere [in Australia], especially where my people are. The degradation, suffering, discrimination, physical and mental hurt my people have felt do not make them bitter or angry. They always come back smiling and laugh at themselves and their own and other Aboriginal sufferings. They turn the other cheek because all they want is peace and justice. Just think, we are at the bottom of Australia's socioeconomic ladder: crisis after crisis, racism, investigations, black deaths, continuous scrutiny. Black people for me must have deep and perfect spirituality to keep going. Time after time when I listen to stories of their lives and what they want to do, I find it is always for their families and communities. I have listened to their stories, their spirituality in the bush, jails, conference rooms, churches and universities; it brings me to tears then I feel so proud and grateful for being Aboriginal. A lot of us don't have to be Aboriginal, but we chose to be Aboriginal because we are custodians of this land, this spirituality, this Dreaming. It keeps me going.

Two hundred years of their destruction and, if nothing else, I believe we still have our spirituality and always will because the super-Dreaming beings, gods, heros and Our Lord is [sic] on our side and with us.

I wrote it this way to demonstrate that I live in two worlds but value *most my* spirituality, my Aboriginality.[10]

This is a long story. In our fast-moving life in this fast-moving world we may become impatient listening to it. But this is a long story made short, and this is only one of such long stories that we begin to hear from the history of the long suppressed people in the world today.

Toward Abolition of the Cross

What overwhelms us is the quiet spirituality of the long-suffering Aboriginals making its way into the world of Christianity that wronged them "without

---

10. See Anne Patel-Gray, *Through Aboriginal Eyes: The Cry from the Wilderness* (Geneva: World Council of Churches, 1991), 113–15.

bitterness and anger" and "with smiling." How different it is from the spirituality of the Christian church that made the cross of Jesus a sign of conquest and the right to claim others for Christ. The spirituality that keeps them going in face of the atrocities and violence inflicted on their persons, on their land, on their culture, and on their humanity is much closer to the spirituality Jesus manifested throughout his life and especially on the cross. "Father," Jesus prayed even though seized with extreme pain, "forgive them" (Luke 23:32). What spirituality!

The spirituality that enables you not to be bitter when your land is taken away from you: Is this not the spirituality of the cross? The spirituality that enables you not to be angry when death is inflicted on you: Is this not the spirituality of Jesus on the cross? The spirituality that enables you to come back laughing when injustice is done to you: Is this not the spirituality of Jesus who on the cross already participates in a new life beyond the cross? It is this kind of spirituality that puzzles the oppressors and frightens the enemies. And is it not spirituality such as this, spirituality that the Aboriginals did not learn from the church but inherited from their ancestors, from their land, spirituality that is "deep in each of them," spirituality that must have come from God who created all human beings including Australian Aboriginals — is it not this indigenous spirituality of theirs that shames white Christians and their churches in Australia, compels them to repent, and inspires them to make good the evil they have committed against their fellow human beings?

What shakes us up in this story is that the "Christian" mission the churches in Australia carried out for the Aboriginals not only failed but proved detrimental. This is a very hard thing to say, but this is what the Aboriginals in Australia are saying to us today. They not only lost their land and culture, but their identity. It is their Dreaming, the stories of their ancestors that they rediscovered, the ruins of their culture that escaped destruction, and the spirituality that survived the violence committed against them that enable them to regain their humanity, give them strength to live, and create in them the courage and vision to live.

Is not, then, their Dreaming part of the Dreaming of God, the creator of heaven and earth? Are they not part of the story of the enslaved people of Israel in Egypt a long time ago? Are they not stories of the women, men, and children with whom Jesus associated himself and of whom, Jesus said, the reign of God is? Are they not also stories of the oppressed people throughout human history and all over the world? And their spirituality, the spirituality that is deep in each of the Aboriginals, the spirituality that enables them not to be bitter and angry but enables them to come back laughing — is it not the spirituality that reveals the noble nature of humanity not entirely destroyed by human lust for power and human propensity for evil?

Questions and questions. We are prompted to ask more questions. Is it, not, for example, because of spirituality such as this, the spirituality that has sustained the Aboriginals in Australia against all "degradation, suffering, discrimination, physical and mental hurt," is it not because of it that we begin to know who God is, why Jesus must suffer and die, and the hope that even the cross, that horrible instrument of death, can bring us? And here is an astonishing irony from which those of us engaged in the hard thinking on the cross and the Christian mission can no longer shy away. The Christian church through its mission brought to the Aboriginals the God who could not recognize their culture, the Jesus who denied their dignity as human beings, and the Spirit who set itself against their spirituality and suppressed it. But now they are disclosing to us the God who created their culture as well as other cultures, the Jesus who is with them in their suffering, and the Spirit who enables them to keep their spirituality active in each of them. This is an irony, but it is also a challenge. It challenges us to reconstruct our "Christian" mission to reflect more of what God has done and is still doing through Jesus in the power of the Spirit.

Sonny Flynn's is a story typical of those being told more and more by the people in those parts of the world that the churches in the West sought to win for Christianity through the missionary expansion. These stories reflect in a profound way the story of Jesus' suffering and crucifixion that "demonstrated the 'solidarity' of the love of God with the unspeakable suffering of those who were tortured to death by human cruelty," the suffering "which has continued down to the present century in a 'passion story' which we cannot even begin to assess, a 'passion story' which is based on human sin, in which we all without exception participate, as beings who live under the power of death."[11] This is an expanded theology of the cross, theology that expands from that particular time and space in which Jesus was crucified backward into the past and forward into the future through the present.

But who, we must ask, wants such a theology of the cross to continue? I do not believe God does. Who wants such passion story to be told again and again? I cannot imagine Jesus, who went through it himself, does. Is this not why black people in South Africa, just to give one example, have been fighting against apartheid, that evil system of racism, to abolish that cross they have carried for three hundred years? How many black people have already died in that struggle, bearing their cross of apartheid to their grave? They must have died dreaming that their children, their grandchildren and their great-grandchildren, will not have to carry it any longer.

Thoughts such as these have profound implications for Christian mission. The mission of the Christian church is to work toward eradication of the cross and the disappearance of it within the church itself, in the society in which it is located, and in the world in which people of different nations strive for justice, peace, and freedom. We are reminded at this point of the empty cross in the churches of the Reformed tradition. The cross is empty, so we are told, because Jesus is risen. True, Jesus is risen. Jesus is no longer nailed on the cross. But this theology of the cross has a lot to explain for itself in face of stories of the

---

11. Martin Hengel, *The Cross of the Son of God,* trans. John Bowden (Philadelphia: Trinity Press International, 1986), 180.

immense suffering in the world, stories reminding us that the story of Jesus' cross is not yet over, that it has not yet come to an end.

Does not this mean that the mission of the church is to work toward the world emptied of the cross, the cross not understood as God's ransom to the devil for our salvation, but the cross as the height of human cruelty and the depth of God's suffering with humanity? And as more and more stories from both inside the church and outside it, and in fact more from outside the church than from inside it, are testifying how people live, struggle, and die in order that human atrocities may cease and human sufferings may end, should not the story of Christian mission be a part of those stories? The world emptied of the cross: this is an apocalyptic dream. But is it not God's vision of "a new heaven and a new earth" (Rev. 21:1), which the seer on the island of Patmos is allowed to envision when the world around him was in turmoil?

Christian mission is not "Christian" if it is not part of the mission of Jesus "to bring good news to the poor, . . . to proclaim release to the captives and recovery of sight to the blind, to let the oppressed go free, to proclaim the year of the Lord's favor" (Luke 4:18–19). Christian mission is not "Christian" if it is not inspired by God's mission of "making all things new" (Rev. 21:5). And Christian mission is, again, not "Christian" if it is not born of the Spirit that "blows where it wills," even where stories such as Sonny Flynn's are told and heard. Christian mission is "Christian" insofar as it serves the mission of God to create a world in which Jesus would no longer be crucified and the power of the Spirit curtailed and suppressed.

Christian mission is carried out in between times, between the time of crucifixion and the time of resurrection, between Good Friday and Easter Day. Its goal is not the fulfillment of the "great commission" (Matt. 28:19) of making all nations members of the Christian church, but the "new commandment" (John 13:34) of loving one another just as Jesus has loved us. Its vision is not expansion of Christianity in the world but the fulfillment of God's will "on earth as it is in heaven." In the meantime, Christian mission is shaped by what Jesus said and did during his life and ministry. And it moves toward the day when the cross, that reality and symbol of divine-human suffering, will be abolished forever, the day when God's will is done on earth as it is in heaven.

Contributors

Walter Altmann, Brazil, Professor of Systematic Theology, Escola Superior de Teologia, São Leopoldo, Brazil.

James H. Cone, United States, Briggs Distinguished Professor of Systematic Theology, Union Theological Seminary, New York, U.S.A.

Jean-Marc Éla, Cameroun, Professor, Department of Sociology, Faculty of Letters and Social Sciences, University of Yaounde, Cameroun.

Simon S. Maimela, South Africa, Professor, Department of Systematic Theology and Theological Ethics, University of South Africa, Pretoria, South Africa.

Elisabeth Moltmann-Wendel, Germany, feminist theologian.

Winston D. Persaud, Guyana, Associate Professor of Systematic Theology, Wartburg Theological Seminary, Dubuque, Iowa, U.S.A.

Choan Seng Song, Taiwan, Professor of Theology and Asian Cultures, Pacific School of Religion, Berkeley, California, U.S.A.

Theo Sundermeier, Germany, Professor of Missions and History of Religions, University of Heidelberg, Germany.

Yacob Tesfai, Eritrea, Associate Research Professor, Institute for Ecumenical Research, Strasbourg, France.

Andreas A. Yewangoe, Indonesia, Professor, Faculty of Theology, Christian University, Kupang, Indonesia.

Index

Abandonment, God's, 13-16
Aboriginals, Australian, 144-47
Abraham, 85
Adorno, Theodore W., 94
Africa: contemporary political systems of, 26; the cross and, 17-35; the historical experience of, 20-27; Jesus Christ and, 19, 28-32; Western civilization and, 22
African: independent churches, 19; societies, 25-26; theology, 33
African-Americans, 48-60
Afrikaners, 44
Allah, 66
Altmann, Walter, viii-ix, 75-86
Ambom, Indonesia, 71
A.M.E. Church, the, 56
Anthony, Saint, temptation of, 108, 109
Apartheid, 12, 147
Apostle's Creed, the, 128
Arevalo, C. G., 73
Aristotle, Luther and, 101
Art, Western Christian, theology and, 106. *See also* Isenheim altarpiece, the
Asia, religions of, 63-66, 69-70
Assmann, Hugo, 5-6
Augustine, Saint: on the incarnation, 29; Martin Luther and, 101, 105
Ayacucho, Peru, 2

Biko, Steve, 38
Black Code, the, 23
Black power, black theology and, 55-60
Black religious thought, 48-60
Black Skins, White Masks (Fanon), 26
Blacks, Latin American, 79
Boesak, Allan, 12
Boff, Leonardo, 7, 8
Bonhoeffer, Dietrich, 80, 95

Brahman, 64
Brazil, 79
Brock, Rita Nakashima, 92
The Brothers Karamazov (Dostoyevsky), 104
Buddhism, 64-65, 133
Bunyan, John, *Pilgrim's Progress*, 142
Buthelezi, Manas, 38

Carmichael, Stokely, 57
Carr, Anne, *Transforming Grace*, 96
Casaldáliga, Dom Pedro, and Pedro Tierra, "Mass of the Earth without Evils," 75
Castres, P., 22
Catholic Action, 123
Césaire, Aimé, 24, 25, 27
Chemparathy, G., 64
Christianity, colonial, 33-34. *See also* Colonial theology
Church, the: Asian, 69-73; neo-colonial, 33; the unity of, 111-29
Cicero, 31
Civil Rights Act, the, 53
Civil rights movement, the, 52-55
Classism, 59, 60
Colonial theology, 42-43
Columbus, Christopher, 3-6
Community, Christian, 127-29
Conditionedness, historical, 113-17
Cone, James H., viii, 48-60: on the crucified people, 11-12; on the death of Jesus, 5; on structural injustice, 13
Confucianism, 65
Constantine the Great, 32, 41-42, 130-31, 132
Contextuality, theological, 99

Cross, the: critiques of, 90-94; Luther's theology of, 99-110; as symbol, 62-63, 96-98, 131-32; theology of, 58; transformation of, 7
Crucified people, the, 10-12
Crucifixion, the, 6-7
Crusades, the, 131
Cullmann, Oscar, 32
Culturalism, 18
Culture, black, 59

Darsane, Nyoman, 109-10
da Vinci, Leonardo, "The Last Supper," 109
de Gruchy, John W., 43-44
Desire, 64
Dependency theory, the, 126
Development, Indonesian, 70-73
Diop, David, 24
Disputation against scholastic theology, the (Luther), 102
Divisions, human, 36-47. *See also* Racism
Dolorism, 63
Doshisha University, Japan, 132
Dostoyevsky, F., *The Brothers Karamazov*, 104
Du Bois, W. E. B., *The Souls of Black Folk*, 48
Dutch Reformed Church, the, 44

EATWOT. *See* Ecumenical Association of Third World Theologians
Ecclesiology, liberationist, 119
Ecumenical Association of Third World Theologians (EATWOT), 3
Éla, Jean-Marc, viii, 2-3, 8-9, 12, 17-35
Elizondo, Virgil, 8
Ellacuría, Ignacio, 10
Erutjahra, Raja, 68
Ethnocentrism, 18
Ethnotheology, 19-20
Eucharist, the, 127-29
Evangelical Christianity, 122, 129

Faith: justification by, 39, 47, 58; social dimensions of, 119
Faithfulness, strategies of, 111
Fanon, Frantz, 18: *Black Skins, White Masks*, 26

Feminist theology, 87-98. *See also* Sexism; Women, the cross and
"The Four Noble Truths," 64

Gardet, L., 69
Garvey, Marcus, 56
Gilligan, Carol, 88
Glory, theology of, 45, 58, 99, 113-14
God: abandonment and, 13-16; the image of, 114; the love of, 102, 109, 114; the suffering, 58
Godoy, Carlos Mejía, 83
Goerdeler, Karl, 36-37
Gollwitzer, H., 42
Gospel, the: historical consciousness and, 21; Jesus Christ and, 17; the one, 113-17; particularity of, 117-26
Great commission, the, 132, 148
Grünewald, Mathias, 106, 108
Gutiérrez, Gustavo, 2, 58

Haight, Roger, 117, 118, 119
Haiti, 5
Hardjoprakoso, Sumantri, "*Indonesisch Mensbeeld als Basis Ener Psycho-Therapie,*" 68
Hebga, Meinrad, 29
Heidelberg disputation, the (Luther), 39, 99-110
Heyward, Carter, 92
Hinduism, 63-64
Historical consciousness, 21
Historical experience, African, 20-27
Hope: in black religious thought, 50-51; Latin America and, 84-85; Martin Luther King and, 55
Humanism, Luther and, 101

Ihsan, 67
Ikhlas, 67, 68
Immanence, 94
Imperialism, British, 43
Inculturation, 114
Indigenous peoples, 4, 76-80
Indonesian Council of Churches, the, 71
"*Indonesisch Mensbeeld als Basis Ener Psycho-Therapie*" (Hardjoprakoso), 68
Indulgences, Luther and, 100, 101
Industrialization, Latin American, 79-80

Industrial Revolution, the, 23
Injustice: social, 71; structures of, 12-13
Institute for Ecumenical Research, the, vii
Isenheim altarpiece, the, 106-10
Islam, 42, 56, 66

Japan, Christianity and, 133
Jesus Christ: Africa and, 28-32; as
    celestial monarch, 81-82; the crucified
    people and, 10, 11; the gospel and,
    17; the humiliation of, 31-32; identity
    of, 18, 20; imperial image of, 33;
    Latin American images of, 80-84; the
    passion of, 29-32; the powerless and,
    32; redemption and, 93; the story of,
    6-7; the suffering of, 81
John, Saint, 107
John Paul II, 4, 25
John the Baptist, 103
Judaism, 106
Judas, 90
Justice: the church and, 80; God's, 49-50;
    interhuman, 115
Justification by faith, 40

Karma, 64
Kassel, Maria, 91
King, Martin Luther, Jr., theology of,
    52-55
Kitamori, Kazoh, *Theology of the Pain of
    God,* 69-70
Kodjo, Edem, 26-27
Kyoto, Japan, 132-33

Land structure, Latin American, 79
"The Last Supper" (da Vinci), 109
Latin America, evangelical and
    Pentecostal Christianity in, 122-26
Liberation, black religious thought and,
    50, 58
Liberation theology, 70, 72-73, 124-26
Louis XIV, 23
Love, black religious thought and, 51
Luther, Martin, ix: Disputation against
    scholastic theology, the, 102; Heidel-
    berg disputation, the, 99-110; theology
    of the cross, 39-41, 46-47, 99-110
Lutherans, modern, 58

Machismo, 79
Magdalene, Mary, 108
Maimela, Simon S., viii, 36-47
Malcolm X, 56-57
Mandela, Nelson, 38
Mark the Evangelist, 106
Martin, David, 122-25
"Mass of the Earth without Evils"
    (Casaldáliga and Tierra), 75
Mbembe, Achille, 25
Mbiti, John, 19
McGrath, A. E., 100
Meditation, 65
Meincke, Sílvio, 85
Meredith, James, 57
Messianism, Asian, 68
Míguez Bonino, José, 12
Minjung theology, 70
Missiology, theology and, 138-39
Mission, Christian, 127, 130-48
Mofokeng, Takatso, 9, 10
Moksha, 64
Moltmann, Jürgen, 34, 37, 41, 58, 105
Moltmann-Wendel, Elisabeth, ix, 87-98
Moralism, 40
Muhammad, Elijah, 56
Mveng, Engelbert, 26, 28

Nagasaki and Hiroshima, 69
Narimo, 66-67, 68
Nationalism: Afrikaner, 44; black, 55-57
Nation of Islam, the, 56
New Testament, the, 17, 18
Nirvana, 65
"Noble Eightfold Path," the, 65
Nolan, Albert, 10
Nominalism, Luther and, 101
Nonviolence, Martin Luther King, Jr.,
    and, 53

Ontology, Aristotelian, 105
Orthopraxis, 119

Pacific School of Religion, the, 132
Passion, the, 19, 29-32
Paul, Saint, 32, 139, 140: on God's love,
    114; on hope, 84-85; theology of the·
    cross and, 39, 105-106
Pematang Siantar, Indonesia, 71

Penance, 100
Pentecostal Christianity, Latin American, 122-26, 129
Persaud, Winston, ix, 111-29
Peter, Saint, 138, 139
Pieris, Aloysius, 62
Pilgrim's Progress (Bunyan), 142
Political systems, contemporary African, 26
Poverty: Asian, 62; Indonesian churches and, 71-72; the passion and, 30-32
Powerless, the, 321
Praxes, plurality of, 122
Praxis, 59, 115, 116, 118
Preaching, Luther and, 108
Purgatory, 100

Racial division as a theological problem, 41-46
Racism, 36-47, 59, 60
Rationalism, 40
Ratu Adil, 68, 69
Reason, violence and, 22
Redemption, 93, 127, 128
Reductionism, doctrinal, 119
Reincarnation, 64
Relics, 100-101
Renaissance, the, 22
Resurrection, the, 8, 15-16
Retief, Piet, 44
Rhodes, Cecil, 43
Righteousness, human, 39, 40
Rila, 68

Sabr, 67, 68
Sacraments, the, Luther and, 108
Sado-masochism, 90-91
Safa, Ikhwan al, 67
Salvation principles, 45-46
Samsara, 64
Sandys, Edwina, 96
Sarah, 85
Sawito, 69
Schüssler Fiorenza, Elisabeth, 95
Secularization, 136
Setiloane, Gabriel, 11
Sexism, 60. *See also* Feminist theology; Women, the cross and
Sichtermann, Barbara, 91

Sin, 40, 89, 96, 97
Slavery: black religious thought and, 49-52; effects of, 22-28; religious sanction of, 42
Sobrino, Jon, 10
Sobukwe, Robert, 38
Social analysis, 59-60
Solidarity, 95-96, 103
Song, Choan Seng, ix, 130-48
Sorge, Elga, 90
The Souls of Black Folk (Du Bois), 48
South Africa, 43-46
Spirituality, 145-46
Staupitz, Johannes von, 99-100
Strobel, Regula, 92-93
Structures of injustice, 12-13
Subjection, the ethic of, 92-94
Suffering: African-Americans and, 48-60; Asia and, 61-74; in black religious thought, 52; the church and, 111-29; human divisions and, 36-47; an Indonesian view of, 66-69; Latin America and, 75-86; Luther on, 102-103; nonviolent, 53; solidarity in, 95-96; Taoism and, 65-66; types of, 38
Suksma Kawekas, 68
Sundermeier, Theo, ix, 99-110
"Superiority," racial, 42-45
Surabaya, Indonesia, 72
Sura Yusuf, the, 67
Sword and cross, the, 77-80
Syrian religion, the, 106

Taoism, suffering and, 65-66
Tao Te Ching, the, 66
Tat-tyam-as, 64
Taymiyya, Ibn, 67
Tesfai, Yacob, vii-viii, 1-16
Thailand, Christian mission and, 134
Theodicy, black oppression and, 36
Theology: African, 33-35; colonial, 32-33, 42-43; culturalism and, 18; ethnocentrism of, 18; feminist, 88-89; of glory, 39; missiology and, 138-39; mission and, 135
Theology of the Pain of God (Kitamori), 69-70
Transformation, 125
Transforming Grace (Carr), 96

Treatise on the Predictions of Djajabava, 68
Triumphalism, religious, 45
Turner, Henry McNeal, 56
Tutu, Desmond, 2, 46

Universality, theological, 99
Universalization, 109
Universal Negro Improvement Association, the, 56

Vallier, Ivan, 123
Verwoerd, Hendrik, 44
Violence, reason and, 22
Voting Rights Bill, the, 53

War on Poverty, the, 53
Watts, California, 57
Western civilization, Africa and, 22
Wilson Schaef, Ann, 88, 89
Wolff, E., 105
Women, the cross and, 87-98. *See also* Sexism
Works, justification by, 39, 58, 101-103
World Council of Churches, the, 117-18, 135

Yucay, Peru, 77-78
Yewangoe, Andreas A., viii, 9, 61-74

Zen-Buddhism, 65